An adopted son

We know that the whole creation has been groaning as in the pains of childbirth right up to the present time. Not only so, but we ourselves, who have the firstfruits of the Spirit, groan inwardly as we wait eagerly for our adoption as sons, the redemption of our bodies. For in this hope we were saved.

Romans 8:22–24a

In bringing many sons to glory, it was fitting that God, for whom and through whom everything exists, should make the Pioneer of their salvation perfect through suffering. Both the one who makes men holy and those who are made holy are of the same family.

Hebrews 2:10–11a

D1512929

AN ADOPTED SON

The story of my life

Norman Anderson

O.B.E., Q.C., LL.D., F.B.A.

*formerly Professor of Oriental Laws,
and Director of the Institute of Advanced Legal Studies,
in the University of London*

INTER-VARSITY PRESS

Inter-Varsity Press
38 De Montfort Street, Leicester LE1 7GP

First published 1985

British Library Cataloguing in Publication Data

Anderson, Norman
   An adopted son: the story of my life.
   1. Christian life
   I. Title
   248.4   BV4501.2

ISBN 0-85110-474-6

Typeset in Great Britain by
Nuprint Services Ltd, Harpenden, Herts AL5 4SE.
Printed and bound by
Cox & Wyman Ltd, Reading, Berks RG1 8EX.

*Inter-Varsity Press is the publishing division of the Universities and
Colleges Christian Fellowship (formerly the Inter-Varsity Fellowship),
a student movement linking Christian Unions in universities and colleges
throughout the United Kingdom and the Republic of Ireland, and a member
movement of the International Fellowship of Evangelical Students.
For information about local and national activities write to UCCF,
38 De Montfort Street, Leicester LE1 7GP.*

Contents

Preface

An explanation ＊ *The meditation I had*
in mind ＊ *A suggestion that did not work*

An explanation

I never intended to write an autobiography. To begin with, the very idea seemed far too egotistical. Who would want to read it? I have certainly had a far more variegated and interesting life than I ever expected; but, although I am reasonably well known in some circles, I am certainly not a public figure. I have never kept a diary other than one for engagements, have preserved very few letters, and have a notoriously bad memory for names. In biographies, moreover, I have always preferred those which depict a man's character and life 'warts and all', but that is a much more difficult task in an autobiography.

A biographer can objectively record a man's successes and failures, his virtues and his vices, as they are seen from the outside – and these may, of course, include some defects of character which the person himself did not recognize, or of which he was only dimly aware. But the writer of an autobiography should be well aware not only of most of the defects visible to his friends and acquaintances, but also of inward fail-

7

ures and sins of which no-one else may do more than guess (and then, very often, be wrong!). These lie in his thought life, his desires and ambitions, his negligences and unfulfilled intentions. How much of this is he to parade before the public? To hide his faults and failures would be disingenuous, while to describe them in full detail would smack of the confessional; so it is far from easy to know where to draw the line.

This is the eighteenth book that I have written, along with about a hundred articles and papers; and it will very likely be my last. A number of subjects had been proposed to me, including several suggestions of an autobiographical nature; but none of them appealed to me. What I wanted to write about was how faithful God is to those who have whole-heartedly accepted his salvation and committed themselves to his service, but have all too often failed fully to appropriate the one or to live out the other. I am convinced that it is true of all Christians that 'we are God's handiwork, created in Christ Jesus to devote ourselves to the good deeds for which God has designed us' (Ephesians 2:10, NEB). So I picture him having what one might describe as his 'original' or 'ideal' plan for our individual lives, from which we may so easily stray and in which we so often stumble. But our omniscient Creator knew all this in advance and, in his unfailing love, must continually be adapting that 'ideal' plan to the exigencies of our condition. It cannot be his *will* that we should sin, falter or fail; but he never gives us up. Sometimes, indeed, he shows us that he is able to 'restore the years that the locusts have eaten' (*cf.* Joel 2:25), and how, as we look back, he has in fact brought good even out of what is basically sin or failure.

8

The meditation I had in mind

What I first intended was to write a book centred on one of my favourite verses in the Bible: 'In bringing many sons to glory, it was fitting that God, for whom and through whom everything exists, should make the Pioneer ['author'] of their salvation perfect through suffering' (Hebrews 2:10). The phrase 'bringing many sons to glory' gives us a glimpse of the universal scope of this purpose of his, which will be fulfilled only when a multitude 'from every tribe and language and people and nation' are gathered round 'the throne of God and of the Lamb' who purchased them with his blood (Revelation 5:9; 22:1). It would be difficult to find a grander picture of world evangelization anywhere in the Bible.

The phrase 'bringing many sons to glory' does not, however, point only to the vast number and infinite variety of these 'adopted' sons (*cf.* Romans 8:15). It also points to the goal to which he is going to bring them – and to all that this involved for him, and would involve for each of them. That goal is not simply the wonder of being acquitted and accepted on the day of judgment, marvellous though this in itself will be. Rather it consists in the supreme glory of God's immutable purpose that all these adopted sons will finally 'be conformed to the likeness of his [eternal] Son, that he might be the firstborn among many brothers' (Romans 8:29).

On God's side, as the letter to the Hebrews clearly teaches, this could be achieved only by 'the Pioneer of our salvation' being made 'perfect through suffering' (2:10). For the primary teaching of this letter is not the status and glory that the eternal Son had, before the world began, in the unity of the triune Godhead –

9

although that is made abundantly clear in the first chapter. Rather, it is the fact that God's supreme purpose for us could be fulfilled only if his Son had first shared our human nature to the full (2:14 and 17). He had to experience our temptations, emotions and limitations and learn that perfect obedience which should have been our happy experience. Since the Fall, even he, 'holy, blameless, pure' as he was (7:26), could learn this perfect obedience only in the school of suffering (5:8, NEB). Then, 'made perfect' in his human character (5:9), he had to die to atone for our sins (2:17) and make us 'holy through the sacrifice of [his] body once for all' (10:10). Only so would he be able, as our great High Priest, to 'sympathise with our weaknesses' (4:15), 'help those who are being tempted' (2:18), become 'the source of eternal salvation for all who obey him' (5:9) and 'save completely those who come to God through him, because he always lives to intercede for them' (7:25) – 'in the power of an indestructible life' (7:16).

It seems to me that it is the letter to the Hebrews, even more than the Gospels, that spells out for us what it meant for the eternal Son to become 'God-in-manhood' – giving both these terms, 'God' and 'man', their full meaning. And the same letter emphasizes our side too. We need to 'pay more careful attention to what we have heard, so that we do not drift away' (2:1). We are to shun 'a sinful, unbelieving heart' (3:12), and not to be 'hardened by sin's deceitfulness' (3:13). Instead, we must 'hold firmly till the end the confidence we had at first' (3:14), and 'come boldly unto the throne of grace, that we may obtain mercy, and find grace to help in time of need' (4:16, AV). In sum, we should avail ourselves to the full of the new covenant, sealed by Christ's atoning death. This includes a forgiveness so complete that God will no longer even 'remember' our sins (8:12), and a personal knowledge of him (8:11) such as only Jesus can mediate (*cf.* Matthew 11:27). Furthermore, this new covenant includes the writing of his 'law' on our minds and hearts (8:10). So, instead of being confronted by two external tablets of stone which challenge an unwilling and even impossible obedience, we begin instinctively to remember his teaching, and genuinely to want to put it into practice.

Even so, there is no promise that it will not be a fight. We are reminded in Hebrews 12:4–7 that very few of us have 'resisted to the point of shedding [our] blood, in our struggle against sin'. We must expect the discipline which our heavenly Father sees we need, whether it comes directly from his hand, from the actions of others, or from our circumstances. We can rest assured 'that in all things God works for the good of those who love him, who have been called according to his purpose': namely, that we may eventually 'be conformed to the likeness of his Son' (Romans 8:28–29). So, if the eternal Son himself had to learn obedience in the school of suffering, then how much more do we!

We are repeatedly told in the New Testament, as a theological fact, that all those who are 'in Christ' 'died to sin' with him. So we must 'not let sin reign in our mortal bodies' but put our sinful inclinations to death (Romans 6:2, 12; 8:13). Here the term 'bodies' clearly includes our brains, instincts and propensities, and so covers both our thoughts and emotions. It is precisely here that God teaches us, through the disciplines of life which he sends (or allows) only 'for our good, that we may share in his holiness' (Hebrews 12:5–10). The promise he gives us is this: 'God is faithful; he will not let you be tempted beyond what you can bear. But when you are tempted, he will also provide a way out so that you can stand up under it' (1 Corinthians 10:13). He has saved us from both the guilt and slavery of sin; but we must not expect to be saved from its presence, or from our struggle against it, until the great day when our Saviour 'will transform our [mortal] bodies so that they will be like his glorious body' (Philippians 3:21). When that day comes we shall sing in a new way the song of the redeemed –

> 'A song which even Angels
> Can never, never sing;
> They know not Christ as Saviour,
> But worship Him as King' –

for then we shall know him both as Saviour to the uttermost (Hebrews 7:25) and King without any reserve.

A suggestion that did not work

I have been thinking a lot about all this in the last two years, so I thought I might write a book about it. My publisher agreed, but suggested that I should include 'autobiographical illustrations' – to show, presumably, how this is applicable, in a practical and down-to-earth way, in the life of an ordinary, busy Christian who is far from a 'super saint'. This seemed eminently reasonable, because I am sure it is true that 'people learn from people'. They learn from the problems others have had to face; from their failures as well as their successes, from the ups and downs in their lives. They also learn from others the way God in his faithfulness has not let them go, but has opened new doors when other ways, for one reason or another, have seemed to close.

So I set out to write a book which could, I suppose, be described as primarily doctrinal (or, rather, a meditation on doctrine) with a number of references to my own life and experience. But this simply would not 'jell'. To write such a book I should need a strong and coherent doctrinal structure to which I could add short, detached illustrations from personal experience, culled from periods in my life which themselves had no coherent sequence. But life is not like that. Nor would such a book give any honest or adequate impression of a life, in both its secular and spiritual facets, which has not by any means run in a straight line, but has included a number of twists and turns – through which, in retrospect, I can trace the guiding and overruling hand of God.

So I came to the conclusion that I should have to reverse the intended structure and write a book which I never meant to write: an autobiography with intermittent digressions and meditations, and with a very grateful testimony to the fact that God has always kept his side of the covenant, even when I have failed to keep mine.

1

My beginnings

*Early childhood * Schooldays * Cambridge and CICCU * The missionary 'call' * Egypt – and Pat*

I was born on Michaelmas day, 1908. My father, half Scots and half English by ancestry, was born and brought up in Cheshire. He was educated at Liverpool College, where he overlapped with F.E. Smith, subsequently to become Lord Chancellor under the title of Lord Birkenhead. His own father had died early, leaving two daughters and several sons, of whom my father was the eldest. Short of funds, the brothers' chief interest was in rugby football, for which one of them was 'capped' for the North; and on Saturday evenings their mother always invited a number of their friends to supper, to discuss and analyse the game. But soon after leaving school my father came to the south to go into business, and my sisters and I scarcely knew any members of his family except his sisters. In London my father lodged at first with my mother's family, who were distant cousins; and it was not long before he and she became engaged.

My mother's grandfather was a German Rabbi, but his son had thrown over the religion in which he had been reared, had come to England and had married a girl of Highland stock who was a nominal Christian.

After marriage, however, both husband and wife were radically converted, and their home became distinctively Christian. My mother often told me how her father, once a Jewish agnostic, used to visit the bedrooms of all his children every Easter morning with the greeting, 'The Lord is risen!' He died when I was still a toddler, and the only grandparent I got to know was his Scottish widow.

She lived to a ripe old age and almost completely lost her memory (to say nothing of her handbag and her spectacles!). I still remember how she would sometimes set herself to do some darning (never one of her favourite occupations) and then suddenly put it aside with the horrified remark, 'Aye, and it's the Sabbath' – quite regardless of what day of the week it happened to be. In somewhat the same vein she would tell my sisters and me what a wonderful place heaven would be, 'like an eternal Sabbath'. I am afraid this description was scarcely calculated to whet our appetites, since at that time we used to find one Sunday a week a somewhat unpalatable foretaste. She seemed to grow increasingly Scottish in her old age, and would constantly remark, 'It's a funny world we're living in the noo.'

My parents could scarcely have been more unlike in their characters and dispositions. My father was quiet, gentle, slow, thrifty and distinctly obstinate, while my mother was talkative, dominant, impatient and somewhat extravagant. She was completely uninterested in clothes or cookery, but had a positive passion for moving house and visiting ironmongers (in which she would buy countless pots and pans and loved the smell of linseed oil). I remember living in two houses in Ealing and at least five in Reigate, and when not contemplating a move she would throw out a bay window or build on an extra wing. One day I got back from playing golf to find that she and my two sisters (one nine and the other seven years older than I) had moved every piece of furniture in my bedroom to a different place, and it took me quite a time to restore it all to its accustomed position! It was my mother, too, who busied herself with the car and chauffeur, as well as domestic servants, while my father preferred to walk or travel by train. It was he who gave me my pocket-money and, later, an allowance, but if I asked him for a penny stamp (how long ago this seems!) I always had to pay for it; whereas my mother would not hear of taking money for such trifles, and could be relied on to pay for the golf balls I so often lost. This was partly from generosity and partly, I suspect, because she did not want to have me hanging disconsolately about the house.

A weekly ritual was when my father went out on his Sunday afternoon walk, on which I would sometimes accompany him. My mother would always see us off, with repeated exhortations to be back by 4.15 for tea. So, since my father nearly always walked in a straight line and then equally straight back, I would begin suggesting, when about half the available time had gone, that we should turn on our heels. 'Oh, I think we'll get to the top of that little hill,' he would say. I would remind him of my mother's exhortations, but receive exactly the same reply – and to the top of that hill (or whatever) we would always go. Inevitably we got home late, to my mother's vociferous reproaches. 'Oh, poor darling', he would say soothingly; and precisely the same thing would happen the next Sunday.

Early childhood

But golf and Sunday afternoon walks with my father are to anticipate. As a small boy my parents used to take me to a Presbyterian church, for which I was at first dressed in a sailor suit and later in a kilt and its accompanying regalia. The minister there was somewhat pompous (and was commonly referred to as 'The Bishop'), and I had to be kept quiet during his sermons by mother's exceedingly amateur drawings of cats and rabbits. I remember being continually tempted to pick an artificial cherry which adorned the hat of a little girl who sat in the next pew. In those far-off days girls always wore hats in church.

For a short time I shared a governess with a girl cousin, who used periodically to disappear under the table in a flood of silent, and to me quite unaccountable, tears. Then I was sent for a time to the kindergarten of the girls' school to which my sisters went – some fifteen minutes' walk from home. Unhappily, this school had a few boarders who, after breakfast each morning, went for a walk in a 'crocodile', and day girls used to have a positive horror of passing this. So whenever my sisters saw the crocodile approaching they would take me, one by each hand, and run – with my feet never so much as touching the ground. My younger sister would also, at times, keep pushing me off the kerb, which infuriated me, or into the front gardens of houses where there were dogs, which terrified me. But in between she would sometimes play with me.

The First World War broke out just before I was six, when my sisters and I were staying with our grandmother in Aldeburgh (where I had been born, and my parents had a holiday house). I well remember the declaration of war and a telephone call from our parents advising us to return home sooner than we had intended. Back in Ealing, we saw soldiers marching as they sang 'Pack up your troubles in your old kitbag and smile, smile, smile', and at school we made up parcels for prisoners of war. It was ostensibly in connection with one of these parcels that my younger sister, always called Dolly, forced me to go into a small sweet-shop and ask for 'a farthing's worth of chocolate-coated Lily caramels' – a request that she herself must often have made, since the shopkeeper and his wife promptly rushed at me, and I ran away as fast as my small legs would carry me.

In retrospect I had a somewhat lonely childhood. My sisters were much older, and a brother (who would have been two years older than I) had died in infancy. So I was left very much alone with a nurse, who often read to me. This partly accounts, I think, for the fact that I was quite exceptionally slow in learning to read for myself. After all, why try to stumble through a story when someone else will read it aloud much more competently?

Some children of Christian parents seem to grow imperceptibly into a knowledge of God as their Father and Jesus as their Saviour. It was somewhat like this – but in a very faltering way – with me. I heard the gospel when I was very young, and I cannot remember a time when I did not *try* to respond. But my faith was painfully weak, and I went through the process of confession of sin and self-commitment to Christ again and again; it was not until I was about fifteen that I came to what is commonly called 'assurance'. If asked when I was 'converted' or 'born again', I could not reply (and I used at times to wish that I had a more dramatic testimony); but if someone were to quiz me as to when I was 'saved' (as an ardent African once did his minister), I could, with him, give the confident answer: 'At precisely three o'clock on the afternoon of the first Good Friday!' In my case this was, however, a dawning realization rather than a sudden crisis.

Schooldays

After various vicissitudes in early schooling I was sent as a boarder to a preparatory school in Haywards Heath in 1918, just before I was ten. On Armistice Day our scout group marched about singing – and shouting 'Lights up' to every blacked-out window. The teaching was good and I got a sound grounding in Latin, Mathematics and English, and began to write some very immature verse, especially sonnets. On the whole I was happy, and I think boarding-school did me good. I got into the various teams, was captain of rugger, and in athletics used to win the sprints. My parents had my name down for both Rugby and Uppingham, and I was on the point of going to the latter when my mother took a violent dislike to my prospective Housemaster's wife! So instead I went, with two local friends, to St Lawrence College, Ramsgate, which was chiefly known at that time as a relatively small public school with an evangelical foundation and a great reputation for hockey.

I did not enjoy my life there at first, since there was at that time a lot of bullying. I had a number of disappointments in games, too, largely because, for some reason, I lost my speed for some years. I got into the cricket eleven fairly young; but I was made to change the style of batting I had been taught, and proved a failure. So I spent the rest of my schooldays as captain of the second eleven or as a substitute for visiting teams. I got a lot of help, however, from a remarkably strong and active Christian Union, and began to grow spiritually. We had a well-attended meeting every Sunday afternoon, usually led by one of the boys; and on the rare occasions when we had a visiting speaker we managed to drum up an attendance of nearly a hundred. We also had week-night prayer meetings. I remember how three of us – Arnold Lee (later Field Director of what was then the China Inland Mission), 'Dick' Perfect (subsequently Canon R.S. Perfect, for many years Headmaster of the College) and I – once attempted to pray all night, fortified by ginger beer. It was not a success, and we fought against sleep, intermittently, most of the next day!

I spent three years in the Classical Sixth, which at that time seemed to be almost the only alternative to science. I could manage ancient history, but am a shockingly bad linguist. This was far from remedied when an elderly master of the old school, who made us work hard at our classics, was succeeded by a man of wide intelligence but correspondingly little horse sense. We soon came to realize that he could be diverted from almost any subject by being asked an 'intelligent' question. So we thought up a number of these; and whenever he suggested that we should write a Greek prose (which many of us hated), someone would ask him a question about 'the Sanskrit nasal sonant', or some such topic; and he was so delighted that he would discourse about this for the rest of the period, and the proposed Greek prose would pass completely from his memory. As a result, it need hardly be said, I did not sit for an Entrance Scholarship to the University.

Cambridge and CICCU

A year earlier I had flirted briefly with the thought of going to Oxford; but now, on the advice of my Headmaster, I opted for Trinity College, Cambridge. I also decided to read Law – largely at my Housemaster's suggestion. The reason he gave me was that I was the best schoolboy debater he had known (probably because I had once won a debate against him!) and was clearly designed for the Bar; but I have always thought that my propensity for arguing had a good deal to do with his advice. I accepted his suggestion, read Law, and found it suited me admirably; but I confess that I spent a very idle first year.

At that time I had a memory which was quick to remember, but was (even then) equally quick to forget. So I decided that it was scarcely worth reading my text-books (for my memory has always been almost exclusively visual) too early in the year, since I should only forget them before my examinations. I joined the CICCU (Cambridge Inter-Collegiate Christian Union) and found its daily prayer meetings, and weekend Bible Readings and evangelistic Sermons given by visiting speakers, very helpful; but I was revelling in a new-found freedom and was a very lazy Christian. I played some indifferent hockey and did a little debating at the Cambridge Union; but the Union was going through a phase in which almost every speaker tried to be witty, which I found distinctly boring (partly, no doubt, because I was no good at this myself). At the end of the academic year I quite undeservedly came out first in the 'Law Qualifying' examination, to the undisguised amazement of my supervisor, who was poised to reprove me sharply for not attending lectures. So I went home to play golf –

but also to go as an officer to a camp for boys under the aegis of the Scripture Union, which I found a great help spiritually.

Next year I was one of the CICCU 'College Representatives' in Trinity, and I found visiting all the freshmen quite an ordeal. We always tried to see them personally, rather than leave a printed invitation to take its place with a lot of other competing invitations to every conceivable sort of society or club. Sometimes one found the room full of visitors, which was rather embarrassing, and sometimes one was forced to leave a note with an invitation on his table. I remember that on one such occasion I received a reply, written on somewhat exotic notepaper in a still more exotic envelope, thanking me for my invitation but saying that I would no doubt understand that he, as a convinced sun-worshipper, could scarcely accept. I replied that we were going to do our best to welcome sun-worshippers by providing a blazing fire; and I added that, since opportunities to follow his religion were so limited in an English winter, he might like to hear about a religion that was less dependent on the climate! He wrote once more, saying that he really could not come on this occasion, but was glad I had a sense of humour.

I was a contemporary at Trinity with several men whose names have become almost household words because their Marxist views led them to embark on a life of espionage for Russia. They belonged to a highly selective circle known as 'The Apostles', but I never consciously met them or even heard of their doings. Trinity is a very large college, and most of my intimates were CICCU men or old school friends, many of them at other colleges. I managed to scrape into the Trinity hockey team (largely, perhaps, because from my second year onwards I had an elderly car, which was a useful means of transport!). But my activities became more and more centred on the CICCU.

I read some Law during the Easter vacation (except for a few days at a boys' camp), and worked very hard during the Easter term before sitting for Part I of the Law Tripos. I went home before the results came out, and was playing golf when one of my sisters drove up and shouted to me that a telegram had come which apparently read, 'Placed alone in Class I, Division I'; so I thought I could not have heard her correctly. But in the afternoon, after seeing the telegram for myself and receiving a call from a friend who had only just come down from Cambridge, I remember walking round and round the garden with the words of a hymn ringing in my ears:

> And for Thy sake to win renown
>   And then to take the victor's crown
> And at Thy feet to lay it down,
>   O Master, Lord, I come.

Even at that time, however, I really knew what life has taught me again and again: that any 'renown' resultant from having a quick memory in a very limited sphere (together with an aptitude for deluding examiners by suitable padding!) is negligible when compared with all the things in which I am almost totally inept. A Senior Scholarship at Trinity followed; but I was much in doubt about whether I should ever become a barrister, since I was feeling more and more drawn to consider what was then still called 'the mission field' – so I rather foolishly decided not to eat the required dinners at one of the Inns of Court.

The missionary 'call'

World evangelization was taken very seriously indeed in the CICCU at that time. We had at least three 'Missionary Breakfasts' every term, attended by about a hundred men and women (when the University was less than half its present size), at each of which some missionary, or mission secretary, would speak. But behind the claims of particular societies, countries or types of work I discerned two seemingly contradictory attitudes to the missionary 'call' – best exemplified at that time, perhaps, by Mr Hudson Pope and Dr Orissa Taylor. Hudson Pope was an exceedingly gifted evangelist and teacher (especially to the young), whose attitude could be summed up in his advice, 'There are two things you should never do unless you cannot help it: get married, or become a missionary!' (although I can never remember him actually saying this in Cambridge). Dr Orissa Taylor, on the other hand, was himself a medical missionary burdened with the thought that there were 'more doctors in Harley Street, packed like sardines in a tin, than there are doctors with a British qualification in all the mission fields of the world'. So his message, understandably, was that a Christian did not need a special 'call' to be a missionary so much as *not* to be one!

Which of them was right? Their message was not fundamentally, of course, as contradictory as it sounded, for both of them believed in marriage and overseas service. The difference was this: that Hudson Pope insisted that one should act only when the divine imperative became almost irresistible, while Orissa Taylor felt that the need abroad – medical, educational and, above all, spiritual – was so overwhelming, and the proportionate resources so unequal, that one had to have a very good reason, or an insistent sense of God's contrary guidance, before one failed to respond. So what was God's will for me: the Law, an academic career, the home ministry, or overseas service? I remember being so impressed by a talk given by a London City Missionary that I wrote to the General Secretary to ask if I would be a suitable candidate, but the reply was not encouraging! So I went home for another Long Vacation – to a boys' camp, to play golf, and to ponder.

I came back to Cambridge in October to read for Part II of the Law Tripos, but horrified my new supervisor, after some weeks, by telling him I wanted to switch to Theology. He somewhat unwillingly agreed; but it took me only three or four days to decide that it would be better to do one thing properly than to waver. There were, moreover, certain points about ordination in the Church of England (especially the then almost indiscriminate baptism of infants) which gave me grave doubts about ordination, and I was not at all sure about a missionary 'call'. So back to Law I went – although my supervisor concluded (with some reason) that I was an unstable character! But I managed to get a First in my Finals and decided to stay on in Cambridge for a fourth year to read for an LL.B. (now graded as an LL.M.), specializing in International Law. I was aided in that decision by having been asked to be President of the CICCU, and by an invitation to supervise first- and second-year Law students in Clare College. Meanwhile, I went to the Keswick Convention.

A very busy year followed – with CICCU work (for we had a mission that year led by Canon S.M. Warner), International Law, teaching, and pondering about the future. I also got another First. Eventually it

25

seemed right to abandon an academic career, pay a short visit with my father to Egypt, and then (encouraged by the Secretary of what was then the Nile Mission Press) to stay on in Egypt with their missionaries for some weeks, to see their work and pray about the future. I also promised to do three months' deputation work for them in Scotland and the north after Christmas.

But before that visit came my last Long Vacation, in which I had been persuaded to lead a beach mission at Criccieth under the banner of what was then called the Children's Special Service Mission. I accepted this invitation with much trepidation, since my previous experience had been almost exclusively in camps for teenage boys, and I have no aptitude at all for speaking to young children. I was encouraged, however, by having a very good team, including a somewhat older Cambridge friend who had had considerable experience, but was unable to take the leadership because he could not manage the full four weeks.

So we concentrated, during our initial Quiet Day, on the verse: 'For the eyes of the Lord run to and fro throughout the whole earth, to show himself strong in the behalf of them whose heart is perfect toward him' (2 Chronicles 16:9, AV). We determined that, however amateur and faulty our accomplishments might be, we would make it our chief and constant aim to be perfect in heart. This thought did not occupy our minds only during the Quiet Day, but in our prayer meetings throughout the whole mission. We were genuinely cast upon God, and he answered our prayers in a wonderful way – especially, perhaps, in the discussion meetings we held twice a week for those between the ages of sixteen and about thirty-five (for we were by no means concerned *only* with children).

Egypt – and Pat

My subsequent visit to Egypt was decisive. Its purpose was not so much sightseeing as being shown how to go round teeming Egyptian markets with evangelistic leaflets, and in seeing how the Nile Mission Press acted as the handmaid of other missionary societies in producing such leaflets, and books in Arabic for young converts and other Christians. Its leader in Cairo at that time had studied Arabic in Cambridge and had a flair for literary work. But the highlight of those weeks was a fortnight spent in Palestine with the then semi-retired pioneer of the Mission, Arthur T. Upson. He had just had time to learn Arabic before he became stone deaf, so he had concentrated largely on writing leaflets for Muslims – at which he was without rival. When we travelled together he would always ask me questions to which I had to reply in writing; but often, when seated opposite each other in a coffee shop, he would know exactly what I was trying to say from reading a sentence or two upside down, even in my atrocious writing. I remember hearing him give three splendid talks to a Missionary Language School on 'The power of the Arabic language, and how to learn it', 'The power of the written word, and how to use it' and 'The power of a holy life, and how we need it'. His Arabic name meant 'bondslave of the Redeemer', and that was what he truly was.

Shortly before I left Egypt I went to Alexandria to stay with Mr and Mrs Stock Givan, who were British residents in Egypt. I had got to know their elder daughter Pat fairly well on two missions, and her parents, when on holiday in Britain, had been supporters of the mission in Criccieth. I found that Pat (who had gone to boarding-school in England, to a 'finishing school' in Lausanne and then to Ridgelands Bible College) was also praying for guidance about missionary work. I had been becoming increasingly attracted to her, and before I left Egypt she was rash enough to accept my proposal of marriage. Soon after this I had to sail for England, and she followed with her parents in the summer – for another beach mission in Criccieth which we jointly led.

But there were two subjects which greatly exercised our minds at that time – and also those of many of our contemporaries. They are so important that I think both of them merit a special chapter, each of them considered in terms both of God's eternal Son and of his sons and daughters by adoption: namely, the problem of discerning God's call to special service (whatever form this may take) and the problem of personal holiness. I shall devote my next chapter to the first of these, since I had to make an almost immediate decision; and I shall consider the other – an ever-continuing problem – later in this book.

2

The problem of divine guidance

Christian students * *Christ our example* * *The divine plan* * *Missionary service* * *No blueprint*

I well remember an occasion when, in my late teens, I told one of my mother's friends how concerned I was about God's plan for my life. This friend had had a lot of experience with young people who were interested in overseas missions. 'Oh, just ask the Lord about it,' she advised, 'and he will make it perfectly clear.' But this was not my experience, although I asked him repeatedly; and I was confused and somewhat discouraged. Two or three years later I had a talk on the same subject with the Reverend W.H. Aldis (at that time Home Director of what was then the China Inland Mission) which I found much more helpful. He told me that, in his experience, it is often far from easy to know God's will about one's next step, and that it frequently seems to get more difficult as life goes on. 'When one is a very young Christian,' he said, 'God sometimes gives one guidance which is almost dramatically clear; but, as one gets on in the Christian life, he seems to expect one to have learnt more about "the mind of Christ" (1 Corinthians 2:16), and to think things out prayerfully in the light of all the circumstances.'

Christian students

The question of divine guidance was certainly one of the major problems faced by Christian students of my generation. This was particularly true in regard to the divine commission to 'go and make disciples of all nations, baptising them...and teaching them to obey everything I have commanded you' (Matthew 28:19–20). This command was taken to heart among Cambridge men at that time with an insistence and earnestness that is not always characteristic, I think, of students in Britain today – whatever may be the case in America, or, indeed, in those of the younger churches which have matured so fast that they often put us to shame.

But the problem of divine guidance is by no means limited to the question of overseas service. It is just as relevant to those Christians whose circumstances, physical health or psychological make-up point decisively to service at home. They are often equally perplexed about whether God's call is to what is commonly termed 'whole-time' Christian service, or to work and witness for Christ in some 'secular' occupation. Years ago I remember meeting a man at the Keswick Convention who was introduced to me as a 'soul winner by profession, but a commercial traveller to defray expenses'! I have no idea whether he himself approved of this form of introduction, and he was certainly a spiritual giant. But surely the fact was that both his business commitment and his 'soul winning' were at that time an integral part of his Christian service. Strictly speaking, the phrase 'part-time' Christian service is a misnomer, however convenient an expression it may be for special activites after 'office hours'. It is our duty to do God's will, and to live for

Christ's glory, whatever we may be doing – and that includes, of course, proper times of relaxation and rest. So the problem of guidance is really all-pervasive, rather than limited to such vital decisions as a life 'call'. Happy is the man who has the quiet confidence, day by day and hour by hour, that he is doing God's will.

Christ our example

This was certainly true of the eternal Son, who is our supreme example. Unlike us, he could confidently say: 'I always do what pleases him' (John 8:29). But that does not mean that this was something that always came easily to him, without any temptation to act otherwise. On the contrary, we are explicitly told that he was 'tempted in every way, just as we are' (Hebrews 4:15); and at times this absolute obedience must have been supremely difficult and costly. The forty days in the desert at the beginning of his ministry, and the agony in the garden of Gethsemane just before the end, particularly come to mind; but the pressure must have been intermittent. To this his rebuke to Peter at Caesarea Philippi (Mark 8:33), his comportment at the sickness and death of Lazarus (John 11:4,33) and his soliloquy when some Greeks came to see him (John 12:27), for example, bear eloquent witness. But how was it that he was able to know – let alone fulfil – his Father's will?

It seems clear that Jesus came to recognize God as his Father from a very early age. Almost certainly, this was in the basically objective way in which babies habitually come to recognize their parents. But, in Jesus' case, he not only came to know Mary as his mother and Joseph as his father figure, but also 'Abba' as his 'own Father' – and, through this recognition, to grow into a consciousness of his relationship to him. It was this knowledge of God as his Father which, Louis Bouyer insists, is what was unique in the consciousness of Jesus. This consciousness 'was pierced and traversed, from its first awakening, by that intuition, which was to precede, penetrate, and saturate all his states of consciousness, whatever they might be' (Bouyer, pp. 137 and 150).[1] Similarly, Père Galot writes: 'When the Son humanly takes consciousness of himself, he does it as a Son, by taking consciousness of his relation to the Father...' (Galot, pp. 179f.).

How, then, did he come to know what his special mission was to be? It may be, of course, that Mary or Joseph told him something of what Gabriel had said to Mary, the angel had said to Joseph, or Simeon and Anna had said to them both (Luke 1:26–33; Matthew 1:20–21; Luke 2:25–38). But it seems to me more likely that Mary, for some years at least, 'treasured all these things in her heart' (Luke 2:19 and 51). However this may be, it cannot have been long before the boy Jesus discovered from experience 'that nobody else knew the Father with the same intimacy and certitude as he did', and before it began to dawn upon him that it must somehow be his mission, as G.B. Caird puts it, 'to lead others into the sonship which he himself enjoyed'.[2] Then, as he learnt to read and to ponder the Old Testament Scriptures, 'Abba' no doubt showed him, little by little, more of what that mission would mean. It is, of course, possible that at this stage, as he grew from boy into man, Mary confided in him some

[1] For both Bouyer and Galot, see Eric Mascall, *Theology and the Gospel of Christ* (SPCK, 1977), pp. 137, 150, 167.

[2] G. B. Caird, *Saint Luke* (Pelican Gospel Commentaries, 1963), p.38.

of what had been predicted. But, however this may be, he began to see his mission in terms of those prophecies in Isaiah 40 – 66, echoes of which we hear in Simeon's words recorded in Luke 2:32–33. These spoke of the Servant of the Lord who would bring salvation both to Israel and to 'the nations' through treading the path of vicarious suffering. But he evidently waited for 'Abba' himself to indicate when the time had come for any public ministry to begin.

It was John the Baptist's summons to Israel to repent that must have given Jesus the signal for which he was waiting. He himself, uniquely, stood in no need of repentance, but he seems to have known intuitively that he must identify himself with those who did; so he responded to the Baptist's call, as Israel as a whole ought to have done. And the voice from heaven that he heard at his baptism, followed immediately by the fiery experience of the temptation in the desert, served both to confirm and to put to the test what 'Abba' had been teaching him inwardly from the Scriptures.

Many scholars today, of course, discount the authenticity of the accounts in the Gospels of both the baptism and the temptation. But Caird persuasively insists that 'the pious ingenuity of the early Church could no more have created these stories than the parables of the Good Samaritan and the Prodigal Son'. Then, writing of the baptism, he maintains that this experience 'represented the end of a long development, of deepening appreciation of the divine fatherhood and his own filial responsibility, of growing insight into his mission and the world's need, of meditation on the meaning of the scriptures and their application to himself'.[3]

[3] Caird, *Saint Luke*, pp. 76 ff.

The temptations were the direct sequel to the baptism, both in time and in content. Jesus had just heard a voice saying 'You are my Son', and now he hears another voice saying twice: 'If you really are the Son of God, then this is what you should do.' It seems clear that two of the temptations were not primarily to doubt that he was the Son of God, but to draw the wrong conclusions from this conviction. Thus the temptation to turn stones into loaves of bread was, in essence, to side-step the need to 'learn obedience in the school of suffering', as we, God's adopted children, have to do. Jesus had been 'led by the Spirit in the desert', where 'bread' is not available; but surely he could overcome the pangs of hunger by resort to supernatural power? We read that later in his ministry he did in fact 'have compassion' on a hungry crowd, and multiply a few loaves of bread into enough to meet the need of thousands. But to perform a miracle not out of compassion for others, nor as a sign that the kingdom of God (in the person of the King himself) had come, but only to satisfy his own hunger, was a very different thing. He must await God's indication that this particular time of testing was finished.

It was much the same with the temptation to throw himself down from 'the highest point of the temple' (Luke 4:9), as a short-cut to winning men's allegiance, without the suffering predestined for the Servant of the Lord. But the third temptation (placed second in Luke's account) is not, by contrast, introduced in either Matthew or Luke by the words 'If you really are the Son of God'. The suggestion that he should 'bow down and worship' anyone other than God himself, or forsake obedience to God's will in favour of that of another, was plainly incompatible with being God's eternal Son – just as to do this is to act out of his true character for any of his adopted sons and daughters.

We should probably not think of these temptations as articulated, one by one, on some single occasion only, but as recurring to Jesus, again and again, throughout the long hours of those forty days. It must have been he himself who told his disciples about them in this vivid form, so that they could at least begin to understand. In sum they amounted to a prolonged and very severe testing of his obedience to what had already been revealed to him of his God-given mission. Then, when the forty days were over, we read that the devil 'left him until an opportune time' (Luke 4:13). But there must have been many such times, to some of which I have already made passing reference.

The divine plan

When we turn from the eternal Son to God's many sons and daughters by adoption, we find some examples of the divine plan for a man's life being made crystal clear. This is true in the case of Saul of Tarsus, in the vision on the road to Damascus (and the subsequent elucidation through the divinely commanded visit of Ananias) recorded in Acts 9:3–16. Even so, it was some years before Barnabas sought him out in Tarsus, and brought him to Antioch (Acts 11:25–26). Then it was yet another year, at least, before the church in Antioch felt led by the Holy Spirit to commission Paul and Barnabas to set out on their first missionary journey (Acts 13:1–3). But most of us do not experience such clear-cut directions as Paul received in Damascus, and again in Jerusalem (cf. Acts 22:17–21) – even when we seek God's will most earnestly.

It is interesting to note, in this context, that on

Paul's second missionary journey he and Silas were 'kept by the Holy Spirit from preaching the word in the province of Asia' (as they had clearly thought of doing), and then 'they tried to enter Bithynia, but the Spirit of Jesus would not allow them to' (Acts 16:6–7) – although we are not told by what means the Spirit restrained them on either occasion. The result was that they came to Troas, where Paul had a vision, apparently in a dream, of a Macedonian saying to him, 'Come over to Macedonia and help us.' It is also noteworthy that, at a later date, Paul wrote to the Corinthians that he would visit them again 'after I go through Macedonia' (1 Corinthians 16:5). Then he evidently let them know that he intended to visit them both before and after going to Macedonia (2 Corinthians 1:16); and finally he reverted to his original plan. But when some of them criticized him for insincerity or vacillation, he told them that this was not true, since he had a perfectly good reason for changing his plans (2 Corinthians 1:15–23).

It seems clear, then, that God guides us in many different ways – depending, presumably, on the relevant circumstances, our particular temperaments and our spiritual maturity. Our first concern should be to study and obey the basic principles set forth in the Bible; but I do not think we should normally expect to light upon some specific verse to give us personal marching orders. I have no doubt that the Spirit of God sometimes makes a verse or clause in the passage we happen to be reading stand out with a clarity, insistence or particular relevance that seems to clinch our hesitation about the next step. But I am very dubious about the way in which some Mission Councils used to expect every candidate to produce some such verse. When I myself was considering service in Egypt

I happened to be reading through the Old Testament day by day, and I remember not infrequently meeting warnings such as 'Go not down into Egypt' (Genesis 26:2, AV); but I did not feel that constituted a divine prohibition for me!

Missionary service

In this matter of missionary service I agree with Michael Griffiths that it would be very helpful if we could abandon, so far as possible, the 'volunteer system' which largely prevails today, and get back to the more biblical 'church sponsored' method. Under the volunteer system missionary societies are largely dependent for recruits on those who respond to an appeal. This is apt largely to produce those whose emotions are easily stirred, those who have what they consider to be the right qualifications, and sometimes those who have the sort of temperament which is unsuited to overseas service today. These volunteers then have to be weeded out by some selection committee, which may well make mistakes or cause deep disappointment.

Worse still, perhaps, the most suitable people may not apply at all, either from natural diffidence or because they are already doing a good job at home which they do not consider an appropriate preparation for overseas service. How much better it would be if an experienced missionary were to make a direct approach to a suitable person (as Barnabas and Paul did, and as still happens in some cases today), and if local churches and fellowships were sufficiently sensitive to the needs of the international church as to pray, seek out and support suitable persons from their membership for some appropriate task. But, as Michael Griffiths remarks, this is often not realistically possible in the case of students and others whose circumstances militate against prolonged membership of any one church or fellowship.[4]

The problem of divine guidance, as we have seen, is certainly not confined to the question of overseas service or the home ministry, for Christians are needed in practically every profession or occupation. Christian witness should be exclusively from the outside only in ways of life which, by their very nature, involve those concerned in sin, in the exploitation of others, or in temptations that we may feel constrained to 'flee' rather than to 'fight'. So how are we to know what God's will is for us personally? Since I have myself always found this far from easy, I will try to summarize some of the conclusions to which I have come.

No blueprint

As I see it, there is no blueprint on this subject. Some people grow up with an almost intuitive desire to be a doctor or a nurse; some from their schooldays feel strongly drawn towards research, scholarship or teaching; others are deeply impressed with the need for Christians in politics, journalism or social service; and many turn instinctively to agriculture, industry or some family business. These intuitive inclinations may well be an indication of God's will, provided that we always remain open to his restraint or redirection. Those who find themselves already in some position, profession or occupation when they are

[4] Michael Griffiths, *Give up your small ambitions* (IVP, 1970), pp. 14–25 and *passim*.

converted should normally; Paul teaches, accept this as God's 'appointment', unless the way opens up to something different (*cf.* 1 Corinthians 7:20).

Many factors are relevant to a responsible decision: our family circumstances, our abilities, aptitude and qualifications, our sense of a job that needs to be done. The surest indication of all, perhaps, is a growing inward conviction that this is God's present will for us – for it can scarcely be stated too strongly that God guides most of us step by step. This is certainly my experience. Sometimes a door seems to close in our faces, while another door may open. Sometimes, again, we may have to make a quick decision in the light of what *seems* to be right, but about which we have no great assurance – relying on the divine promise: 'If you stray from the road to right or left you shall hear with your own ears a voice behind you saying, This is the way; follow it' (Isaiah 30:21, NEB).

When we are deeply perplexed we can find peace of mind and heart by reminding ourselves that God is 'Abba', our very own Father; so, if we truly want to do his will, he will not let us go far astray. A father sometimes gives his children explicit instructions, sometimes gives them little more than a hint, and sometimes tells them that it is time for them to make up their own minds in the light of what he has told them, and what they have learnt in the past. This is where we need continually to study biblical principles and learn to draw the necessary deductions. God may even let us learn painful lessons from our wilfulness or mistakes. But he will never wash his hands of us or let us go.

I have seldom, if ever, myself received what I would describe as dramatic guidance. Usually it has been a question of much thought, hesitation and prayer leading to a growing conviction. Sometimes doors have shut, while others have unexpectedly opened. Very often, on looking back, I am convinced that some problem about which I have been much concerned (and even sinfully worried) has been solved by some circumstance, outside intervention or sudden thought in which I can thankfully trace the hand of God. But I have often made mistakes.

What is even more of a problem, I find, is that of knowing – and doing – the will of God day by day, or hour by hour. This is, however, so closely bound up with what it means to 'abide' or 'remain' in Christ that it verges on the second basic question which concerned us so much in my student days: the problem of holiness. But this is so central to the whole life of a Christian that I shall reserve it until somewhat later in this book.

3

Off to Egypt

*Two pioneers * The Egypt General Mission *
Language school * First-year problems * Marriage*

The first chapter of this book ended with my explora-
tory visit to Egypt and engagement to be married.
Happily, Pat and I had some days for prayer and
discussion about God's plans for our future work before
I had to leave for England. My own mind had been
turning to Cairo for some months: chiefly, I think, for
three reasons. First, I had got to know the then Secretary of the Nile Mission Press and heard him speak
about their work. He influenced me greatly. Secondly,
I began to read the biographies of some remarkable
missionaries who had worked, mainly among Muslims,
in that great city – especially those of Temple Gairdner
and Douglas Thornton.

Two pioneers

They were exact contemporaries and became close
friends and colleagues. Gairdner went up to Trinity
College, Oxford, in 1892, and Thornton to Trinity,
Cambridge, in the same year. Both had a Christian
background, and Thornton had what was almost certainly a conversion experience at the age of thirteen; so

41

he threw in his lot with the CICCU from the first. Gairdner, a brilliant man, soon became a member of a highly intellectual circle of friends. Then, during his first Christmas vacation, one of his brothers died; and Temple Gairdner gave his life unreservedly to Christ. It was not till the end of the next term, however, that he had such a vivid experience of Christ as to transform his whole life, and he joined the OICCU. While Gairdner read Mods and Greats, Thornton opted for the Mathematical Tripos; but in his second term he had an illness during which he decided that he was not as good a mathematician as some thought him to be, that he was really more interested in people than in pure science, and that evangelism and missionary concerns must take absolute priority in his life.

Both men went to the camp of the Student Volunteer Missionary Union at the Keswick Convention in the summer of 1893 – and it was there that Thornton had an experience of the fullness of the Holy Spirit, and 'immediately seemed to see Jesus'. Both men signed Student Volunteer Missionary Union forms and became outstanding witnesses in their Universities, Gairdner becoming President of the OICCU in 1895. Subsequently, they both travelled for the SVMU, were ordained and went out to Cairo under the Church Missionary Society. Thornton, a fervent evangelist and an outstanding missionary strategist, died there prematurely (humanly speaking), and it was Gairdner who wrote his biography. Gairdner himself lived for some twenty years more: missionary, pastor, writer, wandering scholar, musician and, above all, lover of the Lord Jesus. His biography was written by Constance Padwick while I was at Cambridge, and his memory was still fragrant in Cairo when I got there.

The third reason why my eyes were turned towards

Cairo was a realistic appraisal of my own assets and debits – and chiefly the latter! I should have been absolutely useless as a pioneer missionary: I could never have built a house, kept a car in order, or done anything practical of that sort. Cairo, on the other hand, made no such demands, and it was the intellectual centre of the Muslim world. Islam, moreover, constituted a major missionary challenge (*cf.* W. H. T. Gairdner, *The Reproach of Islam*), and it was primarily a religion of law.

As usual, Pat's approach was more direct. She had gone through a period of thinking that God might be calling her to Dohnavur, in South India. But she had come to the conclusion that her first duty was to the land in which she had been born, in which she had lived until she came to England to boarding-school, and in which she had spent one year between finishing school and Ridgelands Bible College. A further factor was that her parents had been resident there for many years, as Christians but not missionaries. Her father was agent for several insurance companies. It was rumoured among the European community that Mr and Mrs Stock Givan 'have prayer meetings on the tennis court between sets', but this was wholly apocryphal! They witnessed among those who knew English or French, but their Arabic was not good enough to enable them to reach the great majority of Egyptians. Her mother's Arabic, indeed, was almost a byword!

The Egypt General Mission

So it was to be Egypt. But with which society? As we talked and prayed it over, we came to the conclusion that it was not to be the Nile Mission Press, much though we admired their work. We wanted a more all-round ministry, rather than concentrating almost entirely on the production and distribution of Christian literature. We finally decided to offer ourselves to what was then called the Egypt General Mission, an interdenominational evangelical 'faith mission' (*cf.* pp. 74ff.) modelled somewhat on the lines of what was then the China Inland Mission. So I did deputation work for three months for the Nile Mission Press (with which we always co-operated closely), and put in some reading about Islam, before travelling to Genoa by train to meet Pat and her parents, and drive across Europe with them in their car in time to lead another four-week mission in Criccieth.

The next problem was the capacity in which to offer ourselves to the Egypt General Mission. Their practice at that time was that engaged couples, if they were both accepted as such, must delay marriage for some two years, or at least until the wife had passed two language examinations. This was the course they would prefer; but we were given to understand informally that if we married first and then offered as a married couple, we would *probably* be accepted. This was what both Pat's parents and mine would have liked us to do (and so would we!), since she had only just reached the age of twenty-one and I would not be twenty-four until the end of September. But we felt uneasy about taking this short cut, and concluded (somewhat reluctantly) that it was God's will for us to offer singly; and it was as such that we were accepted. Pat had already done two years of missionary training; and the Council decided that they would regard my four years in the CICCU (College Representative, Secretary, Vice-President and President), together with camps and leading beach missions, as the equivalent of a course at a Bible or Missionary Training College. This was, no doubt, a very dubious decision, but we were naturally glad not to have a longer delay. It is true that I have always learnt whatever I may know by personal reading rather than lectures; but a Training College has much more to it than lectures. So we drove in my Ford, in convoy with Pat's parents' car, to Trieste and took ship for Egypt.

Pat was assigned to Ismailia, where the EGM had both a boys' and a girls' school and a branch of the Evangelical Church of Egypt (with an Egyptian evangelist). She was to live with two lady missionaries, give a little help in the girls' school, but concentrate on learning Arabic. Her first task, of course, was to unlearn the little Arabic she had picked up in her parents' home. I, on the other hand, was to live in a suburb of Cairo in the home of Mr and Mrs Swan, and to drive into the centre of Cairo five days a week to the School of Oriental Studies, a semi-autonomous part of the American University in Cairo, to take Arabic lessons.

George Swan was the only survivor in Egypt of the seven young men who had founded the Egypt General Mission just before the turn of the century. They were members of a considerably larger interdenominational fellowship of young men, working in and around Belfast, who had been meeting for some months for a half-night of prayer. One night all those present felt constrained to sign a paper stating that they were willing to go as missionaries wherever it pleased God to send them. As the weeks passed, moreover, the conviction grew among them that God was going to set aside seven of them to go overseas together, with the others in support. In due course God made it plain to them who should go, and that Egypt was to be their

45

goal. It is a remarkable story, reminiscent of Acts 13:1–3. When I got to know him, George Swan had been suffering severely from asthma for a number of years and was concentrating chiefly on study, writing and translation. He was a shy and retiring man who could bring a meeting alive by his joyful love of the Lord Jesus. He was a close friend of Temple Gairdner of the CMS, and they had been accustomed to going out together for a day of prayer in the desert when some crisis occurred, such as the lapse of a convert.

On their arrival in Egypt the seven young men, all very fervent, had spent a whole night in prayer for the gift of Arabic, so that they could begin their evangelistic work at once. But about 6 a.m. one of them stood up and said: 'I'm going to go and buy a grammar!' – and all the rest eventually had to follow suit. In England I myself had been advised not to make a start with Arabic, but to read some books on Islam – partly because it was thought advisable to learn Arabic as a living language with the right pronunciation. Looking back, I think it would have been a distinct advantage to have had a bare outline of the classical language in my mind; but there was really no facility then to do that in the time available.

Language school

At the School of Oriental Languages it was the custom for students to start with Egyptian colloquial Arabic (written at first in a phonetic script), so that we could begin to ask the way or say a few words in a shop as soon as possible, and then be in a position to learn the literary language through the colloquial rather than through English. The method used was distinctly advanced for over fifty years ago, and consisted of the use of a 'conversation grammar' taught by an English-speaking Egyptian, individual conversation and phonetic practice with a sheikh who had been trained in the Azhar University and knew no English, and a few general lectures in English from missionaries. This method was no doubt excellent in itself, but I found the 'conversation grammar' lessons with an English-speaking Egyptian most frustrating at first. Having learnt such Latin and Greek as I once knew by the traditional method, I would ask inappropriate questions (such as what the aorist might be of a verb which occurred in the present in lesson 1), only to be told that I must wait till lesson 15 or so to find the answer. So after a few days I went to see the Secretary of the School (Arthur Jeffery, a superb scholar from Australia who was subsequently Professor of Arabic at Columbia University, New York) to explain that, if my questions were not answered when I was interested, I should probably be bored when the answer at last came! Fortunately he was sympathetic, and told the teacher concerned that any reasonable questions I might ask should be answered at once.

Arabic is a very difficult language and I am an exceedingly poor linguist, but in time I found it much more possible for me than a language like Chinese or Tamil. I could never have learnt a tonal language, since I have (alas) no ear for music. Nor can I remember disassociated sounds, such as names or new words. But Arabic largely consists of words fundamentally based on three radicals, which reappear in a variety of different forms. So, when one gets a little further, it is possible to remember words by tracing them to their roots, and linking them in one's mind with other words from the same root. But that was far ahead; there were new consonants to master first.

First-year problems

I think many new missionaries find their first year
distinctly difficult – a year in which one can scarcely
communicate with anybody. Spiritually, there is the
lonely and frustrating contrast between this and being
very busy at home – probably including a good deal of
Christian speaking (with the preparation that this
always entails). Mentally, there is the effort and tedium
of learning what may be an unusually difficult language
for hours and hours every day. This is especially so if
one has no linguistic gifts, and may, indeed, not be
used to protracted study. And engagement, of course,
brings an emotional awakening which to many is
wholly new.

In spite of all the warnings given at a training
college, Pat found living with two women presented
many problems and some disillusionment. One of
them was going through a difficult time of life and did
not get on at all well with the other. In my case things
were made much harder by months of consistently
bad sleeping. I have a very active – and restless –
mind; and in this time of stress it became positively
obsessed by foolish (and faithless) worries. One of
these was the thought that marriage would probably
entail the advent of children – which, though certainly
desirable in itself, would clearly come between Pat
and the active missionary service in which single
women were so effectively engaged and for which I
believed she was admirably fitted. The very idea of
'family planning' was something of which I had myself,
I think, scarcely then heard. It was at that time
generally frowned upon by Christians, and was never
discussed in the circles in which I had moved or in the
books I had read. And this whole side of life, with its

implications, was something which I had previously shunned and repressed.

In this state of inability to sleep for more than a very few hours, compounded by loneliness, stress and strain, the teaching about holiness I had absorbed did nothing to help me. It got me nowhere to 'surrender' and leave it to Christ (or the Spirit) to remove my worries and still my restless imagination – at the root of which was, in the last analysis, a lack of faith. How greatly I wish I had then realized that what the New Testament teaches is that the Christian, who has been made alive with Christ and is indwelt by the Holy Spirit, is both commanded and enabled actively to resist the temptation to worry, to get obsessed with futile imaginations, or to give way to sin. Sin is certainly not dead in him, nor is its presence in his body and its 'members' removed (as I then believed that, if I were truly sanctified or had genuinely entered on 'The Victorious Life', it should virtually have been). Instead, those who are 'in Christ' have indeed died both to the guilt and slavery (or dominion) of sin. The last thing we should do is to become excessively introspective and subjective (as I did). We should recognize that sin will always remain in our 'mortal bodies' – with all that this term includes – but must, and can, be resisted.

The teaching I had largely embraced had, of course, admitted that the appetites of the 'body' would remain throughout our earthly life. They were both natural and good in themselves, but could always be exploited, so far as we allowed this, by sin or the tempter. But the natural appetites were not, at that time, my problem. What I did not realize was that the New Testament teaching about the 'members' of our 'mortal body' (*cf.* Romans 6:12–13) is by no means confined to these appetites, since 'the term also includes the mental powers, the power of thought, the power of reason, the power of imagination.... All these belong in a sense to the physical man and are parts, therefore, or members of this mortal body. But the term also includes the emotions.'[1]

This clearly applies to worry (which, I constantly have to remind myself, amounts to lack of faith about, and a mental obsession with, future situations one has never experienced and cannot fully understand).

What I needed in such a situation was not the sort of teaching which amounts to 'come to the clinic, to the spiritual hospital, where your sickness can be cured and your tendency to relapse be removed'. Instead I needed 'military commands' such as 'Fight the good fight of the faith' (1 Timothy 6:12); 'Be on your guard; stand firm in the faith; be men of courage; be strong' (1 Corinthians 16:13); 'Put on the full armour of God, so that...you may be able to stand your ground' (Ephesians 6:13).[2]

What actually happened was that a variety of stresses and strains (slogging away at a difficult language, inability to communicate, lack of exercise, loneliness, imagination and obsessional worries) so affected my ability to sleep that in the summer I was sent to Alexandria, to live with a bachelor missionary whose primary work was running a club for young men. I was to help in his work, to cut down on language study and to go for a swim in the sea before breakfast every morning.

One incident from those weeks may be worth recording. It had occurred to my senior missionary to

[1] D. M. Lloyd-Jones, *Romans 6: The New Man* (Banner of Truth, 1972), p.166.
[2] *Cf.* Lloyd-Jones, *Romans 6*, p.174.

start an unaggressive form of Christian witness in a strongly Muslim part of the city. So he bought a little shop leading to an inner room, turned the outer room into a Christian bookshop and furnished the inner room as a place where the books could be read rather than bought. A young Egyptian was put in charge, and all went well for a time. Then, as so often happens, opposition was aroused and things began to look dangerous.

In these circumstances my friend rightly thought that the young Egyptian should not be left alone, and we agreed to take it in turns to keep him company. I happened to be there one Thursday afternoon when the schools closed prior to the Muslim Friday; a large and hostile crowd began to gather outside, and I could not understand what they were saying or intending to do. So, when a number of them came into the shop, I told the young Egyptian to close the shutters, while I managed to get those who had entered to go out, and we shut the shop. The crowd allowed us both to leave (probably because of my presence), but threw a few stones at us. Fortunately they had not played cricket and were very bad shots! But we were glad to mount a passing tram. Later, my senior missionary got a friendly Egyptian carpenter to go to the area and to listen to the gossip. The rumour was that the two Englishmen had hypnotic powers which virtually compelled people to enter the shop, where we proceeded to offer each of them five (or was it ten?) pounds, together with an 'American wife', if they would become Christians! But to provide them with American wives might well have proved even more difficult than the financial largesse.

Marriage

In the event the problem of my health was solved by two decisions of the Field Council of our Mission. First, they agreed that Pat should take the stipulated first two language examinations at one sitting. This she successfully did, being a much better linguist than I am. She was only mildly helped by the fact that, when her Egyptian examiner asked her if she could compare the current position of women in Egypt with that of some decades earlier (none too easy in Arabic for a novice), her American examiner burst in: 'But the lady wasn't in existence at that time!' Secondly, the doctors decided that I must go on leave to recuperate. So the Field Council agreed that we should get married from Pat's parents' home in Alexandria on 31 May 1933 and sail for Europe and England next day – not primarily on honeymoon but on some four months' sick leave.

Incidentally, many members of the European community, as well as a number of missionaries, attended our wedding. Some of the former, although friends or acquaintances of Pat's parents, were quite unknown to either of us. They generously gave us more clocks than we could ever use and a variety of silver pieces wholly unsuited to missionary life. So, before sailing next day, we returned some of the presents which had no sentimental significance for us to the shop from which we knew they must have been bought. In exchange we were given credit from which, when we returned to Egypt, we were able to procure necessities over quite a period!

4

New experiences

*Honeymoon * Money matters * A Cairo flat *
Hazel arrives * Preaching in Arabic*

On the day after our wedding we set sail in the evening
from Alexandria to Genoa, on one of the medium-
sized ships of the Lloyd-Triestino Line. Pat was still
only twenty-two, and I remember how intrigued she
was to find her name on our cabin door as *Signora*
Anderson! Her parents came on board to say goodbye,
and we were off.

Honeymoon

We had a very pleasant trip of some four days to
Genoa and then took a train to Streza, on the west
shore of Lake Maggiore, where we spent the first week
of our honeymoon. We were both pretty tired, so we
did little more that was intrinsically exciting than walk
by the lakeside and sample a few restaurants. Our
chief preoccupation was to get used to our new life. We
started to read the Bible and pray together from the
first, as most Christian couples probably do. But it
took us far, far too long to discover that shared devotional reading and intercession, while vital to any
Christian marriage, can never wholly take the place of

individual study and meditation.

At the end of that week we took the train to Lausanne, to visit the *pension* where Pat had spent a year immediately after her schooling in England. It was run by two great friends, one a devout evangelical Englishwoman, and the other a lively, and by no means devout, Frenchwoman; and Pat had had to learn to stand alone during her year there, since almost all the other girls were set on combining the study of French with a gay and carefree life! They were very kind to us and lent us a car to drive around the lake (and incidentally make up our minds where we should stay on our return journey). The vagaries of memory – or now, in my case, of the faculty to forget – never cease to intrigue me; and I can still remember a simple evening meal in the open air, chiefly consisting of quantities of delicious Swiss peaches, then just at their best.

After two or three days we travelled on to England, to my parents' home in Reigate. Pat had hardly got to know them during the previous summer, when she had been staying with her parents on a visit to England – so she found this first visit quite a strain. Since they had not been able to be present at our wedding in Alexandria, they staged a garden party for some of my relatives and local friends, to take the place of a wedding reception. I was much the youngest of the family and an only son; so we were conscious of a certain tension on the part of my mother when I showed myself absorbed in Pat. This made it difficult for both of us: for Pat, for obvious reasons, and for me, because I had to try to tread somewhat of a tightrope!

After a few days my parents lent us a car and we drove to Streetly, where we stayed for a week in a small hotel right beside the Thames, as the second half of our honeymoon. We were able to sit and read in the garden, drive about, and bathe in the far from pellucid river at a temperature that would horrify me today. I remember one incident when we went shopping in Reading and I inadvertently fell backwards down some stairs. No lasting damage was done, but when we got back to the hotel it seemed wise to call a doctor – and Pat (who thought she had been behaving as one who had been married for years) was quite chagrined when he turned to her and said, 'I'm sorry you are having trouble with him already!'

Soon after getting back to my parents' home in Reigate we set out again, in this somewhat elderly car, for Wales, where we had booked a week as paying guests in a cottage up in the hills reasonably near Criccieth. I cannot remember how we had heard of it, and it proved very far from luxurious; but we had time to walk and think. Pat had been a 'walker' for years, since her father virtually never went a day without a walk; but my walking had been almost exclusively confined to golf courses – where, on one occasion, I had played seventy-two holes in one day. When allowance is made for a very wayward route from tee to green, that must add up to quite a mileage.

Next we stayed with my parents in Criccieth itself for part of the beach mission. It felt odd to attend as outsiders, as it were, a series of services in which we had both been very active during two previous years, when we had truly seen God's blessing as we claimed that he would indeed 'show himself strong in the behalf of them whose *heart* is perfect toward him' (however immature and far from perfect their accomplishments might be). We had also learnt something of the power of united intercession and private heart-searching. But there were still old friends in the team, and it was good to see them again.

I chiefly remember two other items on this visit to England. The first was a short visit to Aldeburgh, the little town where I was born, where my parents had built a holiday house near the top of 'Big Steps', and where we had spent many summer holidays. This was, of course, many years before the town attained fame through its Music Festival. In the cemetery that surrounds the parish church stands a gravestone – with the verse 'He shall gather the lambs in his arms and carry them in his bosom; and shall gently lead those that are with young'. Here my brother, who would have been two years older than I had he not died in infancy, is buried.

Aldeburgh was an old-fashioned fishing town with a steep, shingled beach and Victorian bathing-machines, on wheels. These were pushed well into the sea so that the exceedingly modest middle-aged women of that era could climb down the steps on the seaward side straight into the water – and then, if they could not swim, they could hold on to ropes while they bobbed about in the waves! This beach was furnished with a deep barbed-wire fence and other defences during the First World War, lest the Germans should cross the North Sea and make a landing. I can still remember, from those childhood years, how my two sisters, who were several years older than I, planned to put me into the massive old-fashioned copper in the kitchen when we heard that the Zeppelins were coming. This did not appeal to me at all, and I never actually suffered from such an indignity.

Finally, before leaving England, Pat and I went to see an eminent Harley Street physician who had lectured to Pat at Ridgelands and was very missionary-minded. He passed me as fit to go back to Egypt, provided I first had another three or four weeks' holiday on the continent, and he also confirmed that Pat was now pregnant. So we went to the area of Glion, Vevey and Montreux – descending to lower altitudes, but less economical hotels, as the weather became progressively colder.

Money matters

We had one other 'new experience' before we got back to Egypt. On leaving England I had taken as much money as I thought should suffice till we sailed from Venice to Alexandria, but we found Switzerland unexpectedly expensive, even at the very modest standard of our living. Always by disposition a pessimist, it was not long before I felt we should write to my parents for some more. Pat, by contrast, is a born optimist; she thought we could just about make it, and felt we should not reveal our financial incompetence so soon! Shortly before we left Montreux for Venice, where we planned to spend the last four or five days before sailing, she realized that our situation was becoming somewhat precarious, and agreed that I should ask my father to send a little more money to us poste restante at a major post office in Venice.

We got to Venice, found a quite pleasant and fairly economical hotel, and I went to the post office each day to ask if they had a letter for me. But the answer was always 'No'. This certainly clouded our brief visit to Venice, since it looked as though we should run short by a very small sum, however economically we lived. We even resorted to going to two or three jewellers to ask what they would give for a few pieces of jewellery of no intrinsic or sentimental value to Pat; but we soon found that the price of selling such items is very different from that of buying them. So finally I had the indignity of going to the British Consul, explaining our predicament, and asking him to lend me a few pounds which we would repay by cheque as soon as we reached Egypt.

This he did without undue difficulty, and we found that we could almost, but not quite, have got through without it. When, moreover, I wrote to my father asking him why he had not sent it, I found that he had in fact done so at once, by telegram. I had not been intelligent enough to think of money (or credit) being sent by such means, and the post office had not thought of replying to my questions about a letter addressed to me in terms not of a letter but a telegram! So we had denied ourselves several simple pleasures (and I, in particular, had endured considerable anxiety) while the funds we needed were all the time available. Our prayers had indeed been answered, but in a way which we had neither expected nor recognized. I have no doubt the sense of destitution and indignity taught me a lesson I needed to learn, but I must confess that anxiety, of one sort or another, has all too often got me down.

A Cairo flat

After landing at Alexandria, we paid a very short visit to Pat's parents and then went to the Mission's headquarters at Zeitoun. Our first job was to rent a suitable flat not far from the School of Oriental Studies, furnish it and find a Berber man-servant (as almost all foreigners did then), so that we could get ahead with learning Arabic. The Mission helped us enormously by loaning us the services of one of its most senior and trusted employees, Sheikh Sidraq (the title Sheikh in this context means that he was an elder in the Evangelical Church). It was splendid to have someone with such experience and complete integrity to help us locate, inspect and negotiate the rent for a suitable flat. True, he blackballed several of our ideas as 'too expensive'; but this was really all to the good because we had barely what we needed to live on. On the second or third day we found a flat in a good location, of the right size and with a lift which usually worked – although nothing about it could be regarded as in any way impressive. Besides the front door, it had a kitchen door which opened on to an iron staircase that wound its way round the kitchen doors of all the flats and up to the roof, where some of the tenants kept fowls. Each day a block of ice was brought round to service our 'ice-box', and among other would-be salesmen was one who sold live chickens. The story was told that, on one occasion, he had first gone up to the roof, caught two of the fowls, and then come down and sold them to their rightful owner! All the other inhabitants, except one Englishwoman, were Egyptians.

We got our furniture from a number of sources. Some of it was sent out from England – such as a 'compactum' I had used for years, and sundry items we had bought from wedding-present money. These came by sea and rail to Cairo station, and we then hired a man with an open donkey cart to collect it. I went with him in order to see that things were not stolen en route. The sight of an Englishman, clad in a (comparatively) immaculate white cotton suit, sitting on top of various crates as we wound our slow way through the busy streets of Cairo, seemed to cause considerable amusement! For the most part, however, we bought furniture at auction sales, usually from English or American people leaving the country. This was rather fun, and I soon learnt that, if one showed too much interest in any item, the price would be run up by some colleague of the auctioneer. So one had to put in a sudden, but not too eager, bid – often no more than a languid nod – at the last moment. I remember that we secured quite a nice dining-room table, complete with six good chairs, for about £12! We also bought, or ordered, some bedroom furniture made from cheap wood, and then had it painted green for our room, or blue for the spare room, which suited a hot climate remarkably well and needed little care.

We both went to the School of Oriental Studies for the first few months. The lady missionary responsible for keeping tabs on language students in our mission was very keen that Pat should take the third examination, and did not seem to realize – even a few weeks before Hazel's advent – why Pat said she could not. Pat was then too shy to call her attention to the obvious reason! But this would not have provided any excuse for me, and I went on to take five examinations at the School, and then to read a little Islamic philosophy in Arabic with a group of missionaries and more advanced students. It was during these years of struggling with Arabic that I first learnt the discipline of steady, conscientious work – very unlike my rhythm of almost complete idleness (academically speaking), followed by weeks of unnatural 'swotting', in my Cambridge days – and I think I can honestly say that this discipline has been maintained throughout life. What I still find exceedingly difficult is to divide my time and interests between a number of different duties, rather than become almost completely absorbed in one.

Hazel arrives

It was during our earlier months in the Garden City that we made contact with a well-known English gynaecologist and obstetrician to ask him to take care of Pat's pregnancy and delivery. He was a somewhat elderly bachelor whose rooms were full of lovely oriental rugs, piled almost on top of each other. When we commented on their beauty, I remember, he asked if we would not like to borrow one or two for the baby-to-be to play on – a kindly offer which we thankfully, but unhesitatingly, refused. He told us that some of his patients had accepted this offer; so we wondered what sort of babies they could have had! When Pat's time came, she had a delightful room in the Anglo-American Hospital. The nurse who looked after her was quite a tartar, but *very* efficient; and we remained in contact with her for some years. In those days they kept mothers and babies in the hospital for three weeks, rather than three days or less; and I often had tea there looking out on the Sporting Club golf course, where our much loved Bishop Gwynne was sometimes to be seen.

Hazel was a bright, happy baby, who seemed to conform quite naturally to all that our then textbook on the subject (the now antiquated Truby King) recommended. So Pat and I began to think that parents whose children were fractious and difficult just did not 'know their stuff'. It was only when we had a second daughter, who did not take at all kindly to this regime, that we had to have another think. But that was more than two and a half years ahead. Meanwhile Hazel absorbed most of Pat's time – feeding, bathing and taking her out, and washing endless nappies. I am no adept with children myself, but I do love babies (who do not ask endless questions and will stay where one puts them). I remember carrying or wheeling Hazel about while practising the pronunciation, and trying to memorize the vast vocabulary, of our would-be adopted language. But the burden fell much more heavily on Pat, who spent hours sitting beside Hazel's pram in a nearby garden during the hot weather, often wondering what she had come out as a missionary to do.

This was just what I had dreaded when we were engaged; but she was able to say a few words to other women in French or Arabic, and Hazel was a most rewarding baby. Fortunately our Berber man-servant did the marketing, cooking and cleaning; and now that Hazel had arrived we got a change from the endless *'adas* (Egyptian lentil) soup which we had previously had almost exclusively for the first course of our evening meal (since it was reputed to be particularly good for expectant mothers). We also had a dear old Sudanese woman who came in for a couple of hours some evenings, when Hazel was in bed, in order to 'baby-sit' while we went out for a breather — often in a rickety old *'arabiyya* cab, since Pat had recurrent bouts of fever at that time, and found the Cairo summer very tiring. We would get home to find this woman sitting quietly in the dark; and when we asked her why she never switched the light on, she said she could not read, so why waste our electricity if the baby was sleeping!

That summer we had a holiday in Jerusalem, which we could reach by railway. We stayed for the first two or three days in the American Colony — founded in the last century by people who were convinced that Christ was going to come again almost at once, and

62

who went to Jerusalem to await his advent. Now, however, the second or third generation of these settlers were kind and good, but not noticeably spiritual. Very soon, however, we were invited to share the house and garden of an outstanding Christian bank manager, Stanley Clark, and his wife. They were themselves away on holiday, and had left their house in charge of a young Englishwoman, recently converted through their influence, with whom we stayed.

This was a very happy arrangement in which we simply paid our share of the running expenses, while the garden was a great boon to all of us – Pat, Hazel and myself. We also had some Christian fellowship, chiefly with friends of our hostess. Unhappily, Pat was afflicted, on and off, with bouts of fever from trouble in breast-feeding; but a gynaecologist in Jerusalem encouraged her (probably mistakenly) to persist. So at intervals I had to nurse Pat and do everything (except feeding!) for Hazel. But I managed to read through Luke's Gospel in Arabic, *inter alia*, in that garden. Among other guests we were able to entertain my former Headmaster, then Principal of Wycliffe Hall, Canon Ralph Taylor – subsequently Bishop of Sodor and Man.

Preaching in Arabic

Back in Cairo, I remember preaching my first sermon in Arabic, in the Gairdner Memorial Church in Old Cairo. It is a beautiful little church, where they sang many of the canticles and hymns set to the Eastern music which Gairdner himself had adapted for the purpose. Almost immediately afterwards I was asked to preach in a Pentecostal church in Cairo. This provided me with a salutary lesson; for when I had finished my sermon the Pastor first said what a privilege it was to have a foreigner preach to them in their own language, and in the 'classical' (that is, the literary) language at that, and then added: 'In case some of you did not understand, what he said was....' Whether he really remembered what I had tried to say I could not tell, for I found his torrent of colloquial Arabic almost as difficult to follow as his congregation had found my halting attempts to speak the literary language.

When the next summer came we were to go to England for a half-furlough – since my intended work among students fitted in much better with three months every two years, during their summer vacation, than with the usual six months every four years. But we had been told that we were to move to Ismailia, beside the Suez Canal, when we returned, to understudy the missionary in overall charge of the work there. So we had to put our furniture into store in Zeitoun, travel down to Alexandria, and then go by ship to Italy and by train across the continent. It is never very easy to stay with relatives and friends with a baby in tow, but Hazel was very well behaved and that furlough did us all a lot of good. The major snag about three-month furloughs in the summer, however, is that there is little chance to do any real deputation work.

5

Ismailia

A new home ∗ *Outreach in Abu Sweir* ∗
Sheikh Kamil's story ∗ *Summer holiday* ∗
Two New Zealanders ∗ *A second daughter*

Ismailia was unlike any other town I had seen in
Egypt. Its residential area, with its streets lined by
flowering trees, was dominated by the attractive
bungalows occupied by the Suez Canal pilots and
some of its senior officials. Each was surrounded by
cool and spacious verandas and a beautiful, well-kept
garden. At that time the pilots were almost exclusively
expatriates and largely kept themselves to themselves.
The town lies on the banks of Lake Timsah, a small
natural lake which lies about half-way along the Canal,
where the ships, which continually pass through it,
frequently stop for about ten minutes while one pilot
relieves another. There was also quite a pleasant little
shopping-centre, with a distinctly French flavour and
a number of Indian shops.

The Mission building (with its boys' school, missionary quarters and small boarding department)
stood at one end of a sizeable compound with a small
branch of the Evangelical Church at the other,
separated by quite a large playground. The boys'
school had an Egyptian headmaster and staff, the
church an Egyptian evangelist, and the boarding

department an Egyptian matron. But a senior missionary with his wife were in ultimate charge. A few minutes' walk away stood the girls' school, with its missionaries and Egyptian staff. This school was nearer to the railway line which seemed to divide the Canal area, and the older parts of the town, from the mushrooming medley of smaller, and generally poorer, Egyptian houses. It was in the girls' school that Pat had worked before we were married. Its staff always attended the Evangelical Church, and also came over for other meetings in the main compound.

A new home

Pat and I were able to rent the top flat in a two-storeyed house next to the Mission building. It was a pleasant flat approached by outdoor stairs which led into the middle of a long, rather narrow corridor. The corridor had various rooms on each side and terminated at both ends in a veranda – the one to the north glassed-in, and the one to the south open. We liked it very much. I vividly remember the day when we had gone out for a walk in the cool of the evening and got back just in time to see two missionaries from the girls' school climbing our outside stairs, and we suddenly remembered that we had invited them to dinner that evening. So Pat entertained them while I asked our Berber factotum to water the soup, divide the little available meat into four portions instead of two, interpose a course of scrambled eggs and end with both sweets and cheese! We have never, before or since, had so many – or such minute – courses. We thought it would be rude to say we had forgotten, and they asked no questions; but I think they must have guessed.

While our senior missionary was there I had very few routine duties. I went to school prayers every day and sometimes led them, and attended the church each Sunday morning and occasionally preached. On Sunday evenings we sometimes went to an English service at a pleasant little chaplaincy church. Twice a week I took the boys to a football field for a game of football in the early evening. This was sometimes rather difficult, since the ground was not private and boys of mixed ages from the town would often come, shout, and even invade the pitch.

Outreach in Abu Sweir

For the rest of my time I tried to get ahead with my Arabic reading and take as many opportunities as possible to converse with Egyptians. I regularly accompanied the Egyptian evangelist on his visits to a village named Abu Sweir, where there was a Royal Air Force station. Here we would go round paying calls on the villagers and the numerous Egyptian employees of the RAF, and gather as many as we could to a meeting. Most of those who came were Copts, but we tried to reach as many Muslims as possible. There was no local Coptic priest. Although we were always exceedingly careful not to raise any points of denominational controversy at these meetings, the Coptic bishop in whose diocese the village fell would occasionally send an emissary to try to stop the Copts from attending our meetings. But his threats did not seem to have very much effect, partly because we (unlike the bishop's emissary) were not interested in collecting money. I noticed, however, that our evangelist would almost always buy a dozen or so small Egyptian eggs (which he would then tie up in a handkerchief) just before we left, since, he told me, they were marginally cheaper than in Ismailia. I always, of course, travelled with him third class (which is very uncomfortable, noisy and often insalubrious on Egyptian trains); but it was the paltry saving on the eggs which made me think.

The next year, when I was elected to the Field Council of the Mission, I took this matter up. A senior lady missionary who came from a different part of Egypt was greatly concerned that none of our Egyptian employees should be paid more than the pittance that the lower grades of government clerks of a similar educational background received, since she insisted that to go into Christian work should always represent a material sacrifice rather than any financial advantage. To this my reply was that we expected our evangelist to produce a worth-while sermon nearly every Sunday. How could he do this if he could not afford to buy a few books and study by electric light in the evenings—besides meeting the needs of his wife and growing family? Quite an argument ensued, which went substantially my way. All the same, I still felt uneasy on the rare occasions when the evangelist and his wife insisted on entertaining us with the hospitality Egyptians love to show.

One more incident about Abu Sweir may be worth recording. During the visits we paid prior to the meeting, I had always been warned to drink only coffee or tea (since then one could be tolerably certain that the water had been boiled). One hot summer day, however, I was sitting in a little shop talking to the owner (who was a cobbler who made shoes to measure) when a man came past selling bottles of fizzy lemonade. So, when my host urged me to have one, I succumbed. I was intrigued and greatly impressed, however, when he went to the back of the shop and washed the glass, into which he was going to pour it, with a care which exceeded my wildest expectations. It was only when I had half finished the glass that I noticed a number of very small, dark objects sticking to its inner circumference — and it was some minutes more before I realized what they were. The fact was that my host had previously been using the glass for a belated shave, and the specks were such remnants of his beard as he had not been able to wash away. But I comforted myself with the thought that they seemed to be fairly static!

On the road from Ismailia to a British army camp there was a Soldiers' Home, run by a delightful elderly Irish woman with two younger helpers. They provided simple refreshments, comfortable chairs and games of draughts or chess, and, above all, acted as confidantes and advisers to men long separated from their wives, mothers, children and girl-friends. They did a splendid work, and had the tribute, on one occasion, of a marching column facing right in salutation as it passed. Pat and I both accepted fairly frequent invitations to speak at their Sunday evening meetings, and Pat occasionally went to teach some of the men a little French. In any case she was in greater demand than I on Sunday evenings, since it was far more of a novelty for them to meet and listen to a young woman of their own race than to yet another man.

It was during that first year in Ismailia that Pat became pregnant again. She came under the care of a fine French gynaecologist at the local French hospital overlooking the Canal. He was a sincere and practising Roman Catholic who was working there as a vocation. I fancy, too, it was through him that we were admitted to the 'Jardin des enfants' – a French club beside the lake where one could change into swimming wear, bathe, sit about in the shade of little mobile huts, and have a picnic – a great treat from time to time. One day we saw crowded Italian troopships steaming through the Canal to Ethiopia and Eritrea, with the local Italian population mobilized to cheer them at one stage along the Canal and then to leap into cars or coaches to repeat the same performance again at the next stage!

Sheikh Kamil's story

One other memory stands out from the early summer of that year. Our senior missionary, in co-operation with the evangelist and headmaster of the boys' school, had arranged for a week of *Nahdah* (revival or renewal meetings) to be held every evening in the playground. Open-air Christian preaching in the streets or in any public place was forbidden in Egypt, but Christian meetings in or on private property were allowed; and the playground, which could seat two or three hundred easily, was an ideal site on a warm evening. A succession of different speakers had been booked, but far the most impressive and interesting, to me at least, was Sheikh Kamil Mansur. He was formerly a Sheikh of the Azhar (the famous Mosque and University in Cairo), now an evangelist in the Evangelical Church, and beyond question the leading Muslim convert in Egypt.

It was the practice then (and probaby is still) for a convert from Islam in Egypt not only to take a Christian first name but a second Christian name as well – with the regrettable consequence that their families could claim that the convert had renounced them rather than the other way round. The practice pre-

70

sumably grew up from the fact that there are very few names in Egypt which are common to both Muslims and Christians, so one can usually know at once, from a person's very name, whether he or she is a Muslim or a Christian. This total change of name certainly signified a break with the past, but it also meant that the person concerned would be regarded as a Christian by birth by any who were not personal acquaintances – a fact that made life distinctly easier for the convert, but failed to provide, or provoke, a much-needed testimony.

Sheikh Kamil, however, was not that sort of man, and I was thrilled to hear the testimony he gave to a very large audience, many of them Muslims. 'The other day', he said, 'I was walking with the pastor of the village where I was born right past the mosque where I had my primary education. So I asked him to wait a few minutes while I went and found the corner where I used to sit, with the prayer mat I remembered so well. And I could not help, there and then, lifting up my heart to God in praise for bringing me into the light of the knowledge of him that is Christ Jesus.'

Either on that or a subsequent visit to Ismailia he stayed with us, and told us more of his life story. His elder brother, Micka'il Mansur, had been a brilliant young Muslim scholar who had determined to write a book which would finally demolish the Christian faith. He was sufficiently intelligent, however, to know that one could not demolish a faith which one did not understand; so, against all advice, he had asked a local Coptic priest to explain to him what Christians really believed. By the providence of God this priest was intelligent and well taught, and within two or three years the elder brother was convinced and converted. He was so widely known as a rising Muslim theologian, however, that this priest – and others – feared the storm of opposition that his baptism would provoke; so he sought, and received, baptism at the hands of a Roman Catholic missionary.

It was not long before he found that this was not his spiritual home, and he was given employment by the American (United Presbyterian) Mission as a teacher of Arabic in one of their schools. Soon, moreover, he started to hold a weekly meeting, especially designed for students from the Azhar, in their church in Ezbekiah (one of the quarters of Cairo). Each week he would not only proclaim the gospel, but also answer a series of questions – a task for which he was almost uniquely qualified. But the opposition was intense; and his younger brother, then himself a student at the Azhar, told me how he and some other students went along one night, armed with daggers and knives, to kill him. He was urged to avail himself of a comparatively safe asylum through a door at the back of the rostrum which led into the house of an American missionary. But this he refused. Instead, he walked straight down into the audience, opened his outer robe and said: 'Kill me if you wish. I am not better than the One who died for me.' But, whether by the restraining hand of God or by reason of the psychological impact of his courage (or, indeed, both), they did not lay hands on him.

On another occasion, Sheikh Kamil told me, he had been waiting to kill his brother, as a disgrace to the family name, as he was walking home to his house; but again something (or Someone?) restrained him. Somewhat later, he called at his brother's home, expecting to find that the American Mission had made his work and his witness financially worth while. In point of fact, however, he found him living very simply, and burst out: 'You fool, to give up your reputation, your prospects and your family for *this*!' But his brother, Sheikh Micka'il Mansur, quietly replied: 'I would not barter one hour of the peace of heart I now enjoy for all these things you say I have given up.' 'You fool!' the younger brother spat out again, and stormed out of the house. But he could not forget that quiet testimony about peace of heart.

This prompted him to visit his elder brother again some time later and to say, 'Give me one of your Bibles.' This he gladly did, and before very many months had passed my friend too was convinced and converted. He soon became as fearless a witness as his brother, always willing to go to the help of any convert from Islam. I shall always treasure his memory (and, through him, that of his elder brother) as two outstanding examples of the 'many sons' whom God has been 'bringing to glory' from Islam. This is why I have allowed myself this long parenthesis in my story.

Summer holiday

At the height of the summer Pat and I had to send off most of our furniture to mission headquarters in Cairo to be stored, since we were very soon to move into the mission house next door to carry on in the absence of our senior missionary and his wife. Her first child had died in the course of a long and very painful delivery, and she had to go home, soon after she again became pregnant, so that she could be under constant expert care; and her husband went home to Ireland in time for her second (and happy) delivery. But before we moved in we went off for our summer holiday in Alexandria, where we shared Pat's parents' house, during their absence in England, with her younger brother. In the course of the drive down, along the desert road between Cairo and Alexandria, we went over a bump which very nearly caused Pat to have a miscarriage. But this, thank God, was averted.

It was an enormous boon that her parents put their house, servants, tennis court and bathing cabin (and sometimes a car) at our disposal on this and certain other occasions; and after a few days' rest Pat recovered and was able to lounge on the beach and bathe. I too enjoyed bathing and tennis; but I was also able, through the kindness of Sheikh Kamil Mansur, who was on holiday not far away, to read through an Arabic text on Islamic law under his expert guidance. But I must confess that I found that summer, and much of the time in Ismailia, a time of spiritual strain, and all too often of inward defeat, rather than joyful progress.

Two New Zealanders

We were back in Ismailia by the end of July for another 'new experience' – to have first one and then another young man from New Zealand, both even newer missionaries than we were, to live with us for some four months to study Arabic. We found both of them most congenial, and they have remained life-long friends. Through them, too, we learnt at first hand how a so-called 'faith mission' really works. (I have put the term 'faith mission' in quotation marks because it would be monstrous to suggest that missions who deal with financial questions in a rather different way do not also work by faith.) We had not ourselves experienced any practical application of these principles up till then, since my father had given me a little capital in War Loan shares. From the income of

74

this, when free from British income tax, we were just about able to live – with help, I should add, from my parents when we went on furlough, and from the use of Pat's family home for a summer holiday when we did not go to England.

The principles of the Mission were simply these. No money was ever to be solicited, and no collection to be taken at any meeting on the Mission's initiative. Each month the Home Council in London, in concert with Auxiliary Councils elsewhere, would notify the Field Council how much money was available for transmission to Egypt after meeting home expenses. Out of this, together with any income from our hospital and schools, all debts (for the salaries of our Egyptian fellow workers, the rent or repair of premises, and the like) were immediately paid. But no 'debt' as such was owed to any missionary, since they had all joined the Mission on the explicit understanding that they and their families would be dependent on God alone. What they would receive through the Mission, therefore, was the appropriate monthly 'allowance' for each man, woman and child, or such proportion of that allowance as was available. Quite often, at that time, they went somewhat short; and, although this shortage was often made up if sufficient funds came in during the first few days of the next month (or, at times, by specifically designated donation), this was not always the case. In principle, the Mission never went into debt.

When a single missionary, like our two New Zealand friends, came to live with a family, or with other single workers, they would pay so much a month towards housekeeping expenses. So we told our missionary guests what we reckoned their living expenses would come to. But we insisted that they must never feel in the least embarrassed if their allowances were short, since we would gladly meet any deficit. The fact is, however, that month by month they were able to pay. We would, of course, know when allowances were short and would demur. But time after time they would say that they had received some gift straight from a supporter, in New Zealand or elsewhere, and that the Lord had in fact let them 'lack nothing' in regard to the necessities of life. This is one of the great virtues of this form of 'faith principle', because these two young men certainly learnt lessons of financial trust in God in which we ourselves had no practical share – and all such experiences play a valuable part in the training of God's adopted sons and daughters.

All the same, I must confess to a certain uneasiness about the basic desirability of this sort of 'faith principle', except in the case of those who see a special reason to adopt it. George Müller was so strict in his adherence to it that he sometimes refused to publish his accounts, because these might constitute a mute and unintended appeal. We must, however, remember that his stated aim, in running his homes in Bristol, was not only – or even perhaps primarily – to succour orphans, but to prove to an unbelieving world that we still have a God who answers prayer. Again, Hudson Taylor, the founder of the China Inland Mission, adopted very similar principles; but he did this, he said, because he did not want to divert funds from any other work in China, and he had the basic conviction that 'God's work, done in God's way, will never lack God's provision'. Then, in the next few years, a number of small interdenominational missions proliferated, most of which adopted these principles (in varying degrees of stringency) without – I suspect – any deep or independent study of the biblical principles.

Now it is clearly biblical to avoid going into debt

where this is humanly possible – although it is exceedingly difficult on occasions to book passages in advance without at least notionally being under an obligation that, apart from God's intervention, one might not be able to meet. This is, of course, true of all 'faith missions' in so far as rents and the salaries of indigenous fellow-workers are concerned. There is abundant authority in the Bible for the fact that God can, and normally does (but *cf.* Hebrews 11:35b-40), supply our every need; but there is no accompanying injunction (that I know of) that the need concerned is to be made known to God alone. Paul made no bones whatever about pressing his Gentile converts to make contributions towards the fund he was raising to relieve the needs of poor Christians in Jerusalem; and there is, to my mind, something artificial about appealing for new recruits as doctors, nurses, teachers, church builders or whatever, with a studied silence about the funds these new recruits, or some other proposed extension of the work, will inevitably involve.

It seems to me, moreover, somewhat equivocal for a mission, while claiming to be a 'faith mission' in the George Müller or Hudson Taylor tradition, to require its candidates to raise 'sponsored' support. On deputation work it must be exceedingly difficult, or even artificial, for them to avoid making their need known. I myself prefer a system which provides that all needs, financial and otherwise, are frankly made known, but without any such solicitation as is dishonouring to God and his promises. Such a system would avoid going into debt, or even embarking 'in faith' on projects for which funds are not already available, unless God has given reason for corporate confidence – whether by promises from without or deep assurance from within – that they will be provided as they are needed.

Furthermore, it would not claim any degree or definition of faith which some consider superior to that of others, while yet allowing, or countenancing in its fellowship, any practice which comes dangerously near the line.

This said, I must confess that those of us who have certain means of our own miss much of the training and inspiration that those who have to wait continually on their heavenly Father, even for 'pocket money', undoubtedly receive. A radical, but somewhat questionable, solution would be to follow the example of C. T. Studd and his wife who, inspired by the story of the rich young ruler, gave away all their resources. I continually ask myself to what extent we should retain *control* of such capital (while lending part of it, maybe, to a charitable organization that can make full use of its tax-free dividends) as would provide for a long terminal illness of either or both of us, or deprive us of the ability to extend help, regularly or from time to time, to persons or causes that are in special need.

A second daughter

Be that as it may, our second daughter, Janet, was born in December, 1936. At the end she came so fast that we got to the hospital only just in time! Pat was spared the bouts of fever, which beset her intermittently over the first seven months of Hazel's life, by the fact that the doctor in charge responded to a breast abscess by categorically forbidding her to continue breast feeding. With two children, we now indulged in engaging a Christian 'nanny' from Switzerland – but we found that, whether because of her natural disposition or the assiduous attentions of her nurse, Janet did not take at all kindly to the regime recommended by Truby King. She refused to go to sleep at the prescribed times, and made life very difficult when staying with my relatives, or elsewhere, on our three-month furlough when she was between six and nine months old.

But before that our senior missionaries had returned to Ismailia, and we had moved back to Cairo – taking a furnished flat for the few weeks before furlough to save yet another move of our very peripatetic furniture. My chief memory of that flat is that I developed mumps – probably caught in visiting – and that the danger of the children catching this put all our travel plans in jeopardy. So I persuaded Pat to take the girls and the Swiss nurse down to Alexandria to her parents, while I kept pretty strictly in bed, with food provided by our Berber man-servant.

So ended our spell of duty in Ismailia, with many new experiences, sad memories of spiritual defeat in one way or another, but a further testimony to the love and faithfulness of a God who never lets his children go.

6

Cairo University

A student again * *Family law of Islam* * *Student outreach* * *My first book — in Arabic!* * *Impending war*

On our way back to Egypt in the autumn of 1936 we spent two weeks as lodgers in a typical little Swiss chalet, perched comparatively high in the mountains, to look after our two children while their nurse went to her own home for a holiday. Hazel was no trouble at all except at meal-times. She had little appetite; and we found that, after doing our utmost to cajole her into taking spoonful after spoonful of food, she had done no more than produce a primitive sort of 'hamburger' in her mouth! Janet was completely different. She enjoyed her meals all right, but scorned sleep.

In the middle of the morning (when all respectable babies, we had been taught, ought to have a nap), I would take her out and push her in her pram for quite a time until she seemed to be fast asleep. Then I would continue to watch her closely — apparently as peaceful as could be — while I slowed up gradually with the utmost caution, hoping to be able to sit down and read. But as soon as I actually stopped, a small red face would pop up at once with repeated howls of protest. And much the same thing would happen again in her cot in the evening. We had no idea whether she was suffering from claustrophobia or mere petulance; but we eventually had to move Hazel in with Pat while I tried to keep Janet comparatively quiet in the other room. It took us a very long time to realize how much one baby differs from another, and that, whereas Hazel would sleep precisely as our textbook prescribed but was a problem to feed, Janet should have been allowed to eat and play until she had tired herself out.

A student again

When we reached Egypt we soon found a large and pleasant flat in the vicinity of the University of Cairo (then named Jami 'at Fu'ad al-Awwal, after the King, but now Jami 'at al-Qahira). So we proceeded to take our long-suffering furniture out of store again and get settled in. Our new flat, we found, was directly opposite a hostel for girls from other Arab countries who had come to study at Cairo University, which was only some fifteen minutes' walk away. In due course we got to know two or three of them quite well. It did not take very long, moreover, for me to get admitted to the University as a *Talib mustamir* – a student who is allowed to attend lectures without being registered for a degree. In my case this applied to both the Arabic literature section of the Faculty of Arts and to those lectures in the Faculty of Law which concerned the Islamic law of personal status and family relations. My dual purpose was to improve my knowledge of Arabic and to get acquainted with some of the students. It is clearly impossible to walk into a University in a strongly Muslim country and just 'set up shop', as it were, as a missionary; so the obvious course seemed to be to become a student myself and to see what opportunities that might bring.

In the Faculty of Arts I attended a number of lectures by both Dr Taha Hussein and Dr Ahmad Amin – two men who differed greatly in background and style. Taha Hussein had started life as a village boy who became blind at an early age, because his well-meaning mother had rubbed some quack medicament into his sore eyes. Not only had he graduated in the old-fashioned way from the Azhar, but he had won a scholarship to France and become one of the most distinguished literati in Egypt. He had married a French wife; he spoke and wrote beautiful Arabic; and he subsequently became Minister of Education in the Egyptian cabinet. Inevitably I found it impossible to follow his allusions to, and comparisons between, classical Arabic poets whose works I had never read. But I greatly enjoyed listening to the elegant simplicity of the way in which he habitually expressed himself extemporarily in the best modern literary Arabic. Very soon, moreover, I read his autobiography of his early years, entitled *Al-Ayyam*, delighting not only in the quality of his writing but also in his picture of Egyptian life. The book is well worth reading even in its English translation, *An Egyptian childhood*, by E. L. Paxton.

Dr Ahmad Amin was chiefly known, at that time, for his series of books on the history of Islam. The first of these was entitled *Fajr al-Islam* (The Dawn of Islam), and he produced two or three more books on later periods in Islamic history with names from other times of the day – although I fancy he stopped short of writing a book the title of which would amount to 'The Sunset of Islam'! His books, too, were written in a smooth style of straightforward literary Arabic which I could by then read with comparative ease and enjoyment. But his lectures were much less helpful for my purpose, since he turned them into seminars rather than formal lectures, and talked with the students for the most part in Egyptian colloquial Arabic, which I found hard to follow.

Family law of Islam

By and large, much the most illuminating lectures from my point of view were those on the family law of Islam. Unlike all the other lectures in the Faculty of Law, which were always given in French, those on personal status and family law were delivered in Arabic. They were firmly based on the classical Islamic law, the Shari'a, modified only in parts (to make it more congruous with the conditions of modern life) by a series of statutory enactments which were themselves derived, whether directly or indirectly, from the Shari'a. It was fascinating to hear a learned and open-minded Azhar sheikh explain Islamic law to an audience of students which, while predominantly Muslim, included a fair sprinkling of Egyptian Christians and one solitary European. The Egyptian Christians were mostly Copts, with a few Evangelicals, Orthodox and Roman Catholics.

I found it particularly intriguing to hear him enumerate, in considerable detail, the evil effects of polygamy – whether in Egypt or elsewhere – and then set out to explain why Allah himself had seen fit to make explicit provision for it in the Qur'an (4:3). He accomplished this feat by telling a touching story of a judge in Upper Egypt who was deeply devoted to a wife who proved, with the passage of years, to be barren. What was the husband to do, since he felt he *must* have an heir? Was he to divorce the wife he loved and marry another woman? No; with the first wife's agreement he married a second and younger wife, whose first son was then reared by the older woman as though he was her own – with the obvious implication that 'they all lived happily ever after'. The Professor himself clearly disapproved of polygamy except in extreme cases like this; but he did not venture to discuss why the divine law, while it puts certain limits on polygamy, does so in such equivocal terms and leaves so much latitude for abuse.

These lectures were of particular value to me for three reasons. Firstly, they were easy to follow, since they were concerned with a subject that I could understand much more readily than allusions to literature I had never read. Secondly, they were delivered in good, literary Arabic, clearly articulated at a moderate speed, and without the host of synonyms so beloved of many Arab writers or speakers. It was just the type of Arabic, in fact, in which I myself aspired one day to speak and write. Thirdly, the family law of Muslim Egyptians was still firmly based on the Shari'a, although the dominant opinion of the Hanafi school (which the Egyptian courts had previously been required always to apply in such matters) had now been modified by a number of significant reforms. So to hear this law expounded by someone deeply versed in *fiqh* (the scientific study of the sacred law) provided – at one and the same time – an insight into the family lives of Muslims all down the centuries, and also a glimpse of the social conditions, in Egypt and elsewhere, which had occasioned these recent reforms.

Student outreach

To establish any effective Christian contact with the Egyptian students was a much more difficult matter.

84

They were friendly enough, and naturally curious to know what my job was, and why I was interested in Arabic literature and, still more, Islamic family law. It was, indeed, just here that I encountered a moral problem. The word commonly used for a missionary was *mubashshir*, one who was intent on *tabshir* (that is, evangelism). So, on general principles, this would have been the word to use. The difficulty was that this word, as used at that time in the Arabic media and popular speech, had come to have the connotation of proselytization and the machinations of those whose avowed purpose was to lead Muslims astray. It was also the technical term for an Egyptian 'evangelist' who had not reached the status (or, indeed, received the training) of a fully-fledged clergyman or minister.

To have replied bluntly that I was a *mubashshir* without further explanation – in answer, as it would often have been, to a casual question posed by one of a circle of students – would almost certainly have proved a barrier to any easy relationship with them. It might even have provoked a complaint to the University authorities. Yet I clearly did not wish in any way to sail under false colours. So I usually said that I was both 'a man of religion' and 'a member of an English Mission'. The proper term in Arabic for a Christian missionary as such is *mursal* (one who has been 'sent'), and for a mission *mursaliya* or *irsaliya* (although the latter term is also used of a military or trade mission). So I usually added the term 'a man of religion' by way of qualification. I should have preferred the word *mubashshir* in principle, since its basic meaning is 'one who announces good news' (which is, of course, precisely what the gospel is). But the word had so often been used in a derogatory, hostile and aggressive sense that it seemed better to use phraseology which put the major emphasis on the fact that I was a student of religion. Certainly no-one imagined that I was a Muslim.

Opportunities to preach in churches which included a number of students occasionally came my way, and I frequently attended the Sunday services over which the most prominent Christian preacher in Cairo, the Reverend Ibrahim Sa'id, always presided. But for the most part contact was limited to inviting a few students home to tea or coffee, and visiting them in their lodgings – and I cannot say that this was either easy or significantly fruitful. There were quite a large number of Coptic students in the University, and I soon discovered that very many of them seemed to take the attitude that no-one with a good 'Western' education could be expected to accept the New Testament witness to Jesus Christ, his atoning death and his victorious resurrection, at their face value. So it was not long before I set myself to write a book entitled *Al-'Aql w'al-Iman*. Literally, the word *'aql* means 'reason' and *iman* 'faith', but as a title in English one would instinctively reverse the order and say *Faith and Reason*.

My first book – in Arabic!

This took quite a long time to write – and, incidentally, taught me a lot of Arabic. At first I wrote in English and then translated this into Arabic. Before long, however, I came to the conclusion that the English script was more of a hindrance than a help, and I started to write directly in Arabic. But I owe an enormous debt of gratitude to Ibrahim Sa'id for his kindness and patience in reading it, chapter by chapter, and telling me that an Arab would have used another, though largely synonymous, word in this sentence or that, or would probably have expressed the sense of what I had written in a somewhat different idiom. This was an education in itself, equivalent to writing a whole series of Arabic 'proses' – extending, in their printed form, to some 180 small pages.

The book was primarily directed to Christian students who were uncertain, ignorant or sceptical about the foundations of their faith. It included chapters on 'God and man', 'The historic Christ', 'The unique Christ', 'The resurrection', 'Who then was the Christ?' and 'Why did he die?', and it ended with a short testimony about why I was a Christian and with a challenge to the reader. But I was careful also to include, here and there, a number of paragraphs in which I had Muslim misunderstandings and objections particularly in mind. These were designed not only to help a Christian student in his conversation with a Muslim, but also to catch the eye of a Muslim reader. In point of fact, as I soon found, it was sometimes easier for me to offer a Muslim (and for him to accept) a book which set out primarily to convince a nominal Christian that the validity and implications of his faith had by no means been undermined by Western scepticism, than it would have been to get a Muslim to read a book which he felt was specifically designed to question his own convictions.

We had, for some months at least, had it in mind to buy or build a small house close to the University as a centre for any student contacts that might develop, and we had not long been settled in our rented flat before we found a very small plot of land ideally placed in a side road within easy walking distance of the University. So we consulted a young Lebanese architect, who had been recommended to us, as to whether he could design a suitable house on this site.

This was by no means easy, as the plot was very narrow and local by-laws forbade any construction within three metres of its boundaries. We were also insistent that as many rooms as possible should have one window, however small, which faced north and could catch the light breeze which, in Cairo, so often springs up from that quarter in the late evening of a very hot summer day. The result was a strangely shaped house – very modern and distinctive in its yellow bricks, slabs of black stone, flat roof and a very large balcony. What we did not realize, in our ignorance, was that a house which fundamentally rested on concrete pillars connected by only one layer of bricks, and with an open, tiled roof and balcony, would become a positive hot-house in the summer sun. But it looked striking (and in some respects attractive) in a distinctly modern idiom, and we were very pleased with it. So far as we remember it cost us a sum which seems ridiculously cheap today. Even so, we have no clear memory of where the money came from; so we conclude that our parents provided this!

Our next-door neighbour on one side was Maltese, and he kept a fierce dog which barked loudly and, at times, almost incessantly. We certainly did not enjoy this, but it worried us much less acutely than it did a highly-strung English lecturer who lived a little way beyond us. So, when several requests that the dog should be kept quiet fell on empty ears, he walked into the garden one day with a revolver and shot at, and wounded, the offending dog. The ensuing litigation at that time came before the British Consular Court, both parties being British subjects; and our Maltese neighbour at first claimed that the Englishman's original purpose had been to shoot him, not the dog!

This wild accusation was rightly rejected, and the

Englishman was fined for wounding the dog and ordered to pay for such care as it needed. So its owner used to order a taxi to take the dog to a vet at the other end of Cairo and keep it waiting till the vet had treated him; and several such visits ran up quite a sizeable sum. We never really got to know this neighbour, who kept himself much to himself, but we subsequently became very friendly with the Englishman and his wife. He was a Ph.D. who had 'Dr X' on a brass plate beside the gate – with the result that he was occasionally awakened at night by frantic husbands whose wives were in labour!

Impending war

We quite often had student visitors to see us, as we had hoped, and I was able to return some of these calls in the scattered rooms in which most of them lodged. But in 1938 the international position was becoming more and more tense, and we took the opportunity to arrange evening meetings for British Officers and their wives, with people like Lieut.-General Sir Arthur Smith (as he subsequently became) and Pat's father to address them. I also gave a series of lectures in the seminary at which pastors and evangelists for the Evangelical Church were trained – using some of the material I had prepared for my book *Al-'Aql w'al-Iman*, which was published by the Nile Mission Press in 1939. We also entertained missionaries and other guests, including a visit from my parents.

The only trouble about this visit was that my parents would not go anywhere without us; and I felt I must get on with my work, while Pat had to cope with the children. But, besides local sight-seeing, we did on one occasion drive them to Ismailia, Suez and back to

Cairo, visiting mission stations on the way. My mother, I remember, got distinctly apprehensive when our ramshackle car had a minor breakdown on the desert road between Ismailia and Suez – with the wholly unintended result that she insisted on buying us a small second-hand Ford when we got back to Cairo. It had not greatly worried us that our previous car often had to be pushed before it would start. Engineering of any sort is quite beyond me; and one could usually get people to push in Egypt – except, of course, on a desert road.

As the international situation got worse, the British Embassy in Cairo became concerned about the safety of isolated British families in an emergency. The Italians had a considerable foothold in Egypt at that time, especially in King Farouk's Palace; and propaganda about 'Hajj Muhammad Hitler' began to appear (*Hajj* being an honorific title given to a Muslim who has made the prescribed Pilgrimage to Mecca!). So Cairo was divided up into several 'wards', and I was asked to take charge of the ward in which our house happened to fall. This proved to be a fairly large ward geographically, since British residents in our locality were comparatively few and far between. But the work involved was by no means exacting, and involved little more than knowing where British subjects lived so that they could come together, or be assembled, if need arose.

I was still, of course, studying Arabic, and I remember one incident which gives a fairly good impression of the University at that time. When reading a book on Arab history, I telephoned the writer – a noted Arab historian – to ask if I could call on him to ask a few questions. He was very friendly, and asked me round during the course of the morning. On my arrival, moreover, he asked me – with typical Egyptian hospitality – if I would have some coffee. I hesitated, since it was the month of Ramadan, when Muslims are required to abstain from eating, drinking and smoking from dawn to sunset. But he ordered two cups and drank with me while we talked – although I would have abstained, as a matter of courtesy, if he had been fasting. A few moments later a considerable number of students arrived, presumably to pay him a call, and he immediately offered coffee to them too. 'But it's Ramadan,' they exclaimed in horror. 'Oh, so it is,' he replied imperturbably. This, I reflected, was far from strange in Cairo as I then knew it. The sheikhs, the common people and most of the students kept the fast rigidly – at least in public; but the upper classes, and those who had received a 'Western' education, held much more loosely to it.

The missionary attitude – at that time, at least – was to regard any convert from Islam who did not wholly ignore Ramadan as guilty of backsliding. But this attitude, I now believe, needs to be analysed and revised. If a convert keeps the Ramadan fast for theological reasons (because he still believes it is divinely commanded), or in order to give the impression that he has returned to Islam, he would indeed have abandoned the liberty of the gospel for the bondage of a legalism wholly alien to that gospel (cf. Galatians 1:6–9; 2:15–21). But if he quietly confesses the liberty he has in Christ, but is willing to conform to the eating habits of his family to avoid being a nuisance, and not flaunt his new-found freedom in a way that makes life more difficult for them, he would surely be more likely to win them for Christ. This would, as I now see it, be more closely akin to Paul's principle of conforming to other people's way of life, in all that is not sinful, in order to 'win' as many of them as possible (1 Corinthians 9:19–23) – for, after all, there is nothing wrong in going without food for some hours for the sake of others.

In spite of the lowering clouds over Europe no-one could tell, in the early summer of 1939, what was going to happen, so we travelled back to England for three months' furlough. After a visit to my parents in Reigate we went as paying guests to a delightful Sussex farm near Eastbourne, where we were joined by Pat's parents and younger brother. Meanwhile, the threat of war came closer and closer; and one Sunday morning, when I was looking after our little girls while everyone else went to Holy Trinity, Eastbourne, I listened on the radio to the Prime Minister's announcement that we were now at war with Germany – while Canon S. M. Warner at Holy Trinity gave the news to his congregation and then preached on the text 'But all the children of Israel had light in their dwellings' (Exodus 10:23, AV). Next day Pat's brother did his best to enlist, but was temporarily turned down, while we – aided by a letter I had been given about the alleged urgency of the warden's job I had to do in Cairo – set out at once to return to Egypt.

7

Arab guerrillas

More opportunities ✳ *A difficult decision* ✳ *Training for war* ✳ *Recruiting guerrillas* ✳ *The Libyan Arab Force*

Our journey back to Egypt was very different from anything we had experienced before. Although in point of fact the war was to be largely static for the next few months, no-one knew that this would be the case. So when crossing the Channel we were all issued with life-belts, and told to wear them, or at least carry them with us, wherever we might be. Our children thought this rather fun; and the humorous side was brought home to Pat and me by a little charade that happened almost under our noses. Close beside us, sitting on the deck, were various members of a wealthy Jewish family which lived near Pat's parents in Alexandria; and after a time the father and one son went off, a very short distance, to the loo. But they failed to take their life-belts; so the mother, every inch the matriarch, sent her younger son, with his own and two other life-belts, to stand just outside the door – looking distinctly embarrassed – until they emerged in safety.

We were met in Paris, already under a tight blackout, by the curate of the British Embassy church, an old family friend of Pat's; and he drove us, armed with sandwiches, to a train for Marseilles. Everything was topsy-turvy and it was impossible to get a sleeper; but we managed to get a second-class carriage to ourselves at first, and in due course to bed down our two little girls beside us, one on each side. In the middle of the night, however, two Frenchwomen got in, switched on the partly darkened light, and started to talk volubly. This naturally disturbed the children and we were anticipating a lively night when it occurred to me quietly to remove the light bulb. This proved very successful, for – after questioning each other for some minutes as to what could have happened to the electric light – the two women finally relapsed into comparative silence and somnolence; and we eventually reached Marseilles in this unscheduled, and greatly delayed, train.

We went by taxi some seven miles east of Marseilles to quite a pleasant hotel beside the sea, and next day I went into the city to enquire about our proposed passage to Alexandria. I found that the previous ship had been delayed about a week, but that ours might be expected to sail in a few days' time, probably in a convoy. Everything was disorganized and uncertain, and we were much relieved when we did in fact set sail in a heavily darkened ship, which was, we heard, the last to sail without a convoy. The journey proved entirely uneventful, except that the ship was kept rigidly blacked out in the evenings.

More opportunities

In Egypt all was as usual, and there were no shortages – although there were noticeably more British troops. We resumed our meetings for officers and their wives, and I recall that one evening, when General Arthur Smith was due to speak, he had to send news that he was detained elsewhere. It was too late to invite another speaker at such short notice, so I felt that I must, with apologies, fill the gap myself. In God's inscrutable purposes it was the talk I gave that evening which, as a booklet entitled *The Evidence for the Resurrection*, has been widely used and repeatedly reprinted, both in Britain and the United States – and, indeed, in translation into a number of languages.

One other meeting we had in that house taught me a salutary lesson. The 'phoney' war was coming to an end, and there were many speculations about what would transpire. So we invited a doctor friend from Palestine (as it then was), who was on a visit to Cairo, to address a meeting of Egyptian students on the subject. He was a keen student of prophecy, with views largely formulated by 'the Scofield Bible' – and he proceeded to state categorically that Italy would *never* fight against Britain (since these countries constituted two of the ten toes into which the Roman Empire was to be divided in the last days, as depicted in Daniel's image) and that Britain would *never* be allied to Russia, which represented 'the King of the North'. Unhappily, moreover, he did not make these predictions tentatively, as the way in which he personally believed the Bible to point, but as certainties about which the Bible left no room for doubt. I was disturbed about this talk at the time, for I had already come to question Dr Scofield's interpretations of prophecy (on which I had myself been reared), but Pat and I were naturally chagrined that both our speaker's predictions, affirmed as the sure teaching of Scripture, were so soon falsified by the events. The interpretation of prophecy is an outstanding instance of those matters on which dogmatism is not only foolish but positively dangerous.

It was during these months that I came into contact with a Muslim, more a secondary schoolboy than a university student, who wanted to be taught about the Christian faith. So I arranged to meet him at a convenient place, twice a week, to read the New Testament with him in Arabic. I had been carefully warned not to make any gifts of money or goods in such circumstances, because of the danger presented by 'rice-Christians' and the sort of allegations that Muslims are apt to make. But on several evenings when we met he let it be known (whether purposely or as a mere matter of fact) that he had had no food that day. So what could I do but supply him with something to eat, or the money with which to buy it? This only happened occasionally, and we read together for some weeks. Then he suddenly ceased to come, and I never saw him again. He may have lost interest; he may have counted the cost, but found it too high; or he may have been intimidated.

A difficult decision

In the spring or early summer of 1940 I began to run a slight temperature and to have a little pain in my legs. We consulted an able English doctor serving at the CMS hospital in Old Cairo, who decided it must be a very mild bout of rheumatic fever and insisted that I must stay in bed. It continued for some two or three weeks; but if it was rheumatic fever it must have been minimal. Being more or less bedridden, however, I had plenty of time to think – and the war news was getting more and more threatening. So I was in a quandary about whether I should join up. Pat's younger brother had enlisted in the RAF almost as soon as he got back to Alexandria, and had gone off to

Iraq, with a number of similarly placed young men, to train as a pilot. But for me it was a difficult decision.

When a student at Cambridge I had inclined, like many Christians, towards pacifist views. But the Nazi menace to Europe, and especially their brutality to the Jews, now convinced me that they must be resisted; and I became increasingly uneasy about the inconsistency of a Christian saying: 'Yes, fight we must; but I personally could never kill anyone.' As a missionary I should probably have been exempt from compulsory recruitment; but I was not in charge of a hospital or school, I was not ordained, and my desire to work among students had got little further than study, attending lectures, visiting and literary work. I hated the idea of fighting, both on principle and because of what it might mean for Pat and the children in a foreign land. But with General Graziani already menacing Egypt I decided, with many misgivings, to volunteer.

I was immediately asked whether I would be willing to fight with Arab guerrillas. This was because Libyan refugees in Egypt, who had escaped (chiefly from Cyrenaica but also from Tripolitania) from the defeat and savage mauling they had received from Graziani in the First World War, had approached General 'Jumbo' Wilson, then commanding British troops in Egypt, asking for officers, weapons, uniforms and pay to enable them to have another crack at the Italians to 'regain their lands and independence'. This happened at a time when Britain stood alone in the war, except for the beginnings of the 'Free French' movement, so the offer was accepted. But no promises were made about the future, because the memory of the conflicting promises made, some twenty years before, was too recent to be forgotten. They had been made both to Arabs eager to fight against the Turks for their freedom and independence, and also to Jews who aspired to a 'national home' in Palestine. My qualifications for such service consisted solely in a very undistinguished career in the Officers' Training Corps at school, some fifteen years before, and a fairly good knowledge of a spoken and written Arabic.

Training for war

I agreed to this suggestion, was immediately commissioned as a Captain in the Intelligence Corps (since the plans for the guerrilla force were still secret), and told to get my uniform and report to the King's Own Regiment in the desert for some three weeks' weapon training. The situation was dark and full of uncertainties, and I went off wondering what the future held. The King's Own were very good to us, and I was told to sit next to the Colonel – an enormous figure of a man – on the first night in the mess. I cannot remember anything about our conversation, except that I felt no temptation whatever to emulate a young regular soldier whose talk with the Colonel was reputed to have gone something like this: 'Well, my boy, what made you ask if you could join the King's Own?' 'Oh, but I didn't, sir. I tried to get into two or three other regiments first'!

I shared a tent that night with a young Lieutenant in the regular army, and it seemed ridiculous for a complete tiro like me to be technically his senior. I had forgotten to bring any soap, so he lent me a cake of scented soap that reminded me of much more sybarite days; and early in the morning his batman brought us both a large mug of typical army tea – very strong and very sweet. But when the kindly Colonel found that at least two of us had wives and families in Cairo, he asked us if we would not like to sleep at home for as long as this was possible. We jumped at this suggestion, and Captain Hazelden and I left camp about 5 or 6 p.m. each evening in my car, and got back for early morning training by about 6.30 next morning. Hazelden had been born in Egypt, spoke the colloquial language excellently, and was a very congenial companion; and we both greatly appreciated what we expected to be the last taste of home life we were likely to get for a wholly indefinite time.

The training we received was chiefly concerned with the use of the weapons with which we, and the guerrillas we were to command, were to be armed – rifles, bayonets, Bren guns and revolvers (officers in Egypt at that time were under orders to carry revolvers with them wherever they went). But we were also shown how to kill a sentinel silently so that he could not raise an alarm – which brought home to me even more vividly the beastliness of war. Yet I could not see any alternative to resisting Nazi tyranny and genocide by force, nor how a Christian could in such circumstances opt out. I vividly remember deriving comfort from the record in Hebrews 11 of those 'who through faith conquered kingdoms, enforced justice, ... won strength out of weakness, became mighty in war, put foreign armies to flight' (verses 33–34, RSV).

Recruiting guerrillas

When our very brief training was complete, however, I found myself appointed 'Arab liaison officer' instead of commanding a company of guerrillas. This meant being in charge of a tumultuous office in Cairo where sheikhs from Libyan tribes would bring in recruits for whom they could vouch, and would also help me to discriminate between genuine patriots and mere scallywags who clamoured to enlist. But my most interesting duty was regular communication with the future King Idris of Libya, virtually the honorary 'Colonel' of the 'Libyan Arab Force' (as our guerrillas came to be). He was the person whom the vast majority of the people of Cyrenaica, and a significant minority of those of Tripolitania, called 'His Highness the Emir' and looked to as their national as well as religious leader.

But the title of 'King' was then far away, and I had to be careful not even to refer to him as Emir, in case that should be interpreted as an implied promise about the future. The British had at least learnt some lessons from the conflicting – and essentially irreconcilable – promises of the past. The consequence was that, about twice a week, I would receive a polite message from the Libyan 'Major' attached to my office that 'His Highness the Emir would be grateful if you would call on him', and I would reply, 'Will you kindly tell His Excellency the Sayyid (that is, descendant of the Prophet of Islam) that I should be delighted to call on him at four o'clock (or whatever)?'

The selection of Libyan refugees in Egypt was considerably simplified not only by the advice given by sheikhs who knew them or their families, but also by the fact that many of them would bare their legs, arms or shoulders to show the marks of rifle bullets or other wounds which gave substantial evidence of their participation in resistance to the Italians in the past. So recruitment went reasonably well, as did also the payment of the small sums of money I handed out, month by month, to the sheikhs who brought in most of the recruits. They were themselves refugees of long standing who lived on a pittance and were grateful for whatever I could give them; but I got very tired of the tales they continually told me of the capacious bags of gold out of which Lawrence of Arabia was – allegedly at least – both able and willing to distribute largesse.

The Libyan Arab Force

It was not long, however, before the battle of Sidi Barrani radically changed the pattern of recruitment. In that battle in the Western desert the Italians had, I was told, placed their Libyan conscript troops (some 15,000 of them, if I remember rightly) in a forward and exposed position. In the event, however, the British armour swept round them and routed the Italian armour; whereupon the Libyans, sensibly enough, surrendered *en masse* – not only because it would have been suicide for lightly armed foot soldiers to fight against tanks in the open desert, but also because they had no love for the Italians, whom they regarded as usurpers of their country. Before long, therefore, some of these prisoners of war, all of whom were confined in camps beside the Suez Canal, made requests to be allowed to join their fellow-countrymen in the Libyan Arab Force to fight 'for the recovery of their lands and independence'.

In point of fact they had not really enjoyed full independence for a very long time, for the Ottoman Empire had exercised at least nominal control of the coastal strip, which had then been seized and settled by the Italians. Only a limited proportion of the Tripolitanians, moreover, had recognized even spiritual allegiance to Sayyid Idris. The Italians had accorded him the title 'Emir al-Sanusiyya', whose sway they had acknowledged in the interior of Cyrenaica and the hinterland of the Gulf of Sirte, and whom they had accorded a semi-royal salute when he paid periodic visits to his followers in the Italian occupied coastal region. So the prisoners of war were Italian subjects only by *force majeure*.

Even so, it was, perhaps, somewhat questionable in International Law to allow them to fight on the other side. Nor did we in fact accept any volunteers except those who were vouched for by a member of the Sanusi family and some of the sheikhs who accompanied me on the several visits I paid to the camps. There is little doubt that they would have been regarded by the Italians as 'traitors' had they subsequently been recaptured and recognized. So, far from urging them to join the Libyan Arab Force, we accepted only a proportion of those who wished to do so. Finally, however, we formed five battalions and a depot out of a combination of refugees who had been living in Egypt for years and this new influx of those who had only recently escaped from Italian domination.

The concept behind the formation of the Libyan Arab Force – at a time when we stood almost alone against the Germans and Italians – was that when the British Army had advanced as far along the coast as Derna, these guerrilla troops should be let loose in the hill country between there and the plain leading down towards Benghazi. This was country over which armoured fighting vehicles could not at that time have operated. In the event, however, the British armour swept right across the desert south of the hill country and reached the coast near Agedabia. The primary task of the Libyan Arab Force changed, therefore, from the original plan of fighting detachments of the Italians in the 'Jabal' (the Green Mountains), to guarding wells and acting as 'gendarmerie', or armed police, who could deal with such enemy personnel as might be dropped by parachute.

But already one battalion had advanced to the vicinity of Agedabia, and had been dispersed by the German troops, who had now joined (or virtually taken over from) the Italians in North Africa, while another was cut off in the siege of Tobruk. Most of those dispersed near Agedabia eventually found their way back across the desert to rejoin, while those besieged in Tobruk were evacuated by sea to be replaced in the siege by more heavily armed and highly trained troops.

8

Enemy territories

*Cairo under threat * Cyrenaica and Tripolitania *
Planning the future * Visit to Jeddah *
Release leave*

By this time I had been taken over, as a Major, by
Civil Affairs Branch GHQ, Middle East Forces, as
'Secretary for Sanusi Affairs'. The primary task of
Civil Affairs Branch was to take care of the civilian
population of occupied enemy territories. As the bat-
tles rolled on, however, it became responsible for what
was virtually a full 'Colonial' Government in Cyrenaica, Tripolitania, Eritrea and the Dodecanese, taking
over not only the control of food supplies, law and
order, education and political affairs, but also agriculture, roads and ports. But this was, of course, still in
the future. Meanwhile the British army had overrun
Cyrenaica for the second time, only to be pushed back
once more by Rommel before their final victorious
advance.

During one of these interludes I had the interesting
experience of accompanying the Chief Administrator
of Cyrenaica, Brigadier Duncan Cumming, to Trans-
jordan to learn what we could, in regard to the future
of the Libyan Arab Force, from General Glubb's 'Arab
Legion'. Part of this formed the gendarmerie of the
country, as an armed police force, while the other part,

popularly known as 'Glubb's Girls' (because they were all of bedouin stock and wore long hair), formed what was probably the finest indigenous fighting force in the Middle East. Besides seeing Glubb Pasha we also met Mr (subsequently Sir) Alec Kirkbride, the British Resident, and his deputy, Mr Hugh Foot (now Lord Caradon).

Over lunch with the latter we had a fascinating talk about Lawrence of Arabia with two older men who had known him well – and the conversation turned to the question whether he really had such a command of Arabic as would appear to be the case from his books. It was in this context that Foot remarked how easily one can give that impression without meaning to do so. 'An old sheikh may come in from the desert, for example, to see the British Resident, who may ask me to go and find out what he wants. I do so, and later the Resident asks what transpired. "Oh," I reply, "the old boy was most anxious that HMG should do this and that." "So what did you tell him?" the Resident inquires. "I gave him to understand, sir, in the most unequivocal terms, that it was totally out of the question that HMG could entertain any such suggestion at the present time." This may give the impression that I have a reasonably facile command of diplomatic Arabic, when all I may in fact have done was to wag my finger and say (in the way one learnt to say to one's cook from the very first), *"mush mumkin abadan"* (it's quite impossible)!'

There is much truth in this; but I myself learnt a rather different, but most salutary, lesson soon after I had become Arab Liaison Officer with the Libyan Arab Force. I was having one of my regular talks with Sayyid Idris when, after quite a useful discussion, he asked me if I would put to the Commander-in-Chief some personal request – probably on behalf of one of his relatives or friends. I knew that this could not possibly be done, and told him so at once (with, I hope, reasonable courtesy). But this prompted the only letter of complaint he wrote about me, suggesting that perhaps an older and more experienced officer might be appointed in my place; and this taught me that, to an Arab or other Oriental dignitary, a flat negative from a young officer is regarded as almost *lèse-majesté*. To reply that one 'will certainly see what can be done, although it may well be very difficult', causes no such loss of face; and I often found that the subject was then allowed to drop, with no repetition of the request nor question about how it had been received.

Cairo under threat

When the British army had been driven back the second time from Cyrenaica, this time by General Rommel and some of his crack troops, the Germans pushed on into Egypt and the situation became really dangerous. So General Auchinleck, then Commander-in-Chief in Cairo, went down to Alamein (the last really defensible position before the Nile Delta) to take direct command. The guns from Alamein were very audible in Alexandria; and had Rommel broken this line of defence there was virtually nothing with which to stop him. Numbers of civilians left Alexandria; orders were given that all British army wives and children were to prepare for immediate evacuation from Suez to South Africa; and all of us in GHQ were told to be ready to leave within a few hours' notice. Had Pat been evacuated in this way it would have been for the duration of the war. So, after a sleepless night, I managed to get a visa for her and our two small daughters to travel up the Nile to the Sudan, and attempt to get from there to Kenya, where one of her brothers was a missionary.

I was greatly relieved to see them off, since there were considerable fears that, had Cairo been directly menaced, the Egyptians might respond to German propaganda and resort to pillage, riot and violence. But it was a sad parting. We had already learnt that Pat's pilot brother had been killed on patrol duty over the Red Sea, and this had upset her deeply. Happily, we had sold our house and moved into a rented flat, since it had been clear from the time I joined up that I might be sent anywhere at any time. But in the event it was she who had to leave first – in circumstances so black that we could have no idea when (or even whether) we should meet again. Our confidence could be only in God. Pat had a very tiring journey with the children in the full heat of a Sudanese summer; but God was wonderfully good to her in providing help as far as Khartoum from the Governor of the Blue Nile Province, and in Khartoum from 'Uncle' Harper of the Cathedral, who met her and housed her and the children in the bishop's own bedroom. She then managed to get on a Nile steamer and travel – by river, coach and railway – to her brother's mission station in Kenya.

Meanwhile, we in Cairo were busy burning secret documents in preparation for a possible evacuation. We did this so thoroughly that for the remainder of the war we could always parry awkward questions about the origin of this or that by surmising that the relevant records were 'probably burnt in the flap'! I shared our flat for some weeks with a scion of the Huxley family, whose task it was to prepare plans for a possible withdrawal of the British army from the Delta by means of a fighting retreat – in part eastwards towards Suez, and in part southwards up the Nile. Providentially, however, the Highland Division came out from Britain to Suez on the Mauritania, sailing round the Cape at full speed without convoy; a steady build-up of air and gun power began; and General Alexander took over as Commander-in-Chief in Cairo with General Montgomery as Commander of the Eighth Army. Orders were promptly given that all plans for any further retreat should be destroyed, since our troops would stand, fight, advance or die where they stood. This acted like a shot in the arm to morale; but it is all too easy to forget the skill and determination with which 'the Auk' had held the Alamein line with exceedingly slender resources and somewhat dispirited troops.

During 'the flap' the Sanusi family and a number of their followers not unnaturally wished to leave Egypt (since they could expect little mercy from the Italians). Sayyid Idris's first thought was to go on pilgrimage to Mecca and then stay on in Sa'udi Arabia, and he requested the British to pursue the necessary negotiations on his behalf. So it fell to me to inform him that the Sa'udi Government was prepared to accept him and his entourage, but that any books they might wish to bring with them would have to be passed by the Sa'udi religious censorship (which is highly inimical to any literature of a mystical character)! This reply did not please the Sanusis, so the Sayyid, with members of his family and a number of their followers, decided that they would prefer to go to Jerusalem – for which I had to make arrangements through the British High Commission, and subsequently to visit them there.

Meanwhile I was told to take some leave (which I had not had since joining up), while the British counter-attack was being prepared. Naturally enough, I said that I had no desire to take leave in Egypt when my family were in Kenya, and my C.O. was kind enough to say that the next time anything had to be negotiated with the Headquarters in East Africa he would send me to do this. It was not long before an opportunity occurred; so I was flown to Mombasa and took the night train up to Nairobi, where I was met by Pat. Then, after I had finished my job, we had a delightful holiday in Limuru for about ten days. But news came through that the battle of Alamein had begun, and it was only on orders from Cairo that I was able to get a seat, almost immediately, on a seaplane back to Egypt.

I was joined in our flat first by a Christian officer in the RNVR and then by Quintin Carr, formerly a missionary in India but now a Major in the Indian Army. But within a few more months Pat and our two daughters were able to rejoin me, thanks to the fact that Pat had 'resident status' in Egypt, and did not have to apply to Cairo for a re-entry visa (an application which, at that time, would have been referred to the British GHQ and automatically blocked).

Cyrenaica and Tripolitania

After the battle of Alamein the British army had again swept through the desert south of the Green Mountains, and this time had pressed forward right through Tripolitania into Tunisia. We found that almost the entire Italian population of Cyrenaica (quite large at the time of our first occupation, and only slightly smaller at the second) had been evacuated to Tripolitania or Italy. Happily, a number of nuns who were hospital nurses had remained, together with a bishop and a few priests. I believe there were only four other Italians whose presence was winked at – one as a cook who could make an excellent meal out of home-made macaroni and tins of bully-beef, and another as an expert barber. Strict orders had been given that there must be 'no fraternization with the enemy', since the people of Cyrenaica were much more hostile to the Italians than were those of Tripolitania. This order made the letters which our legal adviser sometimes had to write to the Italian bishop appear rather odd, since the former (as a convinced Roman Catholic) always ended such letters with the words 'Your obedient son in Christ Jesus'.

When Tripolitania was occupied, my job was up-graded from being 'Secretary for Cyrenaica', to 'Secretary for Arab Affairs' and then, a few months later, to 'Political Secretary'. Both these appointments carried the rank of Lieut.-Colonel and considerably more responsibility; and I found, to my shame, that the ambition which I had not had any difficulty in renouncing when I opted for missionary service now reared its ugly head much more forcibly.

In 1943 I accompanied Sayyid Idris on part of his triumphant visit to Cyrenaica, and was in far more danger from the shots that Arabs, galloping beside his car, continually let off into the air than I had ever been from enemy fire. I also toured Tripolitania with Wing Commander Mallowan, then Adviser on Arab Affairs in that territory (later Sir Max Mallowan, an arch-aeologist of great personal distinction – besides being the husband of Agatha Christie!). On subsequent visits to the territories I stayed with the British Military Administrator in Eritrea (housed in the villa in Asmara previously occupied by the Duke of Aosta) and with the Military Administrator in Rhodes (housed in its magnificent Castle). But although I paid some five visits to Cyrenaica, three to Tripolitania, two to Eritrea, and one to the Dodecanese, I was thankful to God that I was always centred on Cairo and that I consequently never had to shoot in anger.

One day a letter of more than usual interest to me came, in the ordinary course of business, on to my desk. It was from the Chief Administrator of Tripolitania to my General (the Chief Civil Affairs Officer), and it concerned an English woman who had previously served for some years, with her doctor husband, as a missionary in Tripoli but had been expelled by the Italians just before the war. Her husband was now in the Royal Army Medical Corps; so she had written to the British Administrator asking for permission to return to Tripoli. She had, however, been unwise enough to enclose with her letter a specimen of the leaflets she sent to her prayer supporters about her work – couched in terms of spiritual warfare against the powers of darkness. This alarmed the Chief Administrator, who was disposed to refuse her request; but he wrote to my General about it, lest a question should be asked in Parliament. So I was able to point out that, had she behaved in the way her leaflet might seem to indicate, she would probably have been dead long ago, rather than a veteran missionary! As a result she was allowed back; and I had the pleasure, just before I left Egypt, of receiving a letter from an officer in the Tripolitanian administration saying that he reckoned that she was probably the greatest single influence for good in the whole territory.

Planning the future

It was about this time that I was asked to write papers

about each of the four occupied territories. My instructions were to make suggestions about their postwar future in the light of their ethnic composition, tribal areas, geographical divisions, political aspirations and external connections. We had heard that the Foreign Office had been consulting certain scholars in England on this subject, and were apprehensive that the advice they gave might not be based on an up-to-date knowledge of local realities and the current situation. My papers were then submitted to an internal scrutiny at Civil Affairs Branch and in the territories concerned before being passed to the Middle East War Council – a very high-powered committee presided over by the British Resident Minister and made up of the British High Commissioner in Egypt, the Chiefs of all three services, and a few others.

Not long after this I accompanied Pat and our daughters to Jerusalem, where they were to get a break from the heat of a Cairo summer in company with Pat's parents. I had hoped to spend the first week with them. But within two days I was summoned back to Cairo because the papers I had written were to be considered by the War Council, and I was required to be present to answer any questions. So I caught the night train from Jerusalem to Cairo, only to be turned out at a wayside station, in the early evening, because the line was blocked. This presented me with quite a quandary; so I telephoned to the local Brigadier, explained my plight, and asked if he could possibly get me driven down by car. This he refused, since on two recent occasions drivers bound for Cairo on the long desert road by night, after a day's work, had fallen asleep and crashed; but he said he would send a car to pick me up, give me dinner and a bed, and do his best to get a RAF plane to fly me to Cairo early next morning. This he succeeded in doing, and the situation was saved. But I rather grudged the loss of my one week in the cool of Jerusalem, since some ten hours a day in a small office in Cairo, which caught the full blaze of the afternoon sun (on top of a tempature often exceeding 100 degrees in the shade), leaves one pretty limp.

Next summer I did get some leave in Jerusalem, but under rather different circumstances. I had just been promoted as a full Colonel to the office of Chief Secretary when I went down with infective hepatitis, which affected some 10,000 of our troops, I believe, around that time. This meant some three weeks in the Scottish General Hospital in Cairo, where I was allowed to get out of bed only to go to the loo or to have a bath, but never to sit in a chair! When I pressed to be let out (it was one of the hottest summers I can remember), the doctor said I *must* take some sick leave; so I asked him to let me book a seat on an airplane up to Jerusalem, to which my family had again gone. It was just as well that the seat was booked, since when the time came he was very doubtful whether I was fit to leave the hospital. But walks along Mount Scopus with Pat and her father in the cool of the early evening, with the city in full view on one side and the mountains of Moab on the other, were quite delightful – although one evening I was so weak that I suddenly collapsed and we had to summon a taxi.

The war in Europe (although not, of course, in the Far East) had ended just before I left hospital, but work at the Civil Affairs Branch went on as usual. In the late autumn I heard that my father had bad angina and was not expected to live much longer. If I had got leave to fly home to see him I should probably not, at that time, have got a passage back, so I was sent to the

United Kingdom on duty – for negotiations with the War Office – and then to have a week at home. It was good that this was possible, since my father did in fact die just before we came home on release leave some months later. Incidentally, I had a minor adventure on two on these journeys: on the homeward flight we came across the Channel and landed at Hurn airport with only one engine working and an ambulance waiting, and on the return flight we made such a bad landing in the dark at an airfield near Tobruk that one wing and one propellor were buckled, and we had to wait overnight for a relief plane from Cairo.

Visit to Jeddah

A very pleasant interlude soon came my way in the form of a fascinating visit to Sa'udi Arabia. The Chief of the Imperial General Staff, Field Marshal Lord Alanbrooke, was paying farewell visits, before his retirement, to almost all the countries with which he had been concerned; and General Paget, Commander-in-Chief Middle East Forces, knowing that I was interested in Arabs and Arabic, kindly asked me if I would like to join his party. Besides Lord Alanbrooke, this consisted of General Paget himself, the naval Flag Officer for the Eastern Mediterranean, the Vice-Marshal in command of the RAF in the Middle East, and two or three less senior officers.

We flew to Khartoum for one night, which I spent with the District Commissioner, and then to Jeddah, to which King Ibn Sa'ud had come to meet us. We were first received in audience by the King, who naturally talked politics in terms of post-war relations. Fortunately for me, a Secretary from the British Embassy in Jeddah was there to interpret, since I should have found the King's accent very difficult to cope with. A little later he entertained us all to a banquet in his Palace, at which I sat next to his son and successor, Prince Sa'ud; and after dinner we all sat on the King's right or left on the flat roof of his Palace, while his entourage sat in long rows at right angles to us, to our right and left, and opposite the King stood a magnificent bedouin with a long two-edged sword. It was almost an Arabian Nights' scene, and one could easily imagine that at any moment the King might have pointed to someone and said 'Off with his head'! Next we went to the British Embassy to meet representatives of the British community, while a British cruiser anchored just off Jeddah gave a fire-work display in the late evening.

We were entertained that night at a Sa'udi guest bungalow, where I remember that the baths had only a cold tap (which emitted far from frigid water) at one end and an unplugged hole at the other – so one was always sitting in running water. To sit in water in which one has already washed was apparently considered unhygienic.

Next day the King, some of his fifty-odd sons, and a few other Arabs were invited to lunch on the deck of the British frigate, which was 'dressed overall'. The King himself did not come, but two or three of his sons did, and I sat next to Prince Faisal. As they came aboard a royal salute was fired from the frigate's guns. After lunch the Admiral invited me to travel with him, by sea rather than air, back to Port Sudan. I gladly accepted this invitation, but the Sirius (which was, I believe, somewhat 'heavy on top' from its guns) rolled rather badly when crossing what seemed a perfectly smooth gulf. Unhappily I am a shocking sailor, and the Admiral, who must have noticed this, suggested that I should cut dinner and go to bed. I tried to refuse, but he put me at my ease by saying that he had himself 'catted' for four years on destroyers; so I thankfully, but very regretfully, acted on his suggestion.

Before we left Arabia we had all been given gifts, as was the King's custom. The 'top brass' each received a set of Arab robes made of beautiful camel hair with gold embroidery, an equally splendid head-dress, and a sword in a scabbard embossed in silver. I, and two or three others, were given identical sets of robes and daggers with sheaths completely covered with gold; some of the officers of the Sirius received gold watches; and a number of sheep were loaded on the cruiser to provide the crew with fresh meat. I had quite an argument with the Egyptian customs, when I flew back to Cairo from Port Sudan, about whether they should make me pay duty on a gift given by an Arab monarch; but they eventually gave way!

That year a very nasty pogrom occurred in the market of Tripoli, when well over a hundred Jews were done to death and their shops were looted. Many were duly convicted of looting, but only five or six of murder – in trials which raised a number of somewhat difficult legal problems. By the time their death sentences, with all the necessary details, reached Cairo for confirmation by the Commander-in-Chief, our Chief Civil Affairs Officer, now Major-General Cumming, was in Paris as a temporary member of Ernest Bevin's staff at the Foreign Ministers' Conference of 1946, and I was acting for him in Cairo. So I had the unenviable task of reading all the reports, discussing them with our Legal Adviser, and then giving the Commander-in-Chief the appropriate advice. Duncan Cumming was, in the event, away for some weeks, but I cannot remember any other major worry. Work went on as usual; but I do recall being somewhat amused when I had to sign a letter to the Chief Administrator of Tripolitania authorizing a yearly budget amounting to some millions of pounds! But this was in fact no more than letting him know that a budget, prepared in detail in Tripolitania, had now been scrutinized and approved by the War Office.

Release leave

Almost as soon as Duncan Cumming got back to Cairo the time came for me to return to England on release leave. The army crated some of our belongings, since we did not expect to get back for some three years. My father had died, and I was the only son; our daughters needed to go to school in England; we had all been in the heat of the Middle East for some seven consecutive years, and we had agreed to pioneer a new venture in Cambridge. When I went to pay my respects to the Commander-in-Chief he told me that I was to be awarded an OBE (Military Division) on 13 June, just after we had sailed. Previously I had, to my surprise, been given a MBE (Military Division) in October 1943. I was now due for some months' release leave, since my service had all been overseas.

Looking back over almost six years in the Army, there were reasons for much thanksgiving and also for sincere regret. I was enormously grateful that, through no initiative on my own part, I had first been made Arab Liaison Officer in the Libyan Arab Force and then absorbed into the Occupied Enemy Territories Administration (or Civil Affairs Branch, GHQ, MEF). As a result I had never had to kill anyone. It was hard work, six and a half days a week; but most of it was interesting, and some of it absorbingly so. I had learnt quite a lot about administration in general, and the drafting of official letters in particular, by serving under and alongside men who had been trained in the Colonial Service, the Indian Political Service, and the Sudan Political Service – and also, of course, senior officers from the Regular Army. I had also learnt to be at ease with non-Christians in a way I had never learnt at Cambridge.

I think all who knew me were aware that I was a convinced Christian, with what they no doubt regarded as a few idiosyncrasies. But I do not, to my shame and deep regret, know of anyone during those years whom I personally led to Christ. I was able to live at home throughout the war, except for numerous excursions, and I had no very long absences from Pat and our daughters, except for their months in Kenya. More often than not I was able to attend a weekly Bible Reading with other members of the Officers' Christian Union, and a packed service on Sunday evenings in the Anglican Cathedral in Cairo (which was always evangelical, but only intermittently evangelistic). We got to know some fine Christian friends, and I had occasional chances to speak at meetings, at Soldiers' Homes and elsewhere. But meeting colleagues almost exclusively in the office gave only limited opportunities for intimate talks, and the rush of life in a hot climate was not conducive to adequate times of prayer and Bible study. Much more could, however, have been done.

Only this morning I was reading *Someone who beckons*, by Timothy Dudley-Smith. In his printed prayer about the most important of all life's choices, on the one hand, and the continual minor choices we have to make every day, on the other, he writes:

I *have* chosen. And I have chosen life, and
claimed your covenant, and set my face to
walk your ways, towards that 'destination
which God offers me'.
And then?
THUD
flat on my silly face, miles off-track, enticed
away by some elementary temptation,
the same old world, or flesh, or devil,
and all my choice, and resolution, and
commitment –
all to do again.

  And yet not all.
You take my choices, Lord, for what they are.
I could not choose except your Spirit
prompted me.
And after that, it is in your salvation, not my
choosing
that hope of heaven rests.[1]

This is a fair picture of much of my life. The vital
choice was made, with whole-hearted sincerity, many
years ago; and by God's grace I have never had any
desire whatever to go back on it. God is faithful, the
covenant stands, and all who have been truly redeemed
by Christ are set on a course which must lead, in the
end, to being 'conformed to his likeness', when we 'see
him as he is' (Romans 8:29; 1 John 3:2). But how
slowly (especially at times) some of us grow in grace,
and how often (especially at times) we fall before some
'elementary temptation, the same old world, or flesh,
or devil'.

[1] T. Dudley-Smith, *Someone who beckons* (IVP, 1978), p. 25.

In the war years it was much more 'the world' (mostly in the form of an absorbing job to be done, but also in a desire for, and enjoyment of, the position that went with it) than it was 'the flesh' which was apt to submerge my spiritual life. The pressures of the latter have invaded my mind more insistently at other periods. But, in one way or another, the devil is always active, and contests our spiritual growth at every step. How I wish that I had realized – before, during and after the war – that there is no short cut to holiness. We have been commanded strenuously to 'resist the devil' (James 4:7), to refuse him any foothold in our lives, and deliberately to 'purify ourselves from everything that contaminates body and spirit' (2 Corinthians 7:1) – in the power of him who is at work in us both 'to will and to act according to his good purpose' (Philippians 2:12–13).

9

The problem of holiness

Two baptisms? * *Personal holiness* *
Keswick * *Abiding 'in Christ'*

I have already referred in passing to how deeply concerned a number of CICCU members of my generation
were about the problem of holiness. Many of the visiting speakers at our weekly Bible Readings dealt with
this subject, directly or indirectly; so we were exposed
to the very varied – and even contradictory – teaching
on the doctrine of sanctification which was then
current. It would be no exaggeration to say that what
it really means to be 'sanctified', and how this can in
fact be achieved, were burning questions at that time
among those students who were eager to experience all
that God has for us here on earth.

I have no doubt that this same desire characterizes
many students today; but there is singularly little sign
now of the wrestling with different doctrines on this
subject which then prevailed – although these same
doctrines still exist (in what is, perhaps, a somewhat
more muted form). There is a manifest concern among
the present generation of students about the Holy
Spirit, and he is, of course, the Spirit of holiness; but
this concern seems to have undergone a subtle change.

Two baptisms?

The same differences of view still persist as to whether the baptism 'by', 'in' or 'with' the Spirit, predicted by John the Baptist (John 1:33) and promised by the risen Lord (Acts 1:5), has in fact been experienced by all Christians when they came as sinners to the Saviour, or whether this is a subsequent experience to which some Christians, but not all, can testify. The major argument in favour of the first view is the categorical statement that 'no-one can say, "Jesus is Lord," except by the Holy Spirit' (1 Corinthians 12:3), and the fact that in the same chapter Paul wrote to the church at Corinth as a whole: 'For we were all baptised by one Spirit into one body . . . and we were all given the one Spirit to drink' (1 Corinthians 12:13). The degree to which they in fact 'drank', however, must certainly have differed from one individual to another. The chief argument for the second view is, I suppose, the manifest difference between the experience of most of us contemporary Christians – which scarcely suggests that we have all been baptized 'with the Holy Spirit and with fire' (Matthew 3:11) – and that of the apostolic church, together with the vividness of a post-conversion experience to which many testify today.

The fundamental difference is not so much the use of the word 'baptized' in this context, although it is highly desirable to be precise and biblical in this matter. The vital question is whether a Christian actually inherits all the fullness of Christ at his regeneration, and then enters into this inheritance progressively. (This progression may be either by a comparatively steady growth, or by a series of subsequent crises – one of which may, of course, be particularly vivid.) Or does the full Christian experience normally come in two distinct stages? All would agree that the Bible teaches that it is only through the Holy Spirit's enabling that anyone can genuinely repent and accept Jesus as Saviour and Lord (1 Corinthians 12:3; Romans 8:9); that we are all commanded to 'be filled with the Spirit' (Ephesians 5:18) and to 'keep in step with the Spirit' (Galatians 5:25); and that we all need periodically to be especially 'renewed' by the Spirit (*cf.* Acts 4:31). I myself (like many today, whether they would call themselves 'charismatics' or not) feel that we should reserve the term 'baptized' by the Spirit for the initial Christian experience of being united with Christ in his death and resurrection, of which water baptism is only the outward symbol (Romans 6:3–7), and that we should be wise to use terms such as 'filled' or 'renewed' by the Holy Spirit for any subsequent experience. But that is a comparatively minor point.

Personal holiness

The essence of the difference of approach to this whole subject, by many of my generation and by many today, is that what we were seeking was not only the power of the Spirit to equip us for service, but also, and sometimes chiefly, his sanctifying work in our own hearts. In contrast, the contemporary quest is primarily, I think, in terms of the power and the gifts of the Spirit. I must confess that we in my day did not concern ourselves greatly about these 'gifts'. Nearly all of us at that time assumed, I think, that the more 'dramatic' gifts – such as healing, speaking in tongues and the interpretation of tongues – were given as 'signs' in the apostolic age, and had then been withdrawn. Again, the original apostles and Paul were unique, and would, in a very real sense, have no successors. The New

Testament prophets, we believed, were men especially inspired by God. Their function was either, in some cases, to predict the future or, more generally, to proclaim the word of the Lord authoritatively at a time when the churches were otherwise dependent on the Old Testament Scriptures, on the visit of an apostle, or on one or two apostolic letters. As for evangelists, pastors and teachers (to complete the list in Ephesians 4:11), they, thank God, were with us still.

We would have said much the same, no doubt, about 'the message of wisdom' and 'the message of knowledge' (1 Corinthians 12:8); 'gifts of administration' (1 Corinthians 12:28); and gifts of 'serving', 'teaching', 'encouraging', 'contributing to the needs of others', 'leadership' and 'showing mercy' (Romans 12:7–8). But we did not try to define some of these gifts very precisely, nor did we give much attention to deciding which of them had been 'distributed' to us individually by the Spirit to equip us to fulfil the particular role he had designed for us in building up the body of Christ. On this last point, I feel sure, we did not receive nearly enough teaching or put sufficient emphasis in our prayers. But when it comes to the matter of precise definition, a study of the different lists of spiritual gifts in the New Testament, especially in the Greek, suggests that the gifts mentioned were illustrative rather than exhaustive, and that there was a considerable amount of overlap between them.

My concern in this context, however, is the quest for personal holiness; and about this, as I have observed, the teaching we received at that time was much more insistent than it seems to be today – although it was also, very often, mutually contradictory. Among our visiting speakers there were two or three men, of outstanding personal holiness, who subscribed to the doctrine of the 'clean heart' (taught, for example, by the Japan Evangelistic Band), which is primarily based on Acts 15:8–9. Here Peter, describing his visit to the household and friends of Cornelius, stated that 'God, who knows the heart, showed that he accepted them by giving the Holy Spirit to them, just as he did to us. He made no distinction between us and them, *for he purified their hearts by faith*' (my italics. *Cf*. also Acts 26:18). The doctrine was also, at times, based on what seems to me to be a mistaken interpretation of 1 John 1:7, where we read that 'If we walk in the light, as he is in the light, we have fellowship with one another, and the blood of Jesus, his Son, purifies us from *all* sin' (my italics).

One way in which this doctrine was sometimes explained was by reference to the game of bowls, where each 'wood' has an in-built bias that effectively prevents it from following a straight course – like a Christian who wants to do God's will, but finds that he has an in-built bias that makes him swerve away from it. For this proposition, if my memory is correct, Romans 7:14–24 and Galatians 5:17 were often quoted – although these two passages should probably be distinguished and do not, as I now believe, sustain this doctrine. But the experience of receiving the fullness of the Holy Spirit (by 'surrender' and faith) would, these speakers taught, cleanse or purify the heart not only from the sins of the past and present but from this bias towards sin.

Keswick

On one visit to the Keswick Convention I met a man who went even farther than this. He taught that one could have such an experience of the Holy Spirit's cleansing power that, although still subject to temptations from 'outside', one would no longer be tempted from 'inside'. So far as I can remember he stopped short of asserting that this was a 'once-for-all' experience, but maintained that it could – and should – be maintained by grace through faith. He was a delightful man who impressed me greatly, and I questioned him fairly closely, in spite of my immaturity; but I could never accept his doctrinal position. It seems to me impossible, for example, to deny that the temptation to pride comes primarily from 'within'; yet, all down the ages, the saints have confessed that the temptation to pride – and, worst of all, to spiritual pride – is the most insidious temptation of all.

The concept of the bias towards sin being removed seems, at first sight, much more defensible, for the letter to the Hebrews makes a major point of the superiority of the New Covenant (predicted in Jeremiah 31:31–34 and fulfilled in Christ) over the Old Covenant. This was largely because the New Covenant substitutes a 'law' written on the heart and mind in place of the Mosaic Law inscribed on tablets of stone (Hebrews 8:10ff.; 10:16). This signifies an inward transformation of our affections and ways of thought that is far more effective than any external demand for an often unwilling, and humanly impossible, obedience.

But this surely points to our experience, in embryo at least, at conversion or regeneration, rather than providing any adequate basis for the doctrine of a 'second' work of grace which takes away, rather than promises the power to resist, what Paul terms 'the desires of the sinful nature' (Galatians 5:16). At the Keswick Convention itself, in those days, one could hear two speakers even at one meeting giving talks which, if analysed, really pointed in two different directions. But what came over – to me, at least – from the Convention as a whole was the concept of what I will term 'The Victorious Life', on which one could embark by surrender and faith.

Speaking for myself, I must confess that I have not found this concept helpful, but rather the reverse – for it led, almost inevitably, to a virtual repetition of my childhood response to the gospel (to which I have already referred). I remember, in particular, one night in the Cambridge Camp in Keswick when, stretched out alone in a tent, I surrendered myself yet again, to the very best of my knowledge and capacity, and claimed the fullness of the Holy Spirit. I also searched my heart and wrote a letter (largely unintelligible, I expect, to its recipient) trying to put right something I had said. But I am both very introspective and (alas) impatient by nature; so whenever I detected even the beginning of irritability, for example, I felt that I could not really have entered into the experience of 'The Victorious Life' – and must start all over again, with all that this entailed.

This did not worry me much during my last year at Cambridge. I was very busy, and I had much for which to thank God. But it troubled me greatly in the following year when I went to Egypt to seek God's guidance about the future. I stayed with three bachelor missionaries, all of whom were engaged to be married. Incidentally, they took it in turns to cater, and all of them wanted to save money for the future; so our life-style was pretty Spartan! This did me no harm at all; rather the reverse. But they were also very busy; and although one of them took me out, from time to time, to markets and showed me some of the work they were doing, I had a lot of time alone – to read, think and pray. The emotional upheaval of my own engage-ment followed; and then, after Christmas at home, I spent some months travelling round parts of Scotland and the north of England on deputation work – when again I was much alone, and had a lot of time for prayer and introspection.

Abiding 'in Christ'

Yet I had really been given the secret of what I needed – or at least part of the secret, had I only realized its implications – before the end of my years in Cambridge. I owed a great deal at that time to a somewhat older friend, C. J. B. Harrison, who came as our speaker at a preterminal 'retreat' and at some of the special meet-ings we arranged for freshmen. On one of these occasions I remember consulting him about the diffi-culty I found in 'abiding' in Christ. I would try to do this consciously, for example, during a game of hockey, with the result that I was far from satisfied with the quality either of my hockey or my 'abiding'! In reply, he told me how it had come home to him that a vine branch does not need desperately to hang on to the vine and try to be a branch; it simply *is* a branch. So, provided nothing comes between it and the life of the vine itself, the sap will continue to flow into it.

I also needed to learn what members of the Rwanda Revival subsequently emphasized so insistently: that, as soon as one becomes conscious of any sort of sin, one should immediately confess it, put things right with anyone else who might be involved, and rejoice in God's full and free forgiveness. It is not a case of trying to launch out again on some mental concept of 'The Victorious Life', with the introspection (and thus absorption in oneself) that this entailed; but of picking

128

oneself up as quickly as possible after any fall, and simply getting on with the race – 'looking unto Jesus'.

Later still I came to recognize, largely through the teaching of Dr Martyn Lloyd-Jones, that it is God's fixed purpose that *every* Christian should be 'conformed to the image of his Son'; and that this should proceed progressively here in this world, through the grace of God and the discipline of life, but would be complete only when we see Christ face to face (1 John 3:2). The end result is certain, for it is God's determined purpose which he will himself bring to completion. What remains our responsibility is the pace at which the work proceeds, since we can hinder or hasten it by the way in which we respond to the encouragements and discipline our Father graciously gives us; for it is possible to react to both of these either in the right way or the wrong way. Primarily, however, we should get our eyes off ourselves and on to him:

> In Thy strong hand I lay me down,
> So shall the work be done;
> For who can work so wondrously
> As the Almighty One?

That is one side of 'the problem of holiness'. If we are truly 'in Christ', then it is certainly God's will that we should be sanctified, or made holy; and we can count on him to give us the training and the testing that we need. But there is another side to the problem: the nature of the way in which we should respond. It is at this point that there is such a conflict of opinion. Are we to 'try' to the utmost, or simply to 'trust'; to 'let go and let God', or to 'resist' sin at any cost (*cf.* Hebrews 12:4)? The apostle Paul unequivocally commands us to 'work out, with trembling . . . self-distrust, your own

129

salvation. You have not to do it in your unaided strength: it is God who is all the while supplying the impulse, giving you the power to resolve, the strength to perform, the execution of His good-pleasure' (Philippians 2:12–13, Way's translation).

There is no teaching in the New Testament (as I have now come to realize) that there is a 'second experience', here in this life, by which pride, 'the evil heart of unbelief', or the other effects of the Fall on our minds and bodies can be instantaneously removed, or by which we can launch out into '*The* Victorious Life' by surrender and faith. Instead we are told to 'count' ourselves (or recognize that, theologically speaking, we *are*) 'dead to sin but alive to God in Christ Jesus' (Romans 6:11). So we 'have an obligation' not to live on the level of our fallen nature, but 'by the Spirit to go on putting to death' those remnants of that nature that can still so easily 'entangle' us as long as we live in our mortal bodies (*cf*. Romans 8:13; Hebrews 12:1). By grace we are now adopted sons of God, and the Spirit we have received from him is not one of bondage and fear, but rather 'the Spirit of adoption', enabling us to 'cry, "*Abba*, Father"' (Romans 8:15). As sons, our supreme concern should be our Father's glory and his will, rather than being absorbed in ourselves, whatever form that absorption may take.

How very much I wish that all this had been clearer to me fifty years ago!

10

Tyndale House

When we were about to come home on release leave, in
the summer of 1946, I had already accepted the post of
Warden of Tyndale House, Cambridge. This was a
newly acquired property to provide a residential
library for advanced biblical research. We were to
travel on the Mauritania, then still a troop-ship; and
we had heard stories of the large 'dormitory' cabins in
which a number of women, children and babies were
often herded together. So on the troop-train from Cairo
to Port Said we were wondering what our own fate
would be. In due course a young transport officer
came down the train to give us news.

All husbands and wives were to be separated, but
Pat was greatly relieved to hear that she and our two
daughters had been allotted an inside cabin to themselves, where I could at least go and see them. I was to
share a very nice cabin on one of the upper decks with
three other officers ('Colonel A, Colonel B, and a naval
officer whose name I do not yet know; but I can assure
you, sir, that he will be of an equivalent rank'!). To this
gem of service mentality I replied that I was not nearly
as interested in his rank as in his girth. Where the

question of rank and age did come in was on the deck, for which I had brought a folding tent-chair for Pat, who was already suffering somewhat from her back. When, however, the considerably older wives of Generals or Brigadiers came along and started to talk to her, she felt that courtesy demanded that she should offer it to them; and they almost invariably accepted! There were no deck-chairs or even benches on the decks.

We had never travelled in a ship that sailed so fast, and we reached Liverpool in little more than a week, in spite of calling at Naples to pick up further troops. At Liverpool the customs officers came on board, and I was able to go down into the hold, locate and haul out most of our heavy luggage, and get it put on a train to London. So it was not long before we reached my mother's home in Southborough (a house in which John Wesley had once preached from the staircase).

The Foreign Ministers' Conference

Almost immediately, however, I received a summons to go over to Paris to fill the place on Ernest Bevin's staff at the Foreign Ministers' Conference previously occupied by Major-General Duncan Cumming. The object of this exercise was that, whenever the subject of the future of the occupied enemy territories might come up for discussion by the Foreign Ministers or their deputies, they would have someone available with up-to-date knowledge of the countries concerned and the aspirations of their peoples.

The British delegation was housed, appropriately enough, in the King George V Hotel, and I made the pleasant discovery that I was to share an apartment with Major-General Arthur Dove, the official representative of the War Office and a fellow-member of the Officers' Christian Union. The arrangement was simple: one of the single beds in the bedroom was moved into the sitting-room for me, and we shared the other facilities. The inside walls of the bathroom consisted almost exlusively of mirrors, so wherever one looked one saw nothing but ever-repeated reflections of oneself from every angle. This might, no doubt, have given delight to some; but for me, at least, it was distinctly a shock. It was safer to keep one's eyes turned constantly towards heaven – not, indeed, as a remedy for vanity, but as an escape from a humiliating reality! We had a continental breakfast brought to our respective rooms and our other meals in the dining-room, where the food at that juncture was a mixture of local provisions and British army rations. One of the many Foreign Office members of the delegation remarked one day that he was positively staggered at how many words in a French menu could all mean cod!

Bevin was most courteous, and invited me to lunch the day after I arrived. He himself was rather late, and Mrs Bevin remarked to me: 'It's dreadful how unpunctual "father" has become since he went to the Foreign Office. I suppose it's all this Eton and Harrow business!' But when he came and we sat down to lunch, it was not long before the whole party (of ten or twelve, I believe) gave up any pretence of conversation with their neighbours and addressed their questions to him. After nearly forty years I can still remember one of his replies (which concerned the Foreign Office, appropriately enough – since except for me everyone present was either a member of the diplomatic service or his wife). Bevin had been talking about the conditions in the Ministry of Labour when he had taken this over early in the war. 'But, sir,' said Sir Gladwyn Jebb (then Bevin's Deputy at the Conference, now Lord Gladwyn), 'what we want to know is what's wrong with the Foreign Office? Is it the "old school tie", the Oxford and Cambridge ethos, or the traditions of the past?'

'No, Gladwyn, my boy,' Bevin replied, 'nothing of the sort. I'll tell you what's wrong with the Foreign Office. What's wrong is that for many years now the Foreign Secretary has never been allowed to run his own show without interference from the Prime Minister. First there was Lloyd-George, then there was Baldwin, Chamberlain and Winston. Why, poor Anthony, he had the devil of a life! So when Clem Attlee asked me to take on the Foreign Office, I asked him if that was really the job he wanted me to do. When he said it was, I remarked: "They always say that the Foreign Office is just the other side of the road from No. 10." "Yes," said Attlee, "I suppose it is." "Well, Clem," I told him, "if I'm to take on the job, that's where it's going to stay."' And I think it is probably true that Bevin 'ran his own show' in foreign policy more independently than has been true of any other recent Foreign Minister.

I could tell many stories about Ernest Bevin, but must forbear. He was a great character. He told us, as I remember, that he had been a Methodist Lay Preacher in his youth; but I am afraid little of that remained, to all appearances, except for a rugged integrity of character. We had a meeting of the British delegation as a whole about 10.30 every morning (for the Foreign Office usually seems to get up late and then work far into the night). There were a number of senior people present, including service personnel; but from the moment Bevin came in there was no doubt who was chairman.

'Well, what's the Navy doing?' he would ask. 'Oh, we're negotiating about the former German fleet,' some Rear-Admiral would reply. 'But the First Lord is very anxious, sir, that you should not let the Russians get a foothold in port X.' 'I've no doubt he is,' Bevin would reply; 'the Navy always wants everything. But if I say the Russians can't have any foothold there, they'll only say we mustn't have any right whatever somewhere else. No, I don't think I can stand out for that.' Then he would look round the big table and say, 'Do you think I'm right?' One day I plucked up courage to say that I had been somewhat disturbed by one of the secret telegrams I had seen, since 'the Commander-in-Chief in the Middle East...'. 'Oh, you'd better come and see me about that afterwards,' he said; and when I did he was most reasonable. He was a true patriot, and I can remember him once saying: 'Yes, I think that's right; but I'll find it difficult to put it across to my Party, you know.'

Most Foreign Secretaries, whatever their virtues, have had no experience in bargaining, so what delighted those from the Foreign Office about Bevin was that he had been doing it for years – with the skippers of ships about the wages of their crew, and in a thousand other ways. The Deputies to the Foreign Ministers met in the later part of each morning, while the complete delegations met in the afternoon and early evening. It was very hot, that mid-summer in Paris, especially for those of us who had to wear full winter uniform all the time, and the Conference Chamber became a fume-laden hot-house.

From time to time Mr Byrnes, the American Secretary of State, would, for example, make a long speech which would no doubt make good reading in the American press. Mr Molotov would listen, with eyes which suggested that he sometimes, at least, understood; but he always waited for the translation. Finally he would either pick on some comparative detail for argument (as was frequently the case), or would simply reply: 'We stand by the Yalta Agreement' – shorthand, the experts told me, for 'I can say nothing more about that until I've been on the telephone to Moscow'. The only time when everyone except the Russians would look really happy was when 'Ernie' Bevin would, once in a way, reply to a long speech by Molotov by looking across the table at him and saying: 'I'm sorry, Mr Molotov, I'd like to meet your wishes, but I won't 'ave it!' – accompanied by a loud slap on the table. Complete silence would then reign until one of the Foreign Ministers would say, 'I think we had better turn to the next point on our agenda.' There are usually a number of details which may be challenged or discussed in a long speech, but very little that can be said to one who confines his reply to a proposal to a firm 'I won't 'ave it'!

Occupied territories

As for the occupied territories (which were my concern), there was little difficulty in the decision that the Dodecanese, captured by us from the Germans, should go back to Greece, or that Eritrea should become a semi-autonomous part of the Ethiopian Empire. A good case could, however, have been made, in my opinion, for uniting the largely Christian and Tigrinia-speaking highlands with the Tigrai province of Ethiopia, and the Muslim and Tigre-speaking Western lowlands with the Sudan (possibly including, as a much-needed 'hill station', the semi-highland district around Keren where the people speak a distinct language of their own). Cyrenaica, again, presented only a minor problem: it should become a constitutional monarchy, with Sayyid Idris as King – but possibly, for a time, under British tutelage of some sort.

It was Tripolitania which occasioned much the most controversy. First, the Russians suggested that they should hold a Mandate over it. For this they could produce no possible claim of right – other than that of naked 'power politics'. Next, the Americans proposed that a United Nations Administrator from some neutral State should be appointed, together with an Advisory Council composed, if I remember right, of one American, one Britisher, one Russian, one Italian, one Turkish and possibly one Egyptian member. This suggestion conjured up a positive nightmare of intrigue and 'politicizing' to anyone accustomed to dealing with Arabs, and was firmly rejected. So the only reasonable alternative seemed to be to join Tripolitania and Cyrenaica together (for which there was singularly little historical precedent except under the Italians and, previously, the loose Ottoman hegemony) under the rule of King Idris, with a British Adviser, temporarily, in Cyrenaica and an Adviser from some other country in Tripolitania (where, incidentally, the authority of King Idris would be much less stable). The new Libya seemed destined to be very poor (until its large oil resources were subsequently discovered); so its needs were met, at first, by generous American payments for an air base in Tripolitania, and smaller British payments for facilities for military training in Cyrenaica.

To Cambridge

After I had made what small contribution I could to

the Foreign Ministers' Conference in Paris, I asked if I might return to England and be 'on call' if I could be of any further use. So, after a time by the sea in a small holiday house my mother owned in Bexhill, we took up our appointment at Tyndale House, Cambridge. This was a house that had been bought by the Inter-Varsity Fellowship (now the Universities and Colleges Christian Fellowship) towards the end of the war, to be a 'Residential Library for Biblical Research'. It had been occupied in an unofficial way by two or three people, including – at the time of our advent – the Reverend Henry Chadwick and his wife. Henry Chadwick was then Chaplain and Fellow of Queens' College, Cambridge, but has subsequently been Regius Professor of Divinity at both Oxford and Cambridge and also, between these two appointments, Dean of Christ Church, Oxford. During his months in Tyndale House he had collected the nucleus of what has now grown into a really fine library for biblical research; and he did all he could to help me when I arrived as the first Warden.

When I was offered this appointment while I was still in the Army in Egypt, we had accepted this as our next step, although we were then still hoping to return to the Middle East as missionaries after some three years. My mother had just been widowed; our two daughters had to get settled in English schools; and we needed time to think and pray about our own future.

Tyndale House was a delightful building, with a fine garden, set in an almost ideal position. But much needed to be done to the house, and many additions made, before it could really fulfil its purpose. Pat and I slept in a bedroom so large that it has now been turned into a flat. Another vast room, also now turned into a flat, was bursting at its seams as the beginnings of the present research library; a spacious room was occupied by our two little girls; and a fourth housed two *au pair* girls from Norway. Central heating had been installed in the house by its previous owners but could not be used at this time because of restrictions; and three gas fires that we ordered in the autumn for the three attic bedrooms arrived only in May. We were able to stoke an antiquated boiler in a vast kitchen, light a coke and wood fire in the main reception room, and have a gas fire in our bedroom (round which some of our visitors would occasionally gather). This was the first winter we had had in England for some fourteen years, and it was a quite exceptionally cold one. There was then, of course, no separate Warden's House, and no purpose-built Library with study bedrooms above it; so there was very little room for the Library to expand or to become 'residential'.

The garden was well stocked with plum trees and apple trees, and had quite a variety of vegetables as well as flowers. During the two days when I went ahead of the family to unpack crates of blankets, linen and a few pieces of furniture brought home for us by the army, and to receive and arrange other pieces of furniture given to us by my mother, I lived almost exclusively on plums and apples. But rationing then was at its most stringent (worse even than in the war years, we were told); and visitors had to bring both meat and bread coupons, to say nothing of little pots of butter, sugar and jam. We got half a pint of milk a day for the whole family, and one egg each a week. When I went, one Sunday, to preach morning and afternoon in the Fens, and brought home with me the gift of a chicken and lots of eggs and butter (gifts, but not sales, being exempt from rationing), Pat almost swooned and then said, 'Why don't you go and preach in the Fens every Sunday?'

None of this is intended to be a grumble, for we enjoyed life a lot and had plenty of fun; but it does explain why it was so difficult to get things going. Our elder daughter went away to school at Clarendon (then in Malvern, next in North Wales, and now – years later – near Bedford). Our younger daughter, who had been coached in Egypt with a small boy whose parents wanted him to go to the Dragon Preparatory School, got into the Junior Perse as a day-girl. We all took to bicycles, but we eventually also got a second-hand baby Austin, with enough petrol rations to visit our daughter in Malvern from time to time.

Resident visitors in term-time were few and far between – not primarily because of our lack of space, the minimal character of our Library, fuel restrictions, and the like; but because no scholarship grants were available, and few people just then were in a position to spend much time on research. The one activity we were able to get started, in embryo at least, was a number of Study Groups in the vacations. At these we had some good times, in spite of food restrictions and shortage of accommodation. The Reverend Stafford Wright, I remember, used to put up a tent in the garden! For the latter, indeed, we even had a part-time gardener, Mr Minns by name, who was so short that when he squatted at his work he was almost indistinguishable from a cabbage! His help enabled us not only to profit from fruit and vegetables, but also to invite numbers of CICCU men and women to tea in the garden, when the weather allowed, and sometimes to hear talks from visiting missionaries.

In term-time I first got permission from the Professor of Arabic to attend his classes in the really classical language, and then to attend a few lessons in Biblical Hebrew. This was taught by the direct method: that is, by starting with Genesis 1:1 and analysing each word as it comes, rather than starting with grammar and syntax in the abstract. I think this method was more helpful to me than to the other beginners, since a knowledge of Arabic was a great help; but the lecturer, although by no means a conservative in his attitude to Scripture, spent an inordinate part of our lecture-periods inveighing against the 'documentary theory' of the Pentateuch. Under this, scholars divide up passages and even verses on grounds which, he alleged, no self-respecting philologist could stomach, instead of explaining problems in the text in terms of the different localities in which certain words or titles were in use. But during my first term in Cambridge I was asked if, at the beginning of the Lent term, I would take on the task of giving University lectures on Islam (mostly to recruits to the Colonial Service, but they were also attended during one term by the Kabaka, or King, of Uganda); and soon after this I was asked to give forty lectures a year on Islamic law in the Law Faculty. So I began to realize that I was probably too old a dog to learn wholly new tricks and that I should not lightly jettison such qualifications as I happened to have.

Three years at Tyndale House

Three points dominate all others as I look back at the three years we had at Tyndale House. The first is a purely personal one. I came to Cambridge with a consciousness of my need for spiritual renewal and, thank God, I got it. I had been living a life of great activity marred by considerable failure and dryness of spirit. Then, in an otherwise undistinguished sermon (which, in itself, is an encouragement to those of us who often have to preach), God showed me, from the story in Luke 7 of the 'woman who had lived a sinful life', that the source and inspiration of a true devotion to the Lord Jesus is not years of faithful and fruitful service (much though this should be our goal), but a wondering sense of his matchless forgiveness. That woman was not forgiven because she loved much, but she loved much because she was conscious of how much she had been forgiven.

Her sins may have been 'scarlet', in the colours in which most people assess sin, while mine were more like dirty stains – sins of omission, and sins of the mind, thought and spirit for the most part – but they were, none the less, failure and defeat. And it dawned on me that one way in which God can and does 'restore' to us 'the years the locusts have eaten' (Joel 2:25) is precisely this – the continual sense of the wonder of his forgiveness. Very soon after this renewal, moreover, the church we attended had a mission led by some of the leaders of the Rwanda Revival movement. With one voice they testified, again and again, that there is no such thing as a 'once for all' experience of sanctification, into which one can enter by surrender and faith as a short cut to genuine holiness, but rather a pilgrimage in which one becomes more, not less, conscious of any sin or failure, but learns to look up at once for cleansing, to rejoice again in the wonder of divine forgiveness, and to get on with the war.

The second point that I chiefly remember concerns the CICCU rather than myself, although there was, no doubt, a link between the two. When Pat and I first came to Tyndale House, I think it would be true to say that some members of the CICCU looked at it with mild suspicion. They were so conscious that an intellectual approach to the Bible had, in many cases, led to aridity and a flabby liberalism, that they feared that a 'Residential Library for Biblical Research', even under the auspices of the Inter-Varsity Fellowship, might contaminate 'the simple gospel' which meant so much to them. But in those days it was the custom for CICCU members in almost every college to come together weekly for a Bible Reading led, at least for one term in the year, by someone from outside the group; and I soon found myself leading two or three Bible studies every week, while Pat also led similar Bible studies in Newnham, Girton, or both. All colleges were at that time single sex.

The fact that I had given up my intention to learn Hebrew, moreover, prompted me to go back to the Greek I had studied for a time at school but had almost completely forgotten. I had not, for many years, been a very good sleeper, so at Tyndale House I began to slip out of bed as soon as I woke up (at any time after 4 a.m.), creep along to the Library, wrap myself up in a dressing-gown and rug, and study one of the New Testament letters in Greek with the help of a good commentary. This gave me much spiritual food for my own soul and also, secondarily, for the College Bible Studies. Bible Readings, in fact, became for years the sort of talks I most enjoyed giving (whether at IVF Leaders' Conferences, for the Graduates' Fellowship, or for the Christian Medical Fellowship). Those were, indeed, years of spiritual progress such as I had never previously known.

The third point to which I look back in those years was the way in which my future life seemed to be shaping. As I have observed in passing, Pat and I had hoped to return to the Middle East after some three years, but we could not find any home where we felt we could happily leave our two daughters. None of our relations could take them on, and for one reason or another we could not find a really feasible alternative. Then, a few months before our three years in Cambridge ended, our only son, Hugh, was born.

Meanwhile I had decided that if I was to go back to the academic life I had left when I went to Egypt, I ought to capitalize my resources. I had the academic record which would be acceptable for a teaching-post in Law in some British University; but my English law was rusty, and there are many English lawyers. I also had a reasonably good working knowledge of Arabic, but not of the pre-Islamic poetry (and the like) which would qualify me as an Arabist. Since, however, Islamic law is followed, to some degree at least, by about one in seven of the world's population, there was a real need for it to be taught in this country. So it occurred to me that, whereas very few English lawyers knew any Arabic, and very few Arabists were lawyers, I happened to have both the necessary qualifications – a legal background and a working knowledge of Arabic.

Back to Law

Much though we loved Tyndale House, moreover, it did not seem right to stay there more than three years. In addition to the Library itself, five Andersons and an *au pair* girl, all housed in large rooms, took up too much space; the Study Groups all fell in the vacations, just when our children were at home and could easily become spoilt or neglected; and I had decided to go back to Law rather than start, in early middle life, on a wholly new academic discipline. While still at Cambridge, therefore, I accepted a lectureship in Islamic

Law at the School of Oriental and African Studies in the University of London, to which I travelled two days a week. So we decided to leave Cambridge and move to London – although I continued to teach Islamic Law in Cambridge as a visitor for a few more years.

It is wonderful now to see, nearly thirty years later, how Tyndale House has flourished. A few years after we left it a separate Warden's House and Library complex were built. The latter (with one room in the big house as an Annexe) now houses some 23,000 volumes and a number of special desks at which scholars can do their work in comfort (I am sitting at one of them now), together with some fourteen study bedrooms on the floor above. In addition, most of the vast bedrooms in the old house have now been turned into delightful little flats to accommodate visiting scholars (with their wives and sometimes a child). The number of past readers who now hold teaching-posts in Universities and theological Seminaries – whether in Britain, the USA, Canada, Australia, Africa or elsewhere – grows year by year; and there have been a succession of splendid Wardens, all biblical scholars in their own right, each of whom has made his own distinctive contribution to the community and its activities. The number of Annual Lectures which are given, the size and variety of the Study Groups, and the number and magnitude of the research grants which are available, seem to increase from year to year. And now, as I write, extensive additions are being made to the Library complex to accommodate more books, provide further desks for readers, and make an excellent seminar room available.

Pat and I look back to those years at Tyndale House as some of the happiest of our lives.

11

Learning my trade

*Study leave in Egypt * Family law * Surveys in
Africa * America * Uganda and Nigeria *
Setbacks and opening vistas*

When we left Tyndale House and moved to Ealing, I
had already held the post of Lecturer in Islamic Law
at the School of Oriental and African Studies for two
years – besides teaching that subject in Cambridge.
But I had been much too dependent on textbooks
written in English about what is commonly known as
'Anglo-Muhammadan Law'. This is a system which
had its origin in what was then 'British India', and it
still largely represents in the personal law of Muslims
throughout the Indian subcontinent. It has also had
considerable influence in former British Protectorates
and Colonies in the Persian Gulf, Aden and East
Africa. Its basis is, of course, the Shari'a law of Islam,
but in a form governed by statutory enactments,
moulded by English rules of legal procedure, and
mutilated – on occasion – by judicial interpretation.

If, then, I was now to make Islamic Law my major
academic concern, it was imperative that I should
study it through the standard Arabic texts in the light
of contemporary treatises and handbooks in that language. A matter of particular interest and importance,
moreover, was the attempt that had been made to

146

adapt parts of the Shari'a (or canon law of Islam) to the circumstances of modern life. This attempt had started in the Ottoman Empire, was being actively pursued in Egypt and the Sudan, and was under consideration elsewhere in the Middle East and North Africa.

Study leave in Egypt

Our next step, therefore, was to go on six months' study leave to Egypt, which was at that time the intellectual centre of the Muslim world and in the vanguard of legal reforms. It was also the country in which I should be able to forge the best academic contacts. So at the end of September 1949 Pat and I flew out to Alexandria with a happy little boy who was not quite a year old.

We were able to get rooms in Fairhaven, where Pat's parents were then living. Fairhaven is a fine old building designed years ago by Miss Amy van Somner (a woman of great vision and faith) as a holiday home for missionaries during the summer heat of inland Egypt. Pat's parents had had to move there when her mother's arthritis made it impossible for her to run her own house. So this was an ideal arrangement for us. I could study in the house, and establish academic contacts in Alexandria and with visitors from Cairo. I could also myself travel, with a clear mind, to Cairo, the Sudan, Jordan, Lebanon, Syria and Iraq.

The legislative reforms in Muslim countries, to which I have already referred, were usually of two totally different types. In matters of commercial law, criminal law, the law of procedure and what our continental friends term the 'law of obligations' (chiefly contracts and civil wrongs), the reforms in many of the countries concerned had virtually abandoned Islamic law. In its place they adopted legislation based, for the most part, on French law (although in the Indian subcontinent, and a few other places, principles of English law had been preferrred). To sweep Islamic law on one side in regard to so large a part of life, and to import in its place a basically alien system, might well seem an almost incredible step for a Muslim government such as that of the Ottoman Empire. The fact is that these changes were imposed from above, in the interests of bureaucracy, modernization and the desire to compete on equal terms with other European powers, rather than evolving from below. But at that time Muslims preferred to keep their sacred law compact and inviolate, even if largely replaced in practice through the exigencies of the modern world, rather than to permit any profane meddling with its immutable provisions.

Egypt was the ideal place to study this development, because a new Civil Code had been promulgated in Egypt only the year before, to come into operation in 1949. This was when the Mixed Courts (set up, years before, to deal with litigation between foreigners from two different countries, or between foreigners and native Egyptians) were abolished. The main architect of this new code was 'Abd al-Razzaq al-Sanhuri, now President of the Conseil d'Etat in Cairo; but, fortunately for me, his chief lieutenant was the Dean of the Law Faculty in Alexandria, and he was very helpful. He gave me a series of volumes he had written about this code and was kind enough to elucidate points on which I wanted to ask questions.

Family law

My major interest, however, was in regard to the

family law of Islam. In this field Muslims were not prepared to jettison the Islamic law of Personal Status (or law of the family in its widest connotation) for some alien system. Yet changes in that law, they felt, must necessarily be made. But while law reform is easy enough in regard to man-made law, how could it be done in regard to a law fundamentally based on what they believed to be divine revelation? In the event, in one after another of most of the countries in the Middle East, they managed to do this by one or more of four expedients.

One expedient was a procedural device. Here they made no change at all in the substantive law, but simply provided that certain parts of it were not to be enforced by the courts except in specified circumstances. The second expedient was to promulgate such codes of law (or specific legislative enactments) as they considered necessary by weaving together a miscellany of provisions, for each of which they could claim some Islamic authority. Usually this was from the dicta of well-known jurists of the past, although they sometimes combined parts of two different dicta in a composite whole that neither of the original jurists would have approved. The third device was technically known as reopening 'the door of *ijtihad*': that is, the right to go back to the original sources of the law and interpret them in a new way. This right had previously been regarded, in orthodox circles, as confined to jurists of the first three centuries of Islam. The fourth method was simply to promulgate legislation specifically based on one of these expedients, but occasionally with no more than the bland assertion that this was 'not contrary to Islamic law'.

At that time the latest of these legislative reforms in Egypt concerned the Islamic rules governing the *waqf*

149

system (more or less equivalent to English trusts and endowments). In this the leading figure was Sheikh Faraj al-Sanhuri, who normally visited Alexandria once a week. He had himself written two volumes explaining the provisions in this new piece of legislation, and the grounds on which so many changes had been made in the existing law. So I contacted him, and he was kind enough to spare me time, almost every week, in which I could ask him questions about this law – and, indeed, about several comparable enactments about which he was a positive mine of information. This gave me a most valuable start in my study of these recent reforms, about which I was also able to talk, on my visits to Cairo, with Sheikh Muhammad Abu Zahra and several others who had written extensively on this subject.

But these months of study leave were not confined to Egypt. First, I spent two or three weeks in the Sudan. This was partly in order to work out (with the Egyptian Professor of Islamic Law in the University of Khartoum) the syllabus for an examination in Islamic Law to be taken by their students as one subject in a London LL.B. Unhappily for me, this meant that for some years I had to act as an examiner in that subject. Reading scripts written at top speed in English can be difficult enough, but I found scripts written in Arabic under the pressure of an examination a great deal worse. Much the most profitable part of this visit to me, therefore, was to discover how much progress had been made in the Sudan in effecting reforms in Islamic law. These had frequently followed, and sometimes anticipated, reforms which had been introduced, or were under discussion, in Egypt.

I was also able, in the course of these six months, to visit Jordan, the Lebanon, Syria and Iraq, and to study and discuss similar – although never identical – reforms which had either been promulgated or were under consideration in these countries. These visits gave me the opportunity to get to know a few of the leading jurists – and also, in Baghdad, to venture to give a lecture in Arabic to what was their nearest equivalent to one of the sections of the British Academy.

As a result of this period of study leave I wrote nine consecutive articles on 'Law Reform in the Muslim World' for an American quarterly entitled *The Muslim World*. Subsequently I also wrote a number of articles, in a variety of journals, about reforms in the field of family law which were successively promulgated in the Sudan, Lebanon, Jordan, Syria and (after further visits and consultations) in Tunisia, Morocco and Iraq.

Surveys in Africa

We returned to London at the end of March, 1950; but in the autumn I was off again, this time by myself, for three months of very hard work studying the scope and application of Islamic law in Tanganyika (as it then was), Zanzibar, Nyasaland (now Malawi), Uganda, British Somaliland (now part of Somalia) and Aden (now the People's Democratic Republic of Yemen).

I got home just in time for Christmas, after which I spent the Lent term lecturing at the School of Oriental and African Studies and writing up the information I had garnered, in each of these territories, from Government files, talks with local judges, reported cases and other material. Then I sent what I had written in regard to each country to some knowledge-able person whom I had persuaded to scrutinize my material to see if I had made any mistakes – before setting out again, in the spring of 1952, to spend a similar period of study and research in Nigeria, the Gold Coast (now Ghana), Sierra Leone and the Gambia (as it then was).

The Christmas term that year was almost a repetition of the Lent term – lecturing at SOAS and writing up the material I had collected on my visits, this time, to what were then British Colonies in West Africa. Again I sent my script to some kindly person in each country who had promised to check it for any inaccuracies. Finally, I spent such time as I could spare during the first eight months of 1953 putting all this material into book form. This was published in 1954 by Her Majesty's Stationery Office, under the title *Islamic Law in Africa*, as Colonial Research Publication No. 16, with a Foreword by Lord Hailey. It ran, I believe, to about 250,000 words; and I have just noted with amusement that a casebound copy then sold for 50 shillings (£2.50)! It was republished in 1970 by Frank Cass at a very much higher price.

America

I had been appointed Reader in Oriental Laws in the University of London in 1951, and in 1954 Professor of that subject. I had also succeeded Dr Vesey-FitzGerald as Head of the Department of Law in the School of Oriental and African Studies in 1953; and had been awarded the Cambridge LL.D. in 1955 on the strength of *Islamic Law in Africa* and a number of articles on recent developments in Islamic law in the Middle East and elsewhere. Then, in 1957, I paid my first visit to the United States to take part in a Conference at Dobb's Ferry about Islamic Studies. This was very informative, and enabled me to meet a number of

152

outstanding scholars. The Rockefeller Foundation, which had financed the Conference, had also kindly suggested that I might like to spend two or three weeks in America and make other contacts. Most of these were academic; but I remember being driven, by a missionary friend, to speak at a church in the Amish region of Pennsylvania whose Pastor was Chairman of the American Council of our Mission (now, since the Suez débâcle, re-named the Middle East General Mission, with most of its missionaries deployed in Eritrea rather than Egypt).

After visiting New York University Law School I went with some of its Faculty to part of the annual meeting of the American Bar Association, that year in Washington. Here I was introduced to two or three Justices of the Supreme Court, and also spoke at a 'Prayer Breakfast' arranged by Dr Abraham Vereide, the founder of International Christian Fellowship, with whom I stayed. I also visited Stony Brook, a school that would be described in Britain as a public school, but in America as a 'prep school'. It had, and still has, a fine Christian record, and its founder and then Headmaster, Dr Frank Gaebelein, became a much valued friend. Visits to Harvard and Yale completed a delightful introduction to America, during which I had the opportunity to speak at several meetings and give two or three lectures.

Everyone had to get an exit visa before leaving America at that time, and I remember a middle-aged lady in the appropriate office in Boston asking me sternly whether I had earned any money during my time in the United States. 'Only a few hundred dollars, which I was given in respect of a lecture here and there,' I replied. 'Can you prove that?' she demanded. When I said I couldn't, she told me that in that case she could not give me an exit visa. 'That's too bad,' I remarked, 'since I doubt if the American Government will want me to stay here for the rest of my life!' With this she probably agreed, but did not say so. So I tried a different tack. 'If I had told you that I hadn't earned any money over here, would you have given me a visa?' I asked. She answered this question in the affirmative. 'In that case', I suggested, 'you might as well take my word for it that I have received a few dollars for the odd lecture' – and this, somewhat grudgingly, she did.

In 1958, Pat and I both went to America for some three months, since I had been invited as Visiting Professor by Princeton University, in collaboration with New York University Law School. In Princeton, of course, there is no Law School; but it had an excellent postgraduate department with many students interested in some Muslim country or some facet of Islamics. My job there was not to teach lawyers. Rather it was to show historians, sociologists, linguists and economists that Islamic law is 'the epitome of Islamic thought, the core and kernel of Islam itself' (Joseph Schacht), and that it has been 'the most effective agent...in holding the social fabric of Islam compact and secure through all the fluctuations of political fortune' (Hamilton Gibb). At the Law School of New York University, on the other hand, my primary task was to give five public lectures in the evenings, over a period of some ten weeks, for 'members of the legal and business community' as well as academics, on 'Islamic Law in the Modern World'. These lectures were subsequently published as a book, under the same title, by the New York University Press, with an Introduction by Dr Saba Habachy, KBE – one of the most distinguished Egyptian lawyers and a former Cabinet Minister. It was published also in England.

During these months we visited a number of other universities and churches. At Hertford, Connecticut, I participated in a conference about missionary work among Muslims, from which sprang an invitation to give a lecture at a truly fascinating conference in Asmara, Eritrea, some months later. This conference was to celebrate the union of the American United Presbyterians, who worked primarily in Egypt, and another American Presbyterian Church, which had worked for many years in what was then still called Persia. At this latter conference I met for the first time Bishop Kenneth Cragg, who gave Bible Readings to the members of the conference 'as if a Muslim were looking over his shoulder'. I also met several splendid converts from Islam. One of these, then the leading light in what was, I think, called 'The St Andrew's Brotherhood' in Pakistan, told me the story of his own conversion. His father had been a learned and rigidly orthodox Muslim, who one day called his son into his library and pointed to a book which he 'should *never* read'. Human nature being what it is, the son later took advantage of his father's absence to have a look at this evil book. It was a copy of the New Testament, which he proceeded to read – and this not only led to his own conversion, but to a life spent in bringing the same message to other Muslims.

In Boston I preached and spoke to students at the Park Street Congregational church, and in Los Angeles I gave a lecture at the Von Grunebaum Institute in 'the University of California in Los Angeles', and also spoke at Fuller Theological Seminary. We visited several other places and made numerous friends. American academics in general – and American

Christians in all walks of life – must be among the most hospitable and kindly people in the world.

Just before I left New York University, Dr Russell Niles (the Dean of the Law School), who had just returned from a short visit to England, asked me if I knew who was to succeed Sir David Hughes Parry as Director of the Institute of Advanced Legal Studies in the University of London. When I replied, with complete sincerity, that I had no idea, he told me that the talk he had heard in London concerned 'someone with the name of Anderson'. I regarded this as no more than academic gossip, and did not take it seriously; but he, assuming it to be true, proceeded to give me some very trans-Atlantic advice about 'how it could be built up to become the leading Law School in England'. 'But that', I objected, 'is not the *purpose* of the Institute – nor would it be remotely possible, under our British system, even to contemplate the things you have in mind.' And there our talk ended.

True enough, though, as soon as we reached London I found a note awaiting me from the Principal of London University asking me to call on him at my earliest convenience. I did, and he informed me that he had been authorized, by the selection committee appointed by the Council of Management of the Institute, to offer me the job (subject, of course, to ratification by the University Senate). I replied that my specialization in Islamic law was too exotic for the post, which should, I felt, be held by a scholar in the main stream of English law. But he insisted that 'everyone specializes in something these days', and it didn't matter very much what that 'something' was! So I was duly appointed Director of the Institute, on a half-time basis, from the following autumn. It was also proposed that my established Chair at the School of

Oriental and African Studies should be temporarily 'put on ice' and that I should be given the title of Professor of Oriental Laws in a personal capacity. This would enable me, if I found the two jobs incompatible at some future date, either to resign the Directorship and return to the Chair, or to continue at the Institute and vacate the Chair, which could then be filled by someone else.

Uganda and Nigeria

But I have hitherto omitted from this chapter on 'learning my trade' an important part of that training, as I conceive it. In 1953 I was invited to attend the first 'Judicial Advisers' Conference' in Uganda, and then, in 1956, the second such conference, held this time in Nigeria. Both of these were presided over by Sir Kenneth Roberts-Wray QC, the Legal Adviser to both the Commonweath Relations Office and the Colonial Office, and were attended by the Judicial Advisers of all the then British possessions in Africa. Some of these Judicial Advisers were qualified lawyers and some were not, but the task of each was to supervise the scope and enforcement of 'customary' law in his territory. This 'customary' law in some areas, moreover, had a very close connection with the local form of Islamic law which those Africans who had espoused Islam, or had close family or tribal connections with Muslims, either themselves followed or had to come to terms with. This was, of course, where I came in, with the research I had done for *Islamic Law in Africa*.

The situation was intricate enough in parts of Kenya, Uganda, Tanganyika and Somaliland, for example. But in Nigeria the relations between the Muslim (Emirs') courts and the British courts were extremely unsatisfactory. Several of the Emirs' courts in that country had 'the power of life and death': that is, they were empowered to try cases of homicide under the locally accepted *(Maliki)* interpretation of Islamic law. This law differed from that of the Nigerian Criminal Code, as applied in the British courts, in two vital respects. First, if a man or woman was found guilty in these courts of 'deliberately killing' a Muslim – even in circumstances which might fall well short of 'murder' in the British courts – the 'heirs of blood' might demand the death penalty. Alternatively they might accept 'blood money' instead. Second, the situation was very different if a Muslim 'deliberately killed' a Christian or a pagan. In these cases, the death penalty could never be demanded, but only one-third of the blood money payable if the deceased had been a Muslim could be demanded for a Christian, and only one-fifteenth of that sum, in some Provinces, for a pagan. This meant that a Muslim could, in those areas, murder a pagan for a very small sum, together with a statutory penalty of one year's imprisonment. But one year in prison and a small fine is a remarkably lenient punishment for what might be a foul murder – to say nothing of the gross difference between the value imputed to the blood of a Muslim, a Christian and a pagan.

I was so horrified by this – and also by the fact that, on appeal to the High Court, *some* of these unsatisfactory circumstances were held not to warrant interference – that I wrote to the Colonial Office on the subject. Nigeria was then already moving fast towards independence, and non-Muslims were, very naturally, alarmed. During the days of British rule, injustices of this kind were normally remedied by the local Administrative Officer transferring the case from the

Muslim Emir's Court to the High Court – a power he could exercise at any stage of the case.

I believe that this letter (with the warm and influential support of Sir Kenneth Roberts-Wray) had a decisive effect. The Northern Nigerian Government was asked if it would welcome a Panel of Jurists to discuss these matters with them at the time when Nigeria was almost on the verge of independence. To this suggestion they demurred. Instead, they proposed that they should send missions of their own to three predominantly Muslim countries which had recently attained independence – Libya, Pakistan and the Sudan – to find out how they had managed to reconcile Islamic criminal law with the ethos of the modern world. This done, they said they would welcome a Panel of Jurists to make recommendations, in the light of this information, about their own legal and judicial systems.

In due course this Panel was made up of three expatriates: the Chief Justice of the Sudan, the Chairman of the Pakistan Law Reform Commission (both of them, of course, Muslims) and me. Also on the Panel were three Northern Nigerians: a highly placed Muslim administrative official, an *alkali* (Muslim judge) and a well-respected Christian administrator. I was given to understand, by several very knowledgeable British officials in Northern Nigeria, that, while minor compromises might well be accepted, any radical change was virtually impossible. It took only two or three days, however, to convince the Sudanese Chief Justice, the Pakistani Judge and me myself that the Islamic criminal law and criminal procedure, as applied in the 'native courts', must give way to new codes. Our three Northern Nigerian colleagues were, however, not surprisingly, hesitant about the way in which any such radical proposal would be received.

So we broke off our deliberations for two or three days to have informal talks with the politicians. In these the Chief Justice of the Sudan was supremely effective. He reminded them that they were on the very verge of independence, and presumably hoped to join the United Nations Organization. But this would lead to some very awkward questions being asked, unless radical reforms were introduced. When they suggested going ahead more slowly, he replied that now, *before* international criticism, was the time to act. And he also, in a way I could never have done, put his hand on his heart and said that the Sudan Criminal Code (itself based on the Indian Penal Code drafted largely by Lord Macaulay) was not in any respect contrary to Islamic principles. These informal conversations won the day, and our Nigerian colleagues were given the green light. Then we got to work in earnest.

Nor did it take very long to reach our conclusions. In the main these were that Northern Nigeria should adopt codes of criminal law and criminal procedure modelled on those of the Sudan, with two or three variants on which the Nigerians insisted. It might, indeed, have been more convenient had they been willing to adopt the Nigerian Criminal Code (which was also, fundamentally, based on English law, and would have had the advantage of acknowledging one criminal code as applicable to the whole country). But such had been the disputes about this code in the past that it was much easier for them to accept the Sudanese codes, based as these were on Indian (and therefore Pakistani) codes recommended by both Muslim expatriates. In any case, the differences were marginal. But the adoption of these two codes was only the most fundamental of our proposals.

When agreement had been reached between the members of the Panel, we again departed from normal British practice in such cases. Instead of meticulous care being taken in drafting a Report to be submitted some months later, our Report was drafted jointly by the Secretary to the Panel (Mr S.M. Richardson, formerly of the Sudan Political Service but then serving in Northern Nigeria) and me in a period of some thirty-six hours. It was first approved by my two expatriate colleagues, with very minor revisions, in one session, and then endorsed by the three indigenous members of the Panel almost *in toto*. Finally, it was submitted to the Northern Nigerian Government on the day before we left, and accepted by them, with the solitary exception of one distinctly minor proposal, within two days. The members of the Panel were invited by the Government, moreover, to come back in some three years' time to see how our proposals had fared and to make any further suggestions.

I carried away with me a memory that I cherish. At the very beginning of our work I invited the only other Christian on the Panel, a delightful Nigerian official from the 'Middle Belt', to come round to the Government Rest House, where I was lodged, for a talk. We found that we were in complete spiritual agreement and had some prayer together. As a result I found that, when the members of the Panel greeted each other somewhat formally each morning, this man always added the word 'Brother' (*sotto voce*) when he greeted me!

All this happened very shortly before the semester I spent at Princeton University and the New York University Law School. Both the conferences in Africa and that period in America coincided, rather appropriately, with the two years (1957-59) when I was

Chairman of the United Kingdom National Committee of Comparative Law. Incidently, the chairmanship of this National Committee carried with it membership of the very small International Committee of Comparative Law, which meets year by year and brought me into contact with experts from Western Europe, America, and countries behind the 'Iron curtain'.

Setbacks and opening vistas

As already stated, Pat and I felt that the door to a return to missionary service was temporarily closed by the fact that we could not find any satisfactory home in England for our two daughters, who were aged 15 and 12 when we moved to London in 1949. But it would, of course, have been possible to review the situation a few years later; and there would not have been any problem in having Hugh with us in the Middle East for some years. Pat's back, however, had been somewhat troublesome for a long a time and it became much worse after she had a bad fall shortly before Hugh arrived. We tried one thing after another – an operation performed by Sir Herbert Seddon in search of a 'nodule' which he thought might be causing the trouble, a visit to Dr Cryiax of St Thomas's Hospital to ask if 'manipulation' would do any good, and then, after he had said that surgery alone could avail, Sir Herbert had a final try with a plaster jacket. When this, too, failed we went to Mr Valentine Logue for what he said would be a very serious operation on a thoracic disc, from which recovery would take several weeks.

So, very unwillingly, we sent Hugh as a boarder to a preparatory school years before we had intended to do so. He settled down wonderfully well, and wrote quite good letters for a boy of seven throughout his first year.

But the first letter of his second year, after greetings, read something like this: 'iscuse my spealing, but last yere I had Miss Bond to help me and now I hav no one but God'! So it was clear from this letter that the Almighty expects small boys to learn spelling and grammar in the same way that he expects missionaries to learn Arabic (or whatever); and *not* to rely on divine intervention!

But to return to Pat. She was in intensive care for two or three days, but all went well. For several reasons, however, the surgeon had decided on a laminectomy rather than a fusion, and she still gets pain from that part of her back. She has also, since then, had to have two more laminectomies (one of which also entailed a fusion) lower down her back, at an interval of some years. So return to the mission field was for her virtually out of the question, and the guiding hand seemed to point to an academic life for me in England.

Today many young men and women come up to the university from Christian homes to find themselves in constant contact with those (whose intelligence, learning and academic standing they greatly admire) who adopt, and often propagate, a somewhat cynical agnosticism, or even aggressive humanism. So it may be a help to them – and, indeed, to others who turn to Christ during their years at a university – to know that there are other academics who are convinced of the truth of the Christian faith, and who would always be happy to assist them in any possible way.

I have always found it possible, moreover, to fit in a lot of explicit Christian work alongside my academic duties. During the years of which I am writing in this chapter I was chairman from 1951 to 1954 of what was then the Graduates' Fellowship of the Inter-Varsity Fellowship of Christian Unions and subsequently chairman of the IVF Council for an initial period which extended to six years. It has also been possible to do a lot of Christian speaking for churches, Christian Unions and elsewhere. A certain amount of missionary involvement has been maintained by being chairman of the London Council of the Egypt General Mission from 1947, and then (after the disaster of the invasion of the Suez Canal) of the Middle East General Mission until after it became the Middle East Christian Outreach several years later. But I must sadly confess that an overfull programme has often usurped the place of meditation, prayer and worship, and I have repeatedly been convicted by Bishop Taylor Smith's warning: 'Beware of the barrenness of a busy life.'

When doors have shut, or sadness has overtaken us (of which more anon), I have always wondered whether this was not, in part, because of my need for discipline and correction. But I can gratefully testify that other doors (which I did not even have to push!) have always opened, leading in each case to some post, activity or responsibility for which past experiences have provided a partial preparation. I now realize that reading Law at Cambridge was part of a divine plan of which I then had no idea.

12

The one Son and the many

Christ's temptations and ours ∗ *Positive obedience* ∗
From death to life ∗ *Social implications*

In considering 'the problem of holiness' in chapter 9 of
this book, I deliberately did not allude to the comparable experience of Jesus himself, our supreme ex-
emplar. His experience was indeed comparable with
ours, because he genuinely 'shared our humanity.
(Hebrews 2:14), embodied what 'holiness' (positive as
well as negative) really is, and showed us how we too
ought to live. Yet with this close identification with us
there was always a basic difference between the eternal
Son and the many 'adopted' sons whom he is going to
'bring to glory' (Hebrews 2:10).

It was essential that he should 'be made like his
brothers in every way' if he was to 'make atonement'
for our sins (Hebrews 2:17) and deliver us from the
'fear of death' (verse 15). It was essential if he was to
be in a position, as one who had himself 'suffered when
he was tempted', to help us when we are being tempted
(verse 18). But there was always the fundamental
distinction that he was in himself 'holy, blameless,
pure, set apart from sinners' (Hebrews 7:26). Even so,
he too had to be 'made perfect [mature]' in his human
character and experience 'in the school of suffering'

(Hebrews 2:10 and 5:8, NEB). And while he was 'tempted in every way just as we are', this categorical statement is qualified by the proviso 'apart from sin' (Hebrews 4:15).

This last phrase is commonly translated 'yet without sinning', and it certainly includes that, although this probably does not exhaust its meaning. In asserting the sinlessness of Jesus, the author of Hebrews is postulating what Christians came to believe from a very early date (*cf.* 1 Peter 2:22). It is true that Jesus does not himself make this specific statement in the Gospel records, but he gets very close to it in saying that 'the prince of this world is coming. He has no hold on me' (John 14:30). It seems, however, even more significant that, although he spoke much about sin, the Gospels never record or suggest that he had any personal consciousness either of sin or the need for forgiveness.

In its full significance the phrase 'apart from sin' probably means that, when God sent 'his own Son in the likeness of sinful man to be a sin offering' (Romans 8:3), Jesus not only genuinely became man (*cf.* John 1:14; Romans 9:5; *etc.*), and therefore subject to temptation. He also shared with fallen humanity 'all such needs and infirmities as, not sinful in themselves, are to us occasions of sinning ... because the *victory over sin in its own stronghold* is in question'.[1] Yet in himself there was 'no sin' (1 John 3:5) – either in act or in nature. This is why Gabriel could speak to Mary of 'the holy one' to whom she was to give birth (Luke 1:35).

So Jesus, as our High Priest, can fully 'sympathise with our weaknesses', yet had no need to offer any

[1] Handley Moule, *The Epistle to the Romans* (1893), p.139. His italics.

sacrifice for his own sins, but only for ours (*cf*. Hebrews 4:15; 7:26–27).

Christ's temptations and ours

For Jesus, then, unlike us, there was no 'problem of holiness' in the sense of how to become holy, for he *was* holy. But he did share with us what I may term the problem of how to remain holy, because Satan tempted him in every possible way. It is true that there is one temptation (which most of us know only too well) which he can never have shared: that of slipping once more down the slippery slope of some sin to which we have given way so often in the past. But that does not mean that he did not suffer as severe temptations as we do. On the contrary, if we had to face the ultimate strength of temptation we should give way, which is why we have been given the promise that 'No temptation has seized you except what is common to man. And God is faithful; he will not let you be tempted beyond what you can bear. But when you are tempted, he will also provide a way out so that you can stand up under it' (1 Corinthians 10:13).

The thought here is not that we shall escape the temptation, but may escape defeat. In some cases God will give us the strength to go through it to the very end; but if this is beyond us, he will show us a way out. 'The imagery is that of an army trapped in rugged country, which manages to escape from an impossible situation through a mountain pass.'[2] So it is only the one who was without sin whom God could allow to suffer the *uttermost* temptation. Nor should we think of any temptation whatever as one that Jesus can never have known – unless it is one which

[2] Leon Morris, *1 Corinthians* (IVP, 2nd edition 1985), p.142.

derives its strength from past defeats or from sin in our very nature. We must take literally the statement that he 'has been tempted in every way, just as we are, apart from sin' (Hebrews 4:15).

To ask the old question, whether he was not able to sin, or able not to sin, seems to me to miss the point. I do not believe that Jesus went into temptation with a complete inbuilt consciousness of invulnerability, for that would indeed have robbed temptation of its basic strength. Instead, I believe that Jesus went into temptation, as into all else, in complete dependence on his Father's will and power, and that the Father allowed him to be tempted to the utmost extreme. The worst temptation of all must have been to turn aside from the agony of the cross. This temptation was not primarily in terms of the physical pain (dreadful though this must have been), but in terms of 'being made sin for us', and the horror of the only break in all eternity in conscious communion with his Father that this entailed, summed up in that awful cry, "My God, my God, why have *you* forsaken me?'

It is true, of course, that if Jesus *had* sinned, then he could not have been the very embodiment of God in manhood. It would have been sin for him – as indeed it is for us – to have turned away in any particular from obedience to the Father's will; so it is, in fact, an inept question to ask whether he *could* have come down from the cross. In the garden of Gethsemane he had said to his disciples, 'Do you think I cannot call on my Father, and he will at once put at my disposal more than twelve legions of angels? But how then would the Scriptures be fulfilled that say it must happen in this way?' (Matthew 26:53–54.) To have asked the Father to rescue him, or indeed to have evaded the cross in any other way, would have been to frustrate the basic purpose for which he had come: to make atonement for our sins by dying both 'on our behalf' and 'in our place'. And that, we can say with confidence, Jesus not only would not, but – being who he was – 'could not' do.

Positive obedience

It is vital to remember that holiness is not only – or even chiefly – a negative attribute, but an essentially positive quality. It means to be set apart for God and to do his will. This clearly includes the negative side, to abstain from all that is evil; but it also points inevitably to an obedience that is immediately responsive to every indication of God's guidance and good pleasure. So the eternal Son could say: 'Here I am – it is written about me in the scroll – I have come to do your will, O God' (Hebrews 10:7). And the Gospels tell us the way in which he lived this out, and depict the divine imperative that inspired his every action.

He healed the sick, he released the oppressed, he was 'a friend of tax collectors and sinners' and he 'preached the good news to the poor' (*cf.* Luke 7:34; 4:18). But the most costly element in his life of constant obedience was when he 'resolutely set out for Jerusalem' (Luke 9:51), knowing what would await him there; and when, after the agony in Gethsemane, we read that 'bearing the human likeness, revealed in human shape' (NEB), he 'became obedient to death – even death on a cross!' (Philippians 2:7–8). He died in our place, for 'he himself bore our sins in his body on the gibbet' (1 Peter 2:24); he also died on our behalf, as the representative man.

The basic purpose for which God sent his Son into the world was to save the world (*cf*. John 3:17). This meant that he must 'taste death for every man'; he had to 'be made perfect through suffering', as the Pioneer of the salvation of the 'many sons' God was 'bringing to glory'. Only by his death and resurrection could he free them from the fear of death (*cf*. Hebrews 2:9–14). It stands to reason – and is spelt out unequivocally in these verses – that he could do this only if he 'shared their humanity' in every way (*cf*. Hebrews 2:17). So he died as man for man, and suffered both the physical torture and spiritual agony of being crucified as our sin-bearer – which alone explains his 'cry of dereliction' from the cross. And Paul insists that it was God himself who demonstrated (and still demonstrates) 'his own love for us in this: While we were still sinners, Christ died for us' (Romans 5:8).

But it would not have been God's *own* love which was thus demonstrated unless there had been an ontological link – an essential unity of being – between the Father who sent and the Son who died. The prophet Ezekiel states explicitly, moreover, that 'It is the soul that sins, and no other, that shall die; a son shall not share a father's guilt, nor a father his son's. The righteous man shall reap the fruit of his own righteousness, and the wicked man the fruit of his own wickedness' (Ezekiel 18:20, NEB). So it is unthinkable that God would permit the gross injustice of one who was an utterly blameless man, but no more, being put to a cruel death for the sins and guilt of others. It is only God who can deal with human sin, and only God incarnate who, in an act of almost inconceivable grace, could 'be made...to be sin [or 'a sin offering'] for us' (2 Corinthians 5:21). He, and he alone, could take upon himself our condemnation, and die, 'the righteous for the unrighteous, to bring [us] to God' (1 Peter 3:18). The one who died, truly 'made man' and dying an authentic physical death (*cf.* Colossians 1:22), was essentially the eternal Son, 'the radiance of God's glory and the exact representation of his being'. This is made clear not only in Hebrews 1:1–14, but throughout the whole letter (*cf.* also Philippians 2:6–11; Colossians 1:15–20).

From death to life

So all those who are 'in Christ' have passed out of death into life – 'made holy through the sacrifice of the body of Jesus Christ once for all' (Hebrews 10:10). In him they 'died to sin', and were set free from both its condemnation and its slavery. In him also they were raised from death to 'live a new life' (Romans 6:2 and 4), ultimately 'predestined to be conformed to the likeness of his Son, that he might be the firstborn among many brothers' (Romans 8:29). There is profound truth in the well-known verse of a children's hymn:

> He died that we might be forgiven,
>   He died to make us good,
> That we might go at last to heaven,
>   Saved by his precious blood.

We have been saved by grace through faith. 'It is God's gift, not a reward for work done. There is nothing for anyone to boast of. For we are God's handiwork, created in Christ Jesus to devote ourselves to the good deeds for which God has designed us' (Ephesians 2:8–10, NEB).

In the many sons, as in the eternal Son, holiness is both negative and positive. We are commanded not to 'let sin reign in [our] mortal body so that [we] obey its evil desires' (Romans 6:12). We are no longer to 'put its several parts at sin's disposal, as implements for doing wrong'. Instead, we must 'put [ourselves] at the disposal of God, as dead men raised to life'; and we must 'yield [our] bodies to him as implements for doing right' (Romans 6:13, NEB). In terms of the letter to the Hebrews this means (as we have seen) that we are to 'throw off everything that hinders and the sin that so easily entangles' us, and to 'run with perseverance the race marked out for us' (Hebrews 12:1). Whatever our particular vocation may be, we are to follow the example of Christ (*cf.* 1 Corinthians 11:1), who 'went around doing good..., because God was with him' (Acts 10:38). This means that we must respond to what Christ has done for us by being 'a people that are his very own, eager to do what is good' (Titus 2:14), in what is termed today both 'mission' and evangelism. For in him they were perfectly blended.

Social implications

Holiness, moreover, has a social as well as a personal dimension. In the case of the eternal Son this can be seen in his special solicitude for the poor, the sick and the outcast. So it is ultimately in obedience to his teaching and example that we come to realize our duty to be concerned not only with the needs of individuals, but also with the cause of social, racial and economic justice. In the emphasis put on the latter today there has been an enormous advance in comparison with my own student days, when (I am ashamed to say) we took both the privileges and inequalities of life very much for granted. We would sing, almost without a qualm:

> The rich man in his castle,
>   The poor man at his gate,
> *God* made them high and lowly,
>   And ordered their estate –

(which seems to carry the implication that this is God's will, and so things must remain!). This verse, happily, is omitted in most modern hymnbooks which include this hymn. We were involved to a certain degree in 'charity', of course, and in trying to salvage some of the casualties that had occurred on the 'Jericho road' (*cf.* Luke 10:30–37). But, unlike Martin Luther King, we were not greatly concerned with trying to bring about conditions in which these casualties would be eliminated – or at least mini-mized. This was brought home to me most vividly by our son, Hugh, who died when he was still a student in 1970; for he was passionately concerned with social, racial and economic justice, and with the political action that would foster this.

When I was a student we were, I think, so afraid of the so-called 'social gospel' (on which the Student Christian Movement at that time put such an insistent emphasis) that we failed to realize that the authentic gospel of redemption *must* have social implications. We all too often regarded social relief, education and medical work primarily as means to promote evangelism, rather than causes which are valid and worthy of active support in their own right. As a result we lamentably failed to emulate the example of Lord Ashley (later the seventh Earl of Shaftesbury) who wrote of his future career: 'The first principle God's honour, the second man's happiness, the means prayer and unremitting diligence.' And to these principles, Florence Higham records, 'he remained faithful for fifty-odd years, deliberately devoting himself to helping others, by giving freely of himself to all who asked his aid and by inquiring ruthlessly into every injustice with which he came in contact'.[3]

Jesus, we read, was time and time again 'moved with compassion' for human needs, physical and social as well as spiritual. But his primary mission was to proclaim, by both word and deed, the Good News of the kingdom of God, eternal life and salvation. As himself the King (John 18:37), the giver of life (John 10:10) and the only source of salvation (Matthew 1:21; Acts 4:12), he could do this with unique authority. Yet it is fair to say that we are now in a position to expound this gospel in a more explicit way than he himself could in his earthly life. This is because his Jewish contemporaries had a concept of the role of the promised Messiah which seems to have precluded them from any understanding of what he meant when he said that he was going to 'give his life as a ransom for many' (Mark 10:45), and when he spoke of 'my blood of the covenant, which is poured out for many' (Mark 14:24). It was only after the resurrection that he could explain this, and only after Pentecost that his followers could proclaim it with power (Luke 24:45–49).

So our duty (and privilege) is not only to be deeply concerned about the poverty, malnutrition and injustice which keep so many in different forms of

[3] Florence Higham, *Lord Shaftesbury*, pp.7f.

bondage. It is also, and pre-eminently, to be witnesses to the forgiveness and freedom from the guilt
and power of sin that are now freely available as a
result of his atoning death. Worship, thanksgiving,
evangelism, 'mission' and warm humanity are the
positive aspects of that holiness which basically means
being 'set apart' for God, 'to glorify and enjoy him
for ever'. Jesus himself is our perfect example, and
all Christians can say with the apostle Paul that, as a
theological fact, 'I have been crucified with Christ
and I no longer live [as the person I once was], but
Christ lives in me. The life I live in the body, I live by
faith in the Son of God, who loved me and gave
himself for me' (Galatians 2:20). This means that, as
the Holy Spirit reproduces the life of the eternal Son
in us, God's adopted sons, his holiness (both positive
and negative) will become increasingly ours.

13

The Institute and overseas visits

Across the disciplines ∗ *Raising funds* ∗
To the Middle East ∗ *Other visits*

My appointment (in the autumn of 1959) as Director
of the Institute of Advanced Legal Studies, on a half-
time basis, did not in any way lessen my responsibili-
ties at the School of Oriental and African Studies,
where I was still a Professor and Head of the Law
Department. It merely meant that I had two academic
jobs at the same time. Fortunately, my predecessor at
the Institute, Sir David Hughes Parry, had held the
post only on a part-time basis, and Mr Howard Drake,
the Secretary and Librarian, was accustomed to handling all its routine business. He was primarily a librarian; for the first essential had been to build up, from
scratch, a first-class research library. It was not long,
in fact, before it caught up all the other law libraries in
the United Kingdom, with the solitary exception of
the Bodleian Law Library in Oxford, in the number of
the law books it possessed. Considering that the Institute had been founded only at the end of the Second
World War, and had no claim to a free copy of every
book published in this country (unlike the British
Museum, the Bodleian, the Cambridge University
Library, the Library of Trinity College, Dublin, and

the National Libraries of Scotland and Wales), this was an outstanding achievement. In this it had been greatly helped by two grants from the Nuffield Foundation, first for Commonwealth and then for West European legal literature.

It was in response to the report of the Atkin Committee on Legal Education in England, in 1932, and to advice from another committee under the chairmanship of Lord Macmillan in 1938, that the University of London decided in 1947, 'as part of its post-war policy', to set up this 'Senate House Institute'. As such it was founded not only to serve the University of London as a whole, but also to 'provide a meeting place for teachers and research workers in law for the British Isles and overseas'. So the scope of its library was of primary importance. But the activities of the Institute had not by any means been confined to the provision of its library, for it had also made its mark by the quantity and quality of the bibliographical work it had done or sponsored.

From the first I was most anxious, however, to extend the work of the Institute in new directions. Our first consideration must always be the build-up of our library, as the essential tool for the many research students, and overseas lawyers of great distinction, who came to work there; and this, together with the salaries of our staff, would continue to swallow up almost all the grant we received from the University. Some of our bibliographical work was complete, while some (and especially the *Index to Foreign Legal Periodicals*, edited by Howard Drake under the sponsorship of the American Association of Law Libraries) was in full swing. The Institute was also becoming more and more recognized and used by both committees and individual scholars, from at home and abroad, as their natural meeting-place. Much research was being done in the Institute, but any prospect of engaging research staff of our own was severely limited by lack of funds. So how could we get started?

Across the disciplines

My first step was to arrange a number of inter-disciplinary discussion groups. Thus I took advantage of the temporary presence in Cambridge of Dean Gene Rostow of Yale to launch a group of 'Lawyers and Economists' (since the Yale Law School had done so much to integrate economics and sociology with the study of law). After an inaugural dinner at the Athenaeum to discuss the venture with Gene Rostow and a few key figures, we sent out invitations to both academic and practising lawyers and economists, aiming at a group of some twenty to thirty for each discussion. We always met for sherry at 6 p.m., after which someone opened our discussion and we continued (with only a very brief break for a buffet supper to be served) until about 9.15. Our plan was to have a number of people who came regularly as the continuing core of the group, but also to include some special invitees according to the subject to be discussed.

Lawyers and economists represented a very suitable group with which to start, since they frequently use the same terms with a slightly different meaning. But this first group was soon followed by one which we named 'Lawyers and Sociologists', although in point of fact it also included doctors, psychiatrists and others who were interested in the sort of subjects we discussed. Our first topic, 'The legal process and the ascertainment of facts', stretched over several meetings, in the course of which we examined the whole trial process as it had come to prevail in England. The adversarial procedure between two competing parties (whether the Crown versus an accused person, or a plaintiff versus a defendant) had come to involve protracted delays. There were repeated interviews between solicitors, their clients and potential witnesses; rules about the 'discovery' of relevant documents; and the selection, in some cases, of such expert witnesses as were prepared to support a particular thesis. Then, perhaps months later, there might be a trial in which the witnesses would be cross-examined, counsel would make speeches, the judge would sum up and the jury would deliberate.

Was this really as effective in finding out what had actually transpired as a more inquisitorial form, both of preliminary investigation and eventual trial? This could get under way while people's memories were fresh, and their recollections had not been vitiated or confused by a process of what might well be perfectly innocent attempts (by themselves or others) to rationalize what 'must' have happened. One member of this group was doing whole-time research on the vagaries of human memory, particularly after different periods of time. Another staged an incident in the last lecture of one term, and then got his students to write down, some five weeks later, what precisely had happened; and he found that it was his most intelligent students whose 'evidence' was the least reliable, because they had tried to rationalize the incident concerned.

The third group we formed was that of 'Lawyers and Theologians', and our chief field of discussion was that of law and morality in general, or specific subjects such as marriage, divorce, abortion, euthanasia and the like. In this group we deliberately included participants from a wide range of backgrounds, including serious moralists who would not claim any interest in theology as such. A fourth group was simply termed 'Criminologists', and included lawyers, penologists, civil servants, psychiatrists, policemen and prison governors – everyone, in fact, who was interested in the prevention, detection and punishment of crime, and in the rehabilitation of criminals. Finally, we sometimes turned to subjects in which we felt that members of two or more of our existing groups would not only be interested but prove valuable contributors. Such subjects included genetic engineering, transplant surgery, *in vitro* fertilization, and kindred problems.

We were often asked why we did not record, or publish, any of these discussions. Instead, we preferred to adopt what have come to be termed the 'Chatham House rules'. This enabled those in responsible positions in their respective professions to speak frankly, knowing that nothing they said would be attributed to them personally – although all those present were welcome to use any such facts or ideas in their own work or publications, provided they gave no indication of the source from which they came. This principle no doubt led to a considerable limitation of the value of some of the discussions from one point of view, but made them much more fruitful from another – and we do in fact know of two or three official groups which subsequently benefited not only from including a number of our participants, but also from the knowledge they had thus acquired.

A group set up by Dr Michael Ramsey, when Archbishop of Canterbury, to advise him on the civil law of divorce, for example, included several members of our group of Lawyers and Theologians, and held most of its meetings at the Institute over the same sort of buffet supper; and it was from this group that the publication *Putting Asunder* emanated. Again, one discussion on imprisonment for debt led, virtually directly, to an official Commission on the subject. At another time we were specifically asked by the Chairman of the Law Commission to set up a discussion on matrimonial property in connection with their own examination of this subject.

These discussion groups, each of which met at least three times a year, were much appreciated. Fortunately for us at that time, moreover, these meetings cost very little, for we had no expenses other than the food and drink we supplied, and very occasionally the travel expenses of the one who was to open our deliberations.

Raising funds

My next job – the task of trying to raise funds for specific projects – was far less welcome. I was enthusiastic enough about the projects, but I did not relish the much less congenial task of trying to 'sell' them to various Foundations. What we sought for, and eventually got, were funds to enable us to invite scholars each year from the countries of the 'Old Commonwealth', a number of younger visiting 'Fellows' from the Third World, and a leading Professor of our own choosing from the United States. These funds also enabled us to hold an annual Workshop in the summer to which we could invite all those who taught some selected subject in any British university.

Far the largest project we had in mind, however, was the provision of a new, purpose-designed building to accommodate both our Institute and that of the British Institute of International and Comparative Law. The house in which we ourselves had been accommodated was in many ways an attractive building to which some of us became quite attached; but it was certainly not designed for a library such as ours, which had to be split up between nearly a dozen rooms (with minimum security), or for our ever-increasing number of 'readers'. Meanwhile Lord Denning had succeeded in uniting two existing bodies, the Grotius Society and the Society of Comparative Legislation, into a composite Institute.

This, as its name implies, was devoted both to public and private international law and to comparative law, and it soon developed two particular interests – in West Europe (from which the Economic Community evolved) and in the former British colonies (which often stood in need of advice about proposed legislation, and much else, which they would prefer to seek from a private rather than governmental source). Whereas, moreover, our Institute was essentially academic, the British Institute catered primarily for practising lawyers. So there was no rivalry, and little duplication; but there was a certain inevitable overlap, and we found that many visitors from abroad wanted to visit both Institutes. At first some members of the British Institute felt that to be drawn, as it were, into such close connection with the University of London would jeopardize their intimate links with the Inns of Court and the Law Society; but it was becoming more and more essential for their staff to have ready access to our library.

It seemed to us both, moreover, that an appeal for funds for a building in London to house the activities of both Institutes might prove attractive to possible donors of the large sum of money which would be needed. It was here that the influence of Sir David Hughes Parry, my predecessor as Director of the Institute and now Chairman of its Committee of Management, proved decisive. He secured for us from the University of London an ideal site overlooking Russell Square as an independent unit in a large building stretching back along Bedford Way, the rest of which was to be occupied by the Institute of Education. He also obtained, through one of his former pupils, the promise of generous financial support from the Charles Clore Foundation. The sum involved was raised more than twice, and eventually grew to £650,000.

There were, however, serious delays in the completion of the building, none of them from any fault of ours, and the final cost was more than a million pounds. We made a number of attempts to cover the resultant short-fall, and at one time received a virtual promise that the three floors devoted to the library would be financed by another generous donor, a friend of Sir Charles Clore. But, although we managed to get two or three other gifts, the deficit had eventually to be made up from University funds. The building is owned, of course, by the University; but the British Institute of International and Comparative Law has a continuing lease, for a peppercorn rent, of the floor it occupies, for which it bears its proportionate share of the administrative costs.

The construction of this building brought to the Institute another asset of particular value. When I first became Director Mr Howard Drake held the combined post of Secretary and Librarian; but, to our great loss, he died – suddenly and prematurely of a heart attack – in 1967. Much debate ensued as to whether we should look for an experienced legal administrator, such as a retired Attorney-General from one of our former Colonies, and try to turn him into a librarian; or vice versa. But we finally decided that a fully-trained legal librarian and bibliographer was our primary need. So we appointed Mr Willi Steiner, an experienced legal librarian and expert bibliographer, who soon became Vice-President of the International Association of Law Libraries and General Editor of the *Index to Foreign Legal Periodicals*. The need for detailed planning of the new building, moreover (and later for its furnishing and all the financial and other problems which this involved), enabled me to convince the Principal of the University, Sir Douglas Logan, that we must have a Secretary as well as a Librarian. Happily we were able to recruit Mr John Boxhall, who had had wide experience in the Colonial Service before filling an administrative post in the School of Oriental and African Studies, for this position. What we should have done without him, with his administrative and financial expertise, I should not like to guess.

My own time and activities, throughout these years and well beyond, had to be divided between the Institute and the School of Oriental and African Studies. Looking back, I am amazed at the amount of travelling that was involved. I shall describe only a few of these journeys.

To the Middle East

In the summer of 1960 I paid a visit to Libya and Egypt. In Libya I had been invited by King Idris to his desert palace near Tobruk, where he conferred on me the Libyan Order of Istiqlal (Independence), Class II. I had been warned about this possibility, on my way, by the British Consul in Benghazi, who told me that he had already taken the precaution of writing to Buckingham Palace to obtain the Queen's permission for me to accept this (should King Idris not have forgotten his intention or changed his mind!). What staggered me on this visit was the extent to which an Arab king's hospitality will stretch. I had written him a letter merely saying that I was going to Egypt to lecture and would hope to pay a visit to his country on my way; so I should very much like to see him again if he would give me an audience. But when I arrived at Tripoli airport I was met by a member of his protocol staff who drove me to an excellent hotel, gave me a list of tentative engagements, and told me to 'order whatever I liked' (which meant, as I discovered only when I asked the hotel for my bill, that everything was to be paid for by the Palace).

Almost exactly the same happened a few days later when I flew on to Benghazi, where I was again met by an official, taken to a hotel, given the same instructions, and supplied with a car and driver to take me to Tobruk (some 400 miles) and bring me back for my flight to Cairo. But the final touch came at the end. I had said goodbye to the king on the previous evening, adding that I planned to start very early in the morning on the long drive back to Benghazi. This he approved, and asked me whether I expected to get to Derna in time for breakfast. I said I should like to get a little further, to the hamlet of Shahhata near ancient Cyrene; and he agreed, saying that there was a small inn there. I got there, had my breakfast, and went to pay my bill – only to be told that the Palace had telephoned to say that I must on no account be allowed to pay anything, and that the trifling bill should be sent to the Palace.

In 1961 I paid another interesting visit to the Middle East. In Khartoum I participated in a Conference on 'Traditionalism and Change', at which I read a paper on 'The Modernization of Islamic Law in the Sudan', which was published. I then paid a short visit to Cairo on my way to Kuwait and Bahrein, where I gave two lectures in Arabic under the auspices of the British Council. It was in Kuwait that I heard that my mother had died, at a ripe old age; but I could not get home for her funeral because the chief reason for my whole journey was to investigate (in collaboration with Mr John Gault, a former diplomat in the Gulf) a boundary dispute between the Sheikhs of Qatar and Abu Dhabi. Their main bone of contention was sovereignty over a small island called Halul, although they were also at variance about their land boundary.

The Sheikh of Qatar had told the Foreign Office, which had arranged this arbitration, that he would be delighted to welcome us, would have a brief prepared setting out his case, and would provide witnesses to support it. But he remarked that, in the almost inconceivable event of the decision going against him, he could not, of course, accept it. The Sheikh of Abu Dhabi, on his part, had been much less co-operative. He, too, had said that he would be happy to entertain us; but he added that he had no intention of preparing a brief or calling any witnesses. Every fair-minded person in the Gulf knew that Halul belonged to him, and the British Government must know this better than anyone else!

In point of fact neither Sheikh had any decisive claim to the island. We landed on it by helicopter and could not imagine anyone wanting to live there. Nor had anyone done so other than temporarily, since it was wholly without water. The most that had happened was that parties had camped there for a few days, bringing their own water, in order to fish or catch falcons. The claim of Qatar was chiefly based on propinquity and usage. The island was considerably closer to Qatar than to Abu Dhabi, and visitors from there (including, apparently, the Sheikh's father and grandfather in person) had come comparatively often. The claim of Abu Dhabi, on the other hand, was that in the past their dhows had dominated that part of the Gulf (in which they had been notorious pirates!). In the event we recommended that the claim of Qatar seemed the stronger, and this was accepted by the Foreign Office. No doubt the Sheikh of Abu Dhabi rejected the decision; but, fortunately enough, extensive reserves of oil were at that time being discovered in his territorial waters, and this kept him busy and relatively happy.

Other visits

In 1962 my principal overseas visits were to Ghana and Nigeria. In Ghana I participated in a Conference on Legal Education in Africa. This was held in Accra, and we were housed in the positively palatial University buildings which had been erected a few miles from the city. But my most vivid memory is of a vist to us by President Nkrumah, whose local title was Osagyefo (which can be translated either as 'Deliverer' or 'Redeemer'). It was, no doubt, understood in the former sense by most educated people. But I can still picture some women of his party dancing round on the grass, after he had himself left, extolling their Osagyefo to the tune of a chorus I had often sung as a boy to the one and only 'Redeemer' of mankind.

In Nigeria I took part in the promised return visit of the 'Panel of Jurists' to the Northern Region. This time the Chief Justice of the Sudan was unfortunately unable to come, but otherwise the Panel was the same as before. On this occasion, we had no precise terms of reference; instead, we were asked to take a careful look at what had been done, and give any advice we thought fit. We did, in fact, make a number of suggestions, both general and specific, about further reforms which *might* be introduced; but these informal observations had no such dramatic effect as our previous proposals. For this there were, no doubt, various reasons, both in the nature of the proposals themselves and in what they would involve. But beyond question the chief reason was that independence was now a past fact rather than an imminent event, and that the major defects in their legal system had already been removed. I wrote two articles in the *International and Comparative Law Quarterly*, in July 1959 and January 1963 respectively, describing the work and experiences of the Panel in Northern Nigeria.

Other overseas visits during these years included one to the United States to attend part of the American Bar Association's annual meeting, this time in Washington, and to participate in a conference of American, British and Canadian Law Teachers in New York. I also had the privilege of giving the closing talk at a 'Prayer Breakfast' for members of the Bar Association, sponsored by the International Christian Fellowship. Another interesting occasion was a visit to Tunisia at the personal invitation of President Bourguiba. There I lectured in Arabic in Tunis and Fez under the joint aegis of the Tunisian Government and the British Council, and had an audience with the President. He was unequivocal about the intended implications of the prohibition of polygamy included in the Tunisian Law of Family Rights, 1956, about which there had been considerable controversy. This controversy was subsequently settled, in so far as the law of Tunisia was concerned, by an enactment stating explicitly that a polygamous marriage was invalid *per se*, quite apart from the criminal sanctions to which those responsible were liable. This had previously been denied by many orthodox Muslims.

14

Study leave

It used to be the practice at the School of Oriental and
African Studies to give members of the teaching staff a
period of overseas 'study leave', in some appropriate
area of the Orient or Africa, on a roughly 'sabbatical'
basis. I had myself enjoyed a year's such leave soon
after joining the staff in 1947 – first six months in
Egypt and the Middle East, followed by three months
in East and West Africa, respectively. So in the winter
of 1962-3 I was given some three months' study leave
of a somewhat unusual kind – visiting several countries,
to none of which I had been before, where Islamic law
was at least partially applied and numbers of my
former pupils were working; and then paying a further
visit to East Africa. This tour took me to West Pakistan,
across north India to what was then East Pakistan
(now Bangladesh), back to central and southern India,
and then on to Ceylon (now Sri Lanka), Malaysia and
Singapore; and finally to East Africa on my way home.

My itinerary and engagements had all been made in
close consultation with the British Council, to which I
owe a big debt. Its representatives had made arrangements for me to visit a number of universities, colleges

and societies, to give many lectures, to meet a series of interesting and informative people, and to see some fascinating places. But I must confine myself to a few vivid memories.

Pakistan

In Karachi – a sprawling city of numberless, intersecting streets – my most memorable interview was with the redoubtable Mawlana Mawdudi, the leader of Jama'at-i-Islami. This organization represents what is virtually the counterpart, in the Indian sub-continent, of the Muslim Brotherhood in the Middle East. I was taken to this meeting by Professor Khurshid Ahmad, one of its leading propagandists, who had translated some of Mawdudi's books into English.

Mawdudi himself was an enigmatic figure. He combined a rigid Islamic fundamentalism with an intelligence and originality much greater than that of the average 'Mawlana'. He also had a streak of political realism, somewhat vitiated by occasional lapses. He maintained, for example, that it was mandatory for the Government of an Islamic State such as Pakistan to re-introduce the savage penalties prescribed in the Shari'a for certain specified crimes. These include stoning for illicit sexual intercourse by a man or woman who had ever enjoyed a valid marriage, and the amputation of the right hand for anyone stealing goods from 'safe custody'. He was sufficiently realistic, however, to insist that this should be by no means the first act of a Muslim government, for it was only when the State had been thoroughly Islamized that these penalties could justly be imposed (since the way of life that currently prevailed constituted, in his view, a virtual incitement to immorality and dishonesty). Nor could this state of affairs be remedied until the teachers, rather than their pupils, had experienced a society in which Islamic principles were enforced. So far, so good – from his point of view. But when asked how long this would take, his realism lapsed – and he would say only that this would take 'at least ten years'! It was interesting to contrast Mawlana Mawdudi with Mr A. K. Brohi (formerly Pakistani High Commissioner in India), who struck me as the ablest lawyer I met in West Pakistan.

There was, of course, much else of interest to me in Karachi. There was the University, with its Department of Islamic Studies, and, pre-eminently, there was the Central Institute of Islamic Research. This had been set up, under the aegis of the Advisory Council of Islamic Ideology, to 'undertake research and instruction in Islam for the purpose of assisting in the reconstruction of Muslim society on a truly Islamic basis'. The burning question, then as now, was what it should mean for Pakistan to be an Islamic State – a problem that President Zia al-Haqq is now trying to solve. I had one 'evening off', when I dined with Bishop Chandu Ray (himself a convert from Hinduism) and met some of his friends and supporters.

Peshawar, by contrast, is a fascinating frontier town. Its market was then teeming with a positive medley of races, languages, costumes and merchandise – especially carpets and weaponry (some of it forged or adapted, by loving hands, on the spot). I was the guest of the University, where I conversed with a professor who had previously been Attorney-General, and he told me he had probably had to deal with more homicides than any other living man. The great majority of these, he said, were occasioned by disputes about the ownership or boundaries of land. I was deeply impressed by the Khyber Pass, watched over by the chain of forts on the surrounding hills which had imposed the *pax Britannica* on the highway alone, with its occasional rocks inscribed with the names of the regiments which had served there. Even then the frontier with Afghanistan was officially closed. I had the privilege of spending Sunday with the staff of the CMS hospital, and being asked to preach in its chapel. How different it must all be now – market, pass and hospital – with countless refugees from Afghanistan.

Islamabad was at that time only a capital city in embryo, and Lahore dominated the scene. My host there was the Vice-Chancellor of the University of the Punjab, Mr Justice Mohammed Sharif – my friend and colleague of the Panel of Jurists in Northern Nigeria. He was a fine man, a devout yet open-minded Muslim. His original intention had been that I should stay at his home (where he did, in fact, give a buffet lunch in a marquee in his garden for leading members of the University), but he had realized that it would be easier for people to come to see me if he booked me in at Falettis, a long-established, and very attractive, hotel. The then Chief Justice of Pakistan, Mr Justice A.R. Cornelius, himself lived there, and entertained me to lunch with all the judges of the Supreme Court. Among several engagements at the University I gave a public lecture, over which Mr Justice Sharif presided, which was attended by many judges and other members of the legal fraternity. I was also able to meet a number of my former pupils at a reception given by the Lahore Bar; to make many interesting calls; and to dine with the Anglican bishop and address members of his congregation.

Islam in India

In India Muslims face an entirely different situation from that of their brethren in Pakistan. Numbering more than sixty million, India's Muslim population is one of the largest in the world, yet it represents only some 15% of the total population. Far from wrestling with the problem of what it means – or should mean – to be an Islamic State, the burning question for Indian Muslims is how they can preserve their identity as a comparatively small minority in a 'secular state' in which the vast majority are Hindus. For a variety of reasons they did not emigrate at Partition, the creation of which most of them deprecate. They are loyal to the country of their birth, but they are determined that they, the erstwhile rulers, should not be swallowed up in a secular society dominated by an alien religion.

The great majority of the Muslims in India live in the northern part of the country, and I had the opportunity to pay short visits to Delhi (properly Dehli), Aligarh and Lucknow. Delhi is a divided city, with Old Delhi dominated, architecturally, by its impressive monuments of Mughal power, while New Delhi was designed as a modern capital city somewhat after the manner of Washington. I was granted an interview by Dr Zakir Husain, an outstanding Muslim leader who was then Vice-President of India, and paid visits to the University of Delhi (where I gave a lecture), to the Indian Law Institute, and to a few centres of Muslim culture. My most vivid impression of the roots of Muslim religious thought in India came, however, in the course of a short visit to the Dar al-'Ulum at Deoband, a traditional theological centre some miles from Delhi. I was also able to meet Mr Ben Wati, the Secretary of the Evangelical Alliance in India, to give
194

a talk at the YMCA and to preach on Sunday evening to the Evangelical Church Fellowship.

At Aligarh I was the guest of the Aligarh Muslim University. This foundation was the fruit of the reform started by Sir Sayyid Khan (1817-98), in which he did all he could to get Indian Muslims to learn English and to accept an explicitly Western liberal stance. Himself 'a Muslim gentleman of the old school who knew little English', he had sincerely embraced liberal values – even in regard to the interpretation of the Qur'ān. But while the Indian Muslim community had accepted, with some reluctance, his introduction of English education, it 'insisted that in his College neither his ideas nor the English language should be applied to the study of Islam'.[1]

My time at Aligarh was chiefly devoted to the Department of Law, which had arranged for some lectures and a special symposium. Two law students drove me over one day to Agra, where I found the exquisite lines and perfect symmetry of the Taj Mahal far more charming than any photograph had led me to expect. We also visited the Fort and other Mughal monuments in Agra and drove over to Fatepur Sikri, which was most impressive. In the course of our sight-seeing I made some reference to the Indian Mutiny, to which one of my student guides promptly replied in terms of 'the First War of Indian Independence'; but I forbore to ask him how many such wars there had been. Back in Aligarh, I paid a visit to the centre of the Fellowship of Faith for Muslims, where I conversed with the Director about the perennial question of the Christian approach to Muslims.

[1] W. Cantwell Smith, *Islam in Modern History* (Princeton, 1957), pp.65-68.

Whereas Aligarh University is, in general, both 'Western' orientated and non-sectarian, Lucknow is a predominantly Muslim city in which there has been considerable friction between Sunnis and Shi'is. In the past Lucknow was well known for its culture, wit and frivolity, but I saw nothing of this during my short visit. Unhappily, I know no Urdu, but I gave a lecture in English to the local Law Society on 'Law Reform in the Muslim World' and had been asked to inaugurate a Post-Graduate Law Association in the University of Lucknow. But what gave me the 'feel' of Islam in Lucknow was visiting the strictly Sunni, but reasonably progressive, Nadwat al-'Ulama (Council of Islamic Scholars) with their institute of semi-classical Islamic teaching; the Farangi Mahall (European Centre), where I talked to a man from Dacca who insisted that Pakistan ought to be a secular state, on the basis of a pact between Muslims and Hindus; and the Shi'i community, with their rival college, where I met a man, Mufti al-Sayyid Ahmad 'Ali, who was locally regarded as the only Indian who had attained the status of a *mujtahid*.

Other impressions

If Islam in India was, for me, epitomized by Deoband, Aligarh and Lucknow – for it was not until a later visit that I was introduced to the Iqbal Institute in Delhi – one of the most sacred sites of Hinduism is Varanasi. Here I was the guest of the Benares Hindu University – where, again, some of my former pupils were working. Had I known at that time even the little that I have subsequently learnt about the abstruse and conflicting schools of Hindu philosophy, the religion of Hindu villagers and the various *bhakti* devotional cults. I would have been able to talk much more meaningfully to some of the Hindu scholars there. As it is, my most vivid memory is of being taken down to the Ganges early in the morning to see the pilgrims bathing in its sacred waters and two or three cremations taking place on its banks. This gave me a poignant impression of millions of people who want to be cleansed from their sins (however they may view them) before they die, most of whom have never heard, or had the opportunity to understand, the Good News which it is our duty and privilege to proclaim.

Dacca, the capital of what was then still East Pakistan, gave me my only fleeting glimpse of that region. My stay there was marked by the same courtesy as in Lahore – from the Judges and Bar Association of the High Court, from the 'Law Seminar' and the University (where I lectured to a large audience from the Faculties of Law and Islamic Studies) and from the Madrasah-i-'Alia. This was founded in 1780, when Warren Hastings was Governor-General of India, and claims to be 'the oldest educational institution of the Muslims of the Pak-Indo sub-continent'. I had been warned that the Muslims in Dacca were more 'fanatical' than those in Lahore, but this was not the impression I got. On the contrary, many of those I met seemed singularly open-minded, although there were, of course, a number of 'Mawlanas' of the old school. There are still many more Hindus in East Pakistan than in the West.

In Calcutta, through which I passed twice, the University was closed, but I stayed a night with Cecil Johnston, who spent many years as the leader of the Scripture Union in India. My only visit to the Dravidian south of India was to Madras, where I was the guest of the University. This was also the case in

Hyderabad, where I was given a particularly warm welcome (and two enormous garlands!) by former students. Before Independence Hyderabad had been ruled, as an exceedingly tolerant 'Islamic' State, by its Nizams. At one time the Nizam of Hyderabad had been Viceroy of the Deccan, virtually independent of the Mughal Emperor, and the 'Faithful Ally' of the British. More recently he had been Premier Prince of India, supreme within his boundaries so long as he behaved with reasonable discretion.[2] But the vast majority of the population was Hindu, so Hyderabad was virtually the opposite to Kashmir, where the people were predominantly Muslims. On Independence, however, India was so determined that Hyderabad should not join Pakistan that in 1948 she took it over by force. My concern, however, was not political, but academic, with a primary interest in Islamic law (and its lawyers) in India. So I spent most of my short visit in the Osmaniya University, which stands on a splendid site and is most attractive. I had the opportunity to meet a group of Muslim scholars and a High Court Judge, and to lecture both at the University and its much rougher down-town Law College.

Ceylon (now Sri Lanka) was the first predominantly Buddhist country I had ever visited. In Colombo I was the guest of Mr Justice Tambia, a Christian Tamil, who was both a judge and a scholar. He drove me up to spend one night in Kandy, where he took me to see a Buddhist temple in which an alleged tooth of Gautama the Buddha is treasured. But my primary concern was with the Muslim minority, sometimes called 'Moormans', with the origin of the 'Muhammadan

[2] Cf. Philip Mason, A Shaft of Sunlight, pp. 200–216, for a delightful picture of Hyderabad.

Code' of 1806, and with their present legal position.

Sri Lanka is an island of minorities. The Tamils, themselves a minority of Indian origin, are predominantly Hindus, while the Sinhalese majority are basically Buddhists; but there are also both Christian and Muslim minorities. The 'Muhammadan Code', I was told, represents a translation into English of a Batavian Code which one of the former Dutch Governors of Ceylon had imported – and it was from the Dutch, of course, that the Roman-Dutch law which generally prevails in the island was derived. But this Batavian Code was defective in its scope and highly questionable in its contents; more recent legislation directed towards Muslims was largely concerned with matters of procedure rather than substance; and the personal law applicable in matters of family relations to Muslims in Ceylon (almost all of whom belong to the Shafi'i school of Islamic law) was in urgent need of definition. I was able to converse with some of their leaders, and to attend two Christian churches on Sunday.

Malaya

Malaya is at once attractive, bewildering and authoritarian. The villages are clean, with their houses perched on wooden frames; the population is made up of Malays and Chinese in almost equal proportions; and its law is a mixture of Islamic rigorism and local custom. I was introduced to this in Kuala Lumpur and throughout visits to law courts during a three-day drive from there to Singapore. After giving a lecture in Kuala Lumpur on 'Islamic Law and Modern Life' under the auspices of the British Council, and another in the Department of Muslim Studies in the University, I was told by the Principal of the Muslim College at Klang that he had

199

taken the precaution of getting the consent of the Minister of Religion before inviting me to lecture at his College on 'The Islamic Law of Inheritance'.

When I asked why this was necessary, he replied that the Government of Malaya had been much disturbed by the 'Modernist' views of certain religious teachers who came from, or were trained in, the Azhar University in Cairo (which is usually considered a pillar of orthodoxy); so now no-one was permitted to 'teach Islam' without official approval. I remarked that I, as a convinced Christian, would scarcely be likely to 'teach Islam'; but he replied that any discussion of Islamic law could be construed as purporting to teach a 'doctrine of the Religion of Islam'. Yet much of the law applied in Malay courts would be repudiated as un-Islamic by any Azhar sheikh. The combination of Islamic law, *'adat* (customary) law and local legislative enactments differs from State to State.

I went to supper in Kuala Lumpur with a small group of Christians, most of them teaching in the University, who made a practice of meeting together for mutual encouragement. This was most refreshing. One can speak freely as a Christian to the Chinese element in the population, but any attempt to evangelize a Muslim is prohibited. I was told, moreover, that the law about sexual morality was very strict, making it a criminal offence for a Muslim to be 'found in retirement with and suspicious proximity to' anyone of the opposite sex (except for those within the prohibited degrees of blood or marriage relationship), whether the other party be a professing Muslim or not.

Singapore was throbbing with activity, and I much enjoyed my short stay. I already knew the Advocate-General (a Muslim of primarily Indian extraction who was an expert in Islamic law) and the Solicitor-General (a Chinese who had done excellent work as a research Fellow at the Institute in London), and they could not have been more helpful. I was particularly interested in the work of Mrs M. Siraj, the Woman Social Case Worker in the Shari'a Court, who was having unprecedented success in reconciling married couples who were headed for a divorce. My old friend Arnold Lee (see p.20) had got invitations for me to speak in the University for the Christian Union, which was very active; to preach in a Baptist Church on Sunday morning and in the Anglican Cathedral in the evening.

To Africa and home

The thriving Parsee community in Bombay represents the most accessible remnant of the ancient Zoroastrian religion. So I was fortunate to be able to contact one of its leading lawyers, Professor Irani, during a brief visit to Bombay en route for Nairobi, where I was to join up with Pat and our son Hugh (who had flown out from England to spend Christmas with Pat's parents). I had promised to give a Christmas broadcast in Nairobi that evening, and was preparing this in the plane from Bombay to Aden, where we were so much delayed by engine trouble that it seemed impossible that we could arrive in time. But the plane made up part of the lost time and when I landed I found two cars waiting – one with Pat and Hugh in it and the other ready to rush me to a meeting just in time for the broadcast.

It was delightful to celebrate Christmas in this way, and I much enjoyed it. One day we all went to the game park, where we drove within a few feet of some sleepy lions. Hugh, I remember, was very disappointed when he took what should have been an unusually close-up photograph of a zebra and her foal, only to find that he had forgotten to remove the cover from the lens of his new camera.

In the next few days I was able to renew some contacts in Kenya, Uganda, Tanganyika and Zanzibar, which I had not visited for some years. In Nairobi I had lunch with the leading lawyer in the Isma'ili Muslim communities, who showed me his draft copy of the family code now applied by the 'Agakhan Ismaili Councils of Africa' by decree of the Agha Khan – speaking, as in their view he could, with the authority of God. I was both amused and somewhat shaken to find my own name in two or three footnotes to his draft, all in reference to matters in which they had accepted the interpretation of the meaning or implications of the Islamic sources I happened to favour. These Khojas, as they would have been called in India, are far the most progressive non-European community in East Africa – in regard to monogamy, divorce, hospitals, maternity clinics, schools and their whole way of life. This is partly for the very reason that the Agha Khan can, they believe, introduce reforms even contrary to Qur'anic teaching; and any defiance would entail ex-communication from a very tightly-knit community.

We got back to England in the latter part of January in a very cold spell. Meanwhile the work of the Institute had gone on as usual – and had, in fact, gathered pace as my attempts to raise funds for special purposes began to bear fruit. The 'Butterworth Overseas Legal Fellowship' enabled us to invite a law teacher from the 'Old Commonwealth' to spend part of his sabbatical leave at the Institute; a grant from the Rockefeller Foundation made it possible to offer a number of research fellowships to young scholars from Asia and Africa; and a major grant from the Ford Foundation not only provided a lot of money for our library, but also funded several other activities.

It was not long, however, before I was on the move again. I had not intended to attend the 26th International Congress of Orientalists in New Delhi, but at the last moment an invitation came from the Indian Government to go there as their guest in order to take part in a special Symposium on 'Changes in Muslim Personal Law'. One of the Directive Principles of the Indian Constitution makes it a matter of policy to work towards a uniform personal law. So the Government was anxious to persuade the Muslim minority to introduce reforms in their family law, as the Hindus had already done. Hence the Symposium, in which I was the only non-Muslim on the panel of speakers.

A 'coronary warning'

Further visits to Canada, the United States and Tanganyika followed, and it was about this time that I had my first 'coronary warning'. One evening I got home from the Institute unusually tired, with a tingling feeling in my left arm, which persisted next morning. Our family doctor suspected a coronary and kept me in bed until a consultant cardiologist came to see me. An ECG showed that no actual damage had been done, but he agreed with our doctor's diagnosis that it was a 'near miss'. So he forbade me to travel up to London from what was now our Sevenoaks home (to which we had moved from Ealing some years before, to be nearer my then ageing mother) for two or three weeks, and a secretary came down with correspondence, and to take back my replies, from time to time.

This meant a postponement for some months of my first experience of what Arabs call 'the Maghrib' —

Morocco and Algeria. In Morocco I was able to discuss, in both Rabat and the ancient University of Fez, their new code of family law, and in Algiers to catch a fleeting glimpse of the interaction of Islamic, customary and French law. This was very interesting and reasonably restful.

All the same, we had decided that I must cut down somewhat, and we agreed that if I was to continue with my academic work and Christian commitments (to which being a lay representative of the diocese of Rochester in the Church Assembly had by now been added), the item that could most easily be eliminated was the constant travel from Sevenoaks to the University. This was normally quite simple, although it involved transport to Sevenoaks station, a train to London and further transport to the University – and sometimes a rush to catch the train on the way home. But when there was fog, extreme cold, or engine drivers 'working to rule', it could become chaotic. So in due course we moved to the Hampstead Garden Suburb.

15

Harvard and NEAC

New developments ∗ *Teaching at Harvard* ∗
A special opportunity ∗ *The Keele Congress*

There were several new developments in the work of
the Institute in 1965. The one that I chiefly remember
was in the nature of a 'once for all' effort, since it could
scarcely be repeated for some years. This was a
'Summer School in American Law', for which the
Dean of the Harvard Law School, together with four of
his senior professors, provided the teaching staff. The
Extra-mural Department of the University of London
undertook the practical arrangements, and the Institute assumed responsibility for the academic programme. The course extended over two working
weeks, and the total enrolment was just under 150; but
there was a wide variety in the number of courses each
participant took. In addition, two public lectures on
'Civil Rights in the USA' were given in the Beveridge
Hall. At the first of these well-attended lectures Dean
Erwin Griswold (for many years Dean of the Harvard
Law School, and subsequently Solicitor-General of
the USA) was the speaker, with Lord Morris of Borth-
y-Gest in the chair. At the second Professor Al Sacks
(subsequently Dean of the Harvard Law School) spoke,
and I took the chair.

We also took advantage of the presence in England of Professor Griswold and his four colleagues to arrange a memorable weekend at Ditchley Park, Oxfordshire. To this we invited eight English judges, eight barristers and eight solicitors, together with six members of the Society of Public Teachers of Law, to meet our American guests. Two lively discussions on 'Judicial Control of the Executive in the USA' and on 'Legislation by Judicial Decree' were both presided over by Sir Jocelyn Simon (later Lord Simon), and there was plenty of time for informal conversations.

New developments

After our move to Hampstead I was elected a lay representative of London on the Church Assembly. I retired from the Council of the Inter-Varsity Fellowship of Evangelical Unions under the 'six-year rule', having completed six years as chairman. Meanwhile I had become chairman of the Hamlyn Trust (the chief function of which is to arrange for a series of four or five legal lectures each year and to have them published as a volume) on the death of Dr John Murray, previously Vice-Chancellor of Exeter University, who had been chairman since its inception in 1949. I had also become Dean of the Faculty of Law in the University of London (a largely honorific post which only comes to life at degree-giving ceremonies) for the usual two years (almost always followed by one further period of two years).

In November of that year we welcomed to the Institute a Visitation Committee from the Senate which had been appointed to visit all the Senate Institutes. Their report included this comment:

The Senate visitors were deeply impressed by the quality, vigour and extra-ordinary variety of the work of these Institutes, and wish to convey to the Senate their sense of the uniqueness and importance of the contribution the Institutes are making, not only to University life and studies, but to post-graduate work both in London and in the country as a whole.

In our case the Visitation Committee recognized the need for more space and staff, and noted that my post ought to be made full-time. The trouble was that there was not enough money. This I well understood, but I said I really could not carry on with my present sche-dule. When asked what could be done to help, I replied that I urgently needed a first-class secretary/personal assistant at the Institute. I had previously had to rely on my departmental clerk at the School (fortunately only some fifty yards away) and on occa-sional help from the staff at the Institute, all of whom had their own special assignments. So I was authorized to get a first-class personal assistant as soon as possible. It was not long before I providentially obtained the services of Shelagh Brown (now a deaconess and herself a writer) for four days a week. She had at one time been personal secretary to Sir Edward Boyle (later Lord Boyle) and her appointment made an enormous difference, since she was not only an expert in short-hand and typing, but she was also accustomed to dealing with Government departments, to handling telephone calls and to doing much else on her own initiative.

Teaching at Harvard

After the 1966 annual meeting of the Bureau of the International Committee of Comparative Law, held that year in Nancy and (as always) in early September, Pat and I left England to spend a complete semester in Harvard. It was more than a year since Dean Griswold, on one of his visits to London, had called at the Institute to say he had the authority of the Harvard Law School to offer me a professorship there for life or, failing that, for five years. I thanked him for this attractive invitation, but told him that I had too many roots in England – family, Christian and academic – to make this possible. He then suggested a single year, but I said I could not get away for so long, although a single semester might be possible. His initial reaction was that this would not meet their requirements; but he subsequently wrote asking me to come. He kindly arranged, moreover, for me to give a lecture, followed by a seminar, every Tuesday and Thursday, so that we should be able to make other visits, from time to time, over the weekend. We were fortunate enough to be offered a splendid flat, set aside for visitors, at Quincy House, one of the Harvard colleges. This was most convenient, since it meant we were right in the middle of the University, within some eight minutes' walk from the Law School, and even less from the Faculty Club. So we did not have to buy, license or insure a car.

My pupils were an interesting assortment of post-graduate students. On the one hand these came from the Faculty of Government, from the Middle East Centre, and from other departments, and, on the other, from the Law School. It was impracticable to try to produce the traditional 'case book', or to use the

'Socratic method' of teaching commonly followed in American Law Schools. Instead, I provided them each week with some typescript material on the subject in hand, which they had the opportunity to study beforehand. I then gave a lecture on the basis of this material – not, of course, repeating what was already in their hands, but discussing it, explaining anything that needed elucidation, and generally talking round the subject. Finally, after perhaps fifty minutes, we would use the remaining forty minutes as a seminar, with questions and answers.

In America all Law students have already taken a degree in some other subject first, so in effect they were all postgraduate students. The Harvard Law School at that time, moreover, was made up of some 1,650 students drawn from all over the country, and the other postgraduate schools are very good; so it was interesting to try to bring into a fruitful partnership the Law students (who in general knew nothing of Arabic or Islam) and those who knew no Law but were studying Arabic, Islamics or some related subject. I was particularly interested in a fine young man, who had done exceedingly well at the Harvard Law School a few years previously. Now, after a spell in a New York law firm, he was studying Islamic law in my classes, and Arabic at the Middle East Centre, with a view to becoming a Faculty member specializing in Islamic Law. Next autumn he came to London to continue his studies, before spending some months in Egypt. But it soon came to light that he was suffering from leukaemia; so he returned to America, made a brave fight for some two years, and then, sadly, died.

Dean Griswold kindly allowed me to accept a somewhat urgent invitation from Princeton University to travel down there (by underground, air, taxi and train) every second Wednesday over a ten-week period. This was in order to give a lecture on Islamic law to all who wished to come, and to follow this immediately with a seminar on that subject for those who were taking it more seriously, before travelling back to Harvard. This made a long day, but filled a gap in their curriculum.

On almost all my other excursions Pat was able to accompany me: two or three nights in Montreal at the beginning of an incredible Fall, when I lectured at McGill University on Islamic law; another two or three nights in Durham, North Carolina, when I participated in a Conference on the British Commonwealth at Duke University; and lectures in Pittsburg, Brown and Cornell Universities and the Near East Institute in Washington. For the vast majority of those months, however, we stayed in Harvard. The Harvard Law School is a very friendly place, and we were invited to dinner in many different homes. Our flat included a study/spare room, so we were able to entertain a few friends and our son Hugh during the Christmas holidays of his last year at school. For the first few days he revelled in attending innumerable lectures in the Harvard 'Yard'; but at Christmas he had a big disappointment.

A year earlier, before he had even taken his Advanced level school examinations, his housemaster, realizing he lacked practice, had asked Trinity College if he could sit their Scholarship Examination as a trial spin. To this they agreed, with the proviso that they would 'mark him only after Christmas'. We were greatly surprised, therefore, when he got a letter on Christmas Eve saying that they would offer him a place in Trinity in October without any further examination (provided only that he got the minimum University entrance qualification in his Advanced levels). Alternatively, he could stay another year at school and sit the Scholarship Examination seriously in December. He stayed – and his teachers were confident he would get a scholarship. But over Christmas in America he waited for a telegram in vain, and eventually heard that he had missed it. This was a great disappointment, but he took it well, stayed at school for another year (partly to become Captain of Cricket) and collected three Advanced levels at grade A. Meanwhile we took him to New York to stay with some old friends, Professor and Mrs Garretson; and he enjoyed this so much that he stayed on for two or three days after we had returned to Harvard – visiting museums, art galleries and all there was to see.

A special opportunity

We had many opportunities for Christian witness during that semester. Pat had a Bible study group for girls from Radcliffe (now virtually part and parcel of Harvard) one afternoon a week. This was followed by tea, 'cookies' and peals of girlish laughter which I could hear half-way back from the Law School. I, too, had the opportunity to preach or speak several times. But the most memorable occasion was in January 1967, just as the students were completing examinations and we were getting ready to come home. A committee of students from the Harvard-Radcliffe Christian Fellowship and another student group had asked me to give a public lecture on 'The Evidence for the Resurrection'. They had also persuaded me, somewhat against my will, to agree to their inviting three well-known theologians, of distinctly diverse views, to come as 'Discussants', and to a consultant psychiatrist taking the chair. They were rash enough, too, to book one of the largest lecture theatres, in which I thought the audience, at such an inopportune time, would be positively swallowed up.

The students proved right, however, as a rebuke to my lack of faith. The lecture theatre was virtually full downstairs, with a few even in the gallery, and the psychiatrist was eminently helpful. I spoke from my heart for about fifty minutes. Two American professors from the Divinity School (Lawrence Burkholder and Harvey Cox) were much more restrained and cautious in their comments than I had expected, and the third 'Discussant', Professor Wolfhart Pannenberg (then a visiting professor at the Divinity School) spoke with great authority in support of some of my major points. Then, after I had been given the opportunity for a brief reply, the chairman said that a copy of a booklet I had written on that subject would be sent to any who wrote down their names and addresses on sheets of paper provided at two or three tables – and some two hundred did so. We also heard some interesting re-actions to the occasion during the rest of the week.

When I was washing my hands next day, for example, a somewhat blunt professor in the Law School shot out the question: 'Well, how did you and God get on last night?' Before I could answer, another professor, whom I did not even know by name, remarked: 'I understand that God won' – so I decided to leave it at that. A little later a brilliant young Jewish professor told me that he had come to the lecture, but had chosen a seat at the end of a row so that, in his own words, 'I could get away easily if I was bored'; but he added that he had in fact stayed to the end. Pat and I were particularly sorry that this opportunity had occurred only just before our return to England, since it seems to have aroused considerable interest. The occasion was fully reported in two issues of *Christianity Today*.

The Keele Congress

We got back to London before the end of January 1967, and life could then be summed up largely as 'business as usual'. But early in April I had the privilege of participating in the first National Evangelical Anglican Congress, held at Keele University. For this, nine of us had been asked to write an essay, some 5,000 words in length, on the subject allotted to us; and these nine essays were published by the Falcon Press, before the Congress convened, under the title of *Guidelines*. This was in order that delegates to the Congress could read them (and, in some cases, comment on them) in advance. The speakers could therefore talk around their subject, especially in terms of any points that had been raised, rather than read a paper.

The subject that had been allotted to me was 'Christian Worldliness' (with apologies to Dr Alec Vidler!), with the sub-title 'The Needs and Limits of Christian Involvement'. In retrospect I am most grateful for having been made to give some concentrated attention to a subject that had been sadly neglected by Evangelicals (and certainly by me myself, when I was a student). We had always – in theory at least – recognized 'charity' as a Christian duty; and attempts to help those less privileged than ourselves, in projects like the Cambridge University Mission in Bermondsey, had received a certain amount of support. But for the rest we had largely accepted the inequalities of life as part of the order of things. The urge to evangelize, and to 'witness for Christ', had had signally little counterpart in the sphere of radical social reform.

Pat and I had, however, begun to learn a little from our son Hugh, who developed an exceedingly sensitive social conscience at a very early age. It was not only that he positively scorned social barriers, and was deeply concerned about the underprivileged and disadvantaged both at home and abroad. He felt passionately that these things should not be, and that we ought to do everything possible to change the system which allowed them to persist – rather than merely content ourselves with trying partially to salvage those victims of this system with whom we came into personal contact. So I was glad to write the essay required of me, to speak to it at the Congress, and to spend some two or three weeks in the summer vacation trying to give rather more adequate consideration to such a vast subject in the form of a paperback entitled *Into the World: the Needs and Limits of Christian Involvement*. This was published by the Falcon Press in 1968. Quite a number of invitations to speak about this subject (or on some of its facets) followed, and I accepted as many of these as possible.

Since then, thank God, others – much better qualified than I – have written on this topic more fully and radically, and there has been a palpable change in evangelical thinking. Instead of shrinking from anything labelled 'the social gospel', we have come to see that the basic Evangel of spiritual salvation by faith alone is given its proper place only when we recognize the implications which that gospel should always have had in the field of social, racial and economic justice. In other words 'evangelism' and 'mission' (in more general terms) should always go hand in hand. This has, I think, largely been true, within the terms imposed by the political situation, in times of revival, when the church has been alive and outward looking;

but in times of weakness or stagnation the church has become withdrawn and self-centred.

The outstanding decision taken by that first NEAC was, however, the one which heralded a fundamental change of attitude, by most evangelical Anglicans, about the part they should play in regard to the doctrine, liturgy, policy, practice and administration of the Church of England as a whole. In the days of Charles Simeon evangelical clergymen were a small and widely disregarded band of men who often found it very difficult to get appointed to suitable livings. Then circumstances changed considerably, largely as a result of the Evangelical Revival, the 'Clapham Sect' and the formation of Patronage Trusts which were able to ensure the continuation of an evangelical ministry in a number of parishes.

Still more recently, the number and influence of evangelical leaders had increased significantly. But the tendency had largely prevailed for Evangelicals to stand somewhat apart from the central councils of the church, and to concentrate almost exclusively on the cure of souls in their parishes (together with the outreach of evangelism sponsored by their own missionary societies, both home and foreign). They were fortified by the conviction that they were loyally upholding the Reformation doctrines of their Church, and that it was they, rather than sundry other movements in the Church, who maintained the teaching of the Thirty-Nine Articles. Almost inevitably, therefore, something in the nature of evangelical 'ghettoes', which were largely impervious to the winds of external change, and exercised correspondingly little influence on the Church at large, had developed.

But now a new day had dawned. On the one hand, Evangelicals were in a much stronger position (particularly among the younger clergy). On the other, the Church of England was in a state of flux. New canons had been drafted; experimental liturgies were under consideration; and the Church was on the verge of a new relationship with the State. Evangelicals must either stand on one side and let others debate and decide changes which might – and most probably would – influence them as much as others, or else they must play their part in the synodical government of the future church which was, at it were, just round the corner. It seemed clear to most of us that it was our duty to participate in this, and to do our best to make our distinctive contribution. If we did *not* do this, then we could not really complain if changes were made which were not to our liking. But if we did intend to make our contribution, then we must clearly be ready to listen attentively to those who would, we hoped, listen to us: to receive as well as to give.

This vital decision naturally had many consequences, some of them much more welcome than others. It was wholly good, in my view, that we were shedding any 'ghetto' mentality, and beginning to share some of the riches of our inheritance with others in the Church of which we claimed to be an integral part. Almost inevitably, however, discussion with others – and, indeed, between ourselves – brought to light different shades of opinion, previously in part unrecognized, in our own ranks.

More painful still was the sense of estrangement which became apparent among some of our fellow Evangelicals in the Free Churches, who felt that we were at one and the same time drawing closer to those in our own Church who held different opinions, and farther away from those in other Churches with whom we shared our evangelical heritage. In one sense this was, I suppose, inevitable – although it could (and should) be strictly limited in its effects. Unhappily, however, it was sometimes posed by others in terms which stated baldly that, whereas we had been previously 'Christians first, Evangelicals second, and Anglicans third', we had now become 'Christians first, Anglicans second, and Evangelicals third'. This may have been true of some individuals, but it was a formula to which I would never have subscribed; for most of us still felt a fundamental spiritual unity with our fellow Evangelicals, to whatever Church fellowship they might happen to belong. But we were also loyal Anglicans.

There was one point on which both evangelical Anglicans, and Evangelicals in many of the Free Churches, were equally divided – although there was no need for this difference of opinion to spoil the fellowship that individuals can mutually enjoy. The point to which I refer is sometimes termed the concept of the 'Pure Church': namely that Evangelicals – or, for that matter, any other group – should come out of the 'comprehensive' Churches to which many of them now belong in order to form a new Church in which all would embrace certain fundamental doctrines. There are, of course, a number of arguments which can be put forward for such a concept, which clearly has its attractions. But in this context I always remember a story I once heard about a church which went by the name of 'The Church of God'. Before very long there was a split in its membership about some matter of doctrine or practice, and the splinter group called itself 'The True Church of God'. Once again there was a difference of opinion, and the seceders then chose the title 'The only True Church of God'. So where can anyone go from there?

16

New horizons — and a heavy blow

Visits to the Middle East * *Iran and other places* *
A new departure * *Hugh*

Immediately after this Congress Pat and I went on a
tour of several countries in the Middle East. The plan
was that I should give a lecture or two in each of them
under the joint auspices of the British Council and
some local University, and then that Pat should go on
to Nairobi to see her parents (who had been living
there since the Suez débâcle), while I accepted an
invitation to visit Sa'udi Arabia as the guest of the
Government.

Visits to the Middle East

We started in Libya, where I gave a lecture in Arabic
both in Tripoli and Barce. Then we were picked up by
one of the King's jets to spend some twenty-four hours
with King Idris and Queen Fatima at their desert
palace near Tobruk. Queen Fatima was a charming
and relaxed hostess who told us a number of most
amusing stories. Then, after dinner, a servant brought
in two small packages on a silver tray, which proved to
be a gold 'evening dress' watch for Pat and a larger
one, stamped with the King's crown and name, for me.

My next three lectures, all in English, were in Cairo, Asmara and Addis Ababa respectively. In Cairo my audience was cosmopolitan (including several old friends) at the School of Oriental Studies of the American University, where I had studied Arabic. We spent only one night in Cairo, since I was to give another lecture, and stay two or three nights, on my way home. In Asmara, where I gave a lecture to judges and lawyers, it was a particular pleasure to be able to stay at the headquarters of our mission, now renamed the Middle East General Mission (since most of our United Kingdom missionaries, expelled from Egypt after the Suez fiasco, had been redeployed in Eritrea). Happily, our visit coincided with their 'Annual Gathering', when all those missionaries who can leave their work for a long weekend assemble at headquarters for ministry, prayer and business. So we were able to meet most of them – old friends from Egypt and more recent recruits. I had to spend most of the weekend in bed, however, laid low by a bad attack of what we always used to term 'gyppy tummy'; but I was just able to stagger up to the pulpit of the English Church (normally staffed by a BCMS chaplain) where our missionaries usually worshipped on Sunday when in Asmara. And so to Addis Ababa.

We were met on arrival by Princess Sophie, one of the Emperor's granddaughters, who had been a close friend of one of our daughters at Clarendon School (where the Headmistress could never decide which of the two led the other into mischief!). Far from living a life of idle luxury, she, like her sisters, was doing a splendid job. She contrived, however, to drive us round parts of the city before dropping us at the British Embassy for lunch with the Ambassador – with whom I had stayed when he was Ambassador in Algiers –

before I saw Pat off on a flight to Nairobi.

Next day Princess Sophie had arranged for me to have an audience with the Emperor, a dynamic if diminutive figure. Unhappily this was somewhat spoilt by the fact that he always refused to speak English, although he understood it very well. So it had been agreed that he would speak French and I English, to avoid the need for an interpreter; but my French (if it deserves to be called by that name) was scarcely equal to the strain. I also gave two lectures to the Law Faculty of the Haile Selassie University, met some evangelical students, and went to a tea-party which Princess Sophie had kindly arranged for me to meet several members of the royal family and a few local missionaries.

In Jedda my first appointment was at the British Consulate, which was giving a party to celebrate some occasion or other. Here almost everyone was drinking wine or whisky – a heinous crime in Sa'udi Arabia outside such privileged portals. Both Mecca and Medina are, or course, 'out of bounds' to non-Muslims, so I went on to Riyadh to visit Government officials, judges and lawyers, before flying to Dhahran to confer with the leaders of Aramco (the Arabian American Oil Company). I learnt a lot about the administration of justice in that part of Arabia from reading confidential reports of local trials (compiled by some of their American lawyers who had once been my pupils in London). I was also able to discuss with the Company the minimal degree of religious liberty they enjoyed, and to attend their church on Sunday.

I got back to Riyadh just in time to be taken to see a play performed by some pupils from the 'School for the King's Sons' (who were numerous enough in all conscience, but were somewhat diluted in school by a few privileged commoners). At this I sat just behind the King and briefly conversed with him. But I was acutely embarrassed by the last act of the play – which was, understandably enough, defiant of the Crusades, but also militantly anti-Christian, at least by implication. Finally, after more consultations, a visit to Riyadh University and a fantastic taste of the chaos which at that time reigned in Riyadh airport, I was able, after much delay and confusion, to drag my baggage off a plane bound for some unknown destination and find a seat on an overloaded flight to Cairo. I was not sorry to leave a country where savage punishments are imposed on the generality of men and women for acts which those who are *persona grata* can do with comparative impunity.

In Cairo I dined with a member of the British Embassy who had also invited Hussein Heikal, then quite the leading journalist in the Arab world. He was very interesting to talk to, and offered to get me an audience with President Nasser, had I been able to stay in Cairo a little longer. But I had to get back to London at once, where Pat joined me from Nairobi a few days later. We both had some difficulty with Customs when we declared the gold watches given to us by King Idris, since my Scottish blood prompted me to argue that, unlike a gift from a maiden aunt, one has no option about taking one from an Arab king with whom one had worked during the war – and in due course the money I had paid 'on deposit' was courteously returned, on condition we did not sell the watches!

I had been elected President of the Society of Public Teachers of Law for the academic year 1968-9, and was invited in that capacity to attend the Annual Convention of the Association of American Law Schools in New Orleans. This was only one of several overseas visits in these two or three years, of which the most interesting were, perhaps, those to the Lebanon, Iran and Canada.

I went to the Lebanon in response to an invitation from the Ford Foundation (and its International Legal Centre in New York) to participate in, and contribute a paper to, a conference on 'Law and Social and Economic Development'. This was held at a hotel just outside Beirut; and when it was over I went up into the mountains for two days to join Pat, who had been staying with two missionary friends in Souk al-Gharb – the village on which so much recent fighting in the Lebanon has been centred. Our host, whom we had known for many years in Egypt, was at that time the director of the Lebanon Bible School; and from him and the British Ambassador in Beirut we learnt a lot about the current position in that country.

Iran and other places

The following year I accepted an invitation to make my first visit to Iran to give some lectures – chiefly in Tehran University. This gave me the opportunity to confer with judges, academics and practising lawyers about the interpretation, and implications, of the exceedingly interesting *Family Protection Act*, which had been promulgated in Iran only in 1967. On this trip, too, Pat was able to accompany me. Some of my former pupils were very kind in entertaining us and taking us, *inter alia,* to see the closely guarded display of the Crown Jewels. These were magnificent; but before the end we began to feel we never wanted to see another diamond, emerald or ruby – or certainly not ones of that quality or size. These jewels had at that time become part of the heritage of the nation, I believe; but they gave us some idea of the vast wealth of the Peacock Throne, which was already under widespread criticism. While I was lecturing at the University the wife of the Director of the Iranian branch of the British Council was good enough to drive Pat round Tehran, which easily outdid Cairo or Beirut, to say nothing of Paris, in the menace of its brash and undisciplined driving.

The most noteworthy part of this visit, however, came towards the end, when one of my former pupils drove me down to the sacred city of Qom, where we breakfasted with his brother (a local schoolmaster). The brother then took me to pay calls on two of the most eminent of those 'divines' who had reached the status of a *mujtahid* (commonly referred to in Iran by the more general title of 'Ayatollah'). I found both of them sitting cross-legged on carpets in their reception rooms, wearing fantastically wide turbans; and I was able to talk with them in Arabic. I had been warned beforehand that if I drank any tea or coffee they would probably feel it necessary, after I had left, to break the glass out of which I, as an 'unbeliever', had drunk; but when, in each case, a servant came in on his knees and proffered me a glass, I took it , regardless of the consequences. And I very much doubt if it suffered any worse fate than to be washed.

Although invited by my host to go into the sanctuary itself I naturally refused, since the Shi'is in Iraq and Iran do not permit non-Muslims to enter their mosques; but even in the outer area through which we had to pass I was eyed askance by a number of people, who clearly questioned my companion about me. As I knew no Persian I was none the wiser, but I strongly suspect that he was evasive, if not positively untruthful, both in what he said to them and in his subsequent answers to my questions. It would clearly have been unsafe for Pat to accompany me, which was why she had flown straight to Isfahan to stay with the Bishop of Iran and his English wife, and it was to their house that my former pupil drove me in the evening.

Bishop Dehqani Tafti is himself an Iranian convert from Islam, while his wife's maternal grandparents were medical missionaries in Isfahan whose daughter had married a young Irishman named Thompson. In due course he had become the last British bishop of what was then known as Persia. So it was eminently suitable that his daughter should marry the man who was to become the first Iranian bishop. Pat and I much enjoyed our short visit to them. The bishop is a most interesting man, and his wholly admirable wife, bi-lingual in English and Persian, took us on a tour of what must be one of the most beautiful cities in the world.

Much more recently the Dehqanis have suffered greatly from the 'Islamic Revolution'. One night some would-be assassins burst into their bedroom intending to murder the bishop, and his wife got wounded in shielding him; and some months later their only son was in fact murdered. So now they and their daughters are in England. In present circumstances it is impossible for Bishop Dehqani even to visit Iran; but his appointment as an assistant bishop in Winchester allows him to travel to other dioceses of the province of Jerusalem and the Near East, of which he remains Presiding Bishop.

A new departure

It was in 1969, too, that what I regard in retrospect as a new phase in my life opened up, although at the time

I was wholly unaware of this. It arose from what was, in itself, a single event – welcome indeed, but not particularly significant: an invitation to give a series of four theological lectures in Trent University, Ontario, Canada. In that University there was no Faculty of Theology; so the decision had been taken to invite a visiting speaker once a year to give a series of lectures on this subject, which would be open to all faculties of the University and to local residents. Usually, no doubt, they invite a professional theologian; but they had decided that from time to time they would invite someone from another academic displine. Hence this invitation.

Why this opportunity was so special from my point of view was that it came officially from a university as such. I had given evangelistic or devotional talks, scores of times, in universities or colleges at the invitation of Christian Unions. These were fitted in with professional engagements on my overseas visits, or undertaken *ad hoc* in Britain. But I had always regarded the preparation and delivery of these talks as extra-curriculum activities, and had tried to be strictly conscientious in not letting them detract from the academic work for which I was responsible. But considerable emphasis has, however, been put of late on interfaculty activities and cross-fertilization; so I felt justified in regarding the preparation and delivery of these official lectures as part and parcel of the work for which I was paid. This made a big difference. I also decided to turn the subject-matter of these lectures into a book, which was published by the IVP under the title of *Christianity: the Witness of History* (1969).

What made this the beginning of a new phase in my life was that I received a number of similar invitations in the following years, out of each of which emerged

225

the substance of another book on some aspect of the Christian faith. But just as I had taken the opportunity to give Christian talks 'on the side' when travelling on legal business, I was able on this trip to give lectures on Islamic Law in McGill University, Montreal, in Queen's University, Kingston, in Osgoode Hall, Toronto, and in the University of Toronto itself.

Early in 1970 a somewhat similar invitation came in the form of the annual Church of Ireland Lectures at Queen's University, Belfast (in which all the University chaplains were in some measure involved, and the chair was taken by the Vice-Chancellor). My subject this time was 'Christianity and Comparative Religion', on which I preached on Sunday and lectured on the next three days. Again a book, under the same title, was published by IVP in 1970. It was about this time that I was elected a Fellow of the British Academy.

Hugh

Our most vivid memories of the years 1967-70 are, however, concerned with our son Hugh. In 1967 he and a school friend had won the award of the Observer Mace in a debating competition open to all secondary schools. Pat and I attended the final in a London hall; and I remember that, as we listened, we both thought 'Can this possibly be our son?', for he spoke without notes with a clarity, fluency and conviction that took us completely by surprise. Then, in October, he went up to Cambridge to read history, and from the first found both Trinity and the debating Union eminently to his liking – so much so that he was elected Secretary of the latter at the end of his first academic year. He was also an active member of the Christian Union. In the Long Vacation he first did some teaching, and then went with a school friend to Italy, where they found that £50 (at that time the maximum one was permitted to take abroad) was all too soon exhausted by the museum charges, travelling, photos, Youth Hostels and inexpensive meals. So he reached the hotel where we were going to meet him two days early – bearded because of the discomfort of shaving in cold water. There our kind hotelier had provided a bed in a bathroom (since all his bedrooms were booked) and gave him plenty of good food until we arrived. But he soon had to return to England to go, now permanently bearded, on a cricket tour; and then the blow fell.

By that time we had returned to England, and he came home one night in great pain. He had been struck by a cricket ball in the groin, and this revealed that he had a cancer. It then transpired that he had had a few intermittent twinges of pain previously, but had not consulted a doctor. A major operation was followed by radiotherapy, and we were told there was an 85% chance that there would be no secondaries. But he had to go up to Cambridge rather late, so he resigned his secretaryship of the Union. He was, however, re-elected Secretary for the Lent term, and Vice-President for the Easter term, of the following year. He had planned, moreover, to spend most of the Long Vacation running a pioneer course in Southall to introduce immigrant boys and girls to British life and ways; and he had been having regular medical check-ups. He had in fact had one of these, seemingly satisfactory, just before we left for two weeks in Italy.

It was in the second of these weeks that a letter came from him marked 'Not to be opened' until a specified date (just before the day when we were to come home). This aroused our suspicion, so we opened it at once. It told us that soon after our departure he had received a

227

letter from the hospital telling him that he had developed a secondary cancer, this time on his lung. So he had consulted our son-in-law, John Trapnell, a consultant surgeon in Bournemouth, and the London friend who had performed the first operation. Both were under pledge not to tell us, since he felt we needed our holiday (which was typical of him). Then he had started a further course of radiotherapy. Naturally, however, we came home at once.

He was finding that each radiation made him feel very sick for some two hours, but insisted on continuing with his work in Southall – in which he showed great ability in organization, leadership and improvization. He was lodged in Southall during the week but came home for a time after each radiation; and he stayed with us each weekend. It was then that he read a short commentary on the letter of James[1] by a friend, the Rev. Alec Motyer, lent to him by Pat without any special comment; and as a consequence he told us he would like to follow James 5:14–15 in asking 'the elders of the church' for prayer and anointing. Pat's brother Desmond Givan, a missionary parson, was staying with us, and Alec Motyer agreed to come. He had a private talk with Hugh which he rightly regarded as confidential, but he felt at liberty to assure us, afterwards, that we 'need have no doubt whatever that Hugh is a believer'. This did not in any way surprise us, but it was good to hear it thus confirmed. Then we had a simple service of prayer and anointing (using some kitchen oil), with a full realization that the outcome was subject to the will of God.

[1] Published by the New Mildmay Press. Later re-written and published under the title *The tests of faith: Practical Christianity in the letter of James* (IVP, 1970).

At the end of his course of radiotherapy he was told that the trouble on his lung seemed to have cleared up. So he went for a short holiday with our married daughter Hazel in Bournemouth, and then back to Cambridge for his presidency of the Union in the Michaelmas term. For this he had arranged a phenomenally full programme of debates, lectures and discussions, about which he had written innumerable letters during the vacation. He invited us up to two of the debates: one on the motion that 'Modern man is the loser by his rejection of the Christian faith', and the other his Presidential Debate. I have subsequently been told by Lord Hailsham that he was the out-standing President of the Cambridge Union since the war, and others have paid even more sweeping tributes.

The 'paper' speakers at the first of these two debates were the Vice-President of the Union, Malcolm Muggeridge and Dr Michael Ramsey, then Archbishop of Canterbury, for the motion, and the son of the Indian High Commissioner in London, John Mortimer, QC and Professor Alastair MacIntyre against it. After listening to them I remember thinking to myself, 'What we now need is a speech about the essential validity of the Christian faith.' This thought was prompted by the fact that Professor MacIntyre's central point was that all the speakers for the motion had concentrated on the benefits of Christianity. These included its moral influence, its comfort, and the way in which it had inspired great music, literature, paint-ing, architecture and, in a word, a whole civilization, besides personal sanctity. But these speakers had largely neglected the basic question: 'Is it *true*?' For if it was not essentially true, then – whatever its value in the past – modern man could scarcely be termed a loser by rejecting it.

I could not then myself make the points I felt ought to be made, since I was sitting upstairs in the gallery with Pat. But a few days later the Director of Extra-Mural Studies in the University of London telephoned to ask if he could come over to see me. London University, he told me, had for years been arranging a residential weekend for the Workers' Educational Association, but had never had a lecturer speaking specifically as a Christian (although many who were, no doubt, themselves Christians must have spoken on science, music, literature or a multitude of other subjects). But now, he said, the request was for a conference on 'The post-Christian Era'. For this he had a number of speakers lined up, including an atheist philosopher; so he needed someone who was prepared to argue 'the case for Christian faith'. Would I be willing to do that? In the circumstances, I could hardly refuse.

Back to Hugh. Towards the end of his presidential term he came up to London for another medical check-up, and was to lunch with me afterwards. But he phoned to tell me that he had been asked to wait while some X-rays were examined, and then again to say: 'Father, I have bad news for you. The tumour has come back.' We lunched together, carefully avoiding the subject; but afterwards he asked if he could come back to my office for some prayer. To this I gladly agreed, and asked him if he would start; but he preferred to leave that to me. I don't remember what words came to me in those traumatic moments, but then I heard Hugh's voice saying, 'O God, you know how difficult it sometimes is to say "Your will be done". Help me to say that now.' After that, when kind friends of a strongly 'charismatic' persuasion urged Pat and me to take him to this 'healer' or that, we always refused. He had chosen the path of James

5:14–15 and God had seemed to act; and he had put himself in his heavenly Father's hands. So would it have helped his faith to go hither and thither, and was the power of God limited to any particular individual?

He finished the term, was given chemotherapy, and soon reduced his rooms, which had been chaotic during his presidential term, to apple-pie order. He was President of the Cambridge Labour Club, and then the National Chairman of 'Students for a Labour Victory' in the coming election – for his views were distinctly left wing, although never remotely anarchistic. A close friendship had grown up between him and Bishop Trevor Huddleston, to whom he had owed much at an earlier period when it seemed to him that Christians talked a lot, but *did* very little about social justice, while his left-wing friends had no personal faith, but did a lot. In Trevor Huddleston, on the other hand, he found one who undeniably did a great deal, but as an explicit expression of his personal faith.

It was about this time that Hugh was asked to give a short talk for the Crusaders' Union at the Central Hall, Westminster. He was far from well, and we were somewhat dubious about it. But he said: 'Don't try to stop me. I don't get many opportunities for this sort of thing.' A little later, when he was in hospital in London, he told us that his doctors had said he *might* be allowed to get up after lunch next day to travel to Manchester for the Universities' debating competition for the Observer Mace. He did so, and about 10 p.m. the telephone rang to ask if I would accept a call from Hugh Anderson in Manchester. Almost at once, he quietly said: 'Father, I have just won' – and he was back in hospital by 10.30 next morning. His trophy as the best individual debater stands in my study now.

Chemotherapy, however, did not avail, for (as we

subsequently learnt) his cancer was of the taratoma variety, and very virile. So he had to have a lung amputated – which caused him a lot of pain, and seemed to put paid to his beloved cricket. Back at Cambridge again, he became ill with severe headaches, which his doctor thought were due to influenza. But our surgeon son-in-law was suspicious and telephoned us. Hugh was moved to Addenbrooke's Hospital; and we rushed up to Cambridge. A very kind and skilful surgeon, Mr John Gleave, told us that a scan showed that he had another tumour, this time on the brain. There was not much hope, but he had been asking himself what he would do if it were his own son; and he said that he would opt for a further operation, as the only possible hope. To this Hugh agreed, the operation was done, and ten days later we drove him home. But he again fell sick, and we took him back to Addenbrooke's, where it transpired that he had yet another growth on his brain. A comparison of the new and former X-rays seemed to show, however, that this was a coeval, rather than a progeny, of the first, and Mr Gleave again operated.

Back home he came, and we took him to Italy to recuperate. He bathed with us in Lake Como, and one day insisted on playing table tennis with me; but we noticed that he found difficulty in reading his letters. So when he again felt sick (from what might have been a purely local upset) we rushed him home and back to Addenbrooke's. But there was nothing further that could be done; and when he felt rather better, he went to Bournemouth to stay with Hazel. Sometimes he seemed himself, and enjoyed a meal in a restaurant; but most of the time he lay on his bed upstairs.

I met him at Waterloo and drove him home, and he insisted on coming to church and Holy Communion.

Then he got such bad headaches that we took him into the Mildmay Mission Hospital. After two or three days there he fell into a coma, from which his doctors thought he would never come round. But during the night he did, just when a Christian doctor was standing by his side. 'It must be getting near the end now, isn't it, doctor?' Hugh asked; and the doctor very wisely said: 'Well, Hugh, I think you are drawing near your Lord.' 'Yes', he replied, 'I am drawing near my Lord. I am at peace. I think my work is done.' This from a young man not yet twenty-two years old, who loved life and longed to turn the world upside down, gave us great comfort. After that I slept in the hospital each night while Pat sat there almost all day, and we were both there in the evenings. But the end soon came in his sleep, and I shall never forget the peaceful look on his now painless face. This was about 2 a.m. on the morning of 12 August 1970. There was a talk of some twenty minutes about him on the BBC that same afternoon, and his death was included in the 10 p.m. news bulletin.

I had been booked for weeks to record, next day, one of the 'quarter to eight' talks on the BBC, to be broadcast in the following week. Four different speakers were to talk about the general subject 'Taking a new look', each from his own point of view. From the first I had decided to speak about 'Taking a new look at the essential validity of the Christian faith', particularly in terms of the convincing evidence for the resurrection of Jesus. So it seemed to both Pat and me that I should not cancel this engagement, but end it with a testimony to what this meant to us in the context of Hugh's death. It was not easy, since Hugh and I were very close. But several of my academic colleagues, who had tuned in for the eight o'clock news, were clearly more impressed by this short talk than by anything else I had ever said – since they realized that it must have come from my heart. Many people have subsequently told me that they heard it.

We decided on an almost immediate private cremation (since Pat had been through a two-year-long ordeal of alternating hopes and fears, punctuated by Hugh's four major operations). Our friend and Rector, John Stott, took this for us, and was a great help to us throughout. Then I took Pat away for a few days in the Cotswolds. We had agreed with John to have a memorial service in All Souls, Langham Place, in September; and when I suggested that Trevor Huddleston should be asked to speak, he told me that he was about to make the same suggestion. We also asked John to read the closing verses of Romans 8 (which he had read beside Hugh's bed on the evening before he died) with a few comments. It was a most impressive service, attended by some 700 people – including the Prime Minister and four or five members of the Labour Cabinet, besides many of our friends and relations. Later there was a second memorial service in Trinity College Chapel, at which Bishop David Sheppard spoke. He drew a parallel between Hugh and Martin Luther King, as men who, not content with salvaging victims on the road between Jerusalem and Jericho, were determined to do their best to rid the road of robbers. Among many letters there was one from the President of the CICCU, saying that 'everyone in Cambridge' knew that Hugh was a member, and that his influence had reached people whom few others could touch.

This blow was much harder for Pat to bear than for me, since she had to rest every afternoon (having had a second major operation on her back not very long before). So while I could throw myself into my work, she had long hours in which to think. Not surprisingly, she underwent a 'chemical depression'. She also found it very difficult at first to talk about Hugh. It is comparatively easy for a Christian to be triumphant in a crisis, but a reaction is almost bound to follow. To grieve is a perfectly natural human experience, in which our Lord himself shared. But, thank God, we do not grieve as 'those who have no hope'. Less than five years later our two daughters also died, so invitations to speak about bereavement began to flow in – and Pat, after a struggle, told the Lord that she was willing to say yes, if this was his will. In this way, as I have often been told, she has brought consolation – and, indeed, new life – to many. But this is to anticipate.

17

The General Synod

*A new job * A new procedure * International
links * A miscellany*

I shall not try to describe the blank that Hugh's death
left in our lives. He had always been so full of vitality
and plans for the future, and his life was one of such
outstanding promise. Some years later my former
supervisor in Cambridge wrote me a note saying that
Lord Butler, then Master of Trinity, had just remarked
at a dinner for Trinity parliamentarians that in Hugh's
death Trinity had 'probably lost its first Labour Prime
Minister'! Almost immediately after his death a letter
had been published in *The Times*, over the signatures of
Lord Butler, the Prime Minister (Harold Wilson), the
Archbishop of Canterbury (Michael Ramsey), Bishop
Trevor Huddleston and several members of the
Cabinet, appealing for a memorial fund. Out of this a
scholarship was established for a black South African
to be brought to England, under Trinity auspices, for
a University education – whether at Trinity itself or
elsewhere. This would, I am sure, have pleased Hugh
greatly. Another continuing memorial, set up under
the same fund, was for an annual Lecture to be given
in Hugh's honour at the Union. This is normally given
by a leading Labour politician, or some similar figure;

but in 1981 it was given by the Prince of Wales, with whom Hugh had been a contemporary at Trinity.

Immediately after Hugh's death we received a large number of letters about him, from friends, relations, politicians, academics and others who had known him, as well as many of our own personal friends. These we greatly valued – particularly those which mentioned not only his talents, achievements and prospects, but his character, compassion and personal faith. We gave his pocket Bible to Trevor Huddleston, his watch to another friend, and his library to the Cambridge Union.

People used continually to ask us why a young man of such promise, and with such a zest for life, should be allowed to die so young. To this the only reply, we both feel, is that we do not, and cannot, know. The vital question to ask God in such cases is not, 'Why did you allow this?' (to which he seldom, I think, vouchsafes an answer), but, 'What do you want to teach me through this?' There is one blessing in such circumstances to which we can all aspire. It was spelt out in the message Jesus sent to John the Baptist: 'Blessed is he who takes no offence at me' (Matthew 11:6, RSV). Or we could express it in Samuel's words: 'He is the LORD [our Covenant God]; let him do what is good in his eyes' (1 Samuel 3:18).

The Christian can have peace of heart only by accepting such things from God's hands (in the sense that he has permitted them to happen, whatever their immediate cause may be, and for whatever reason he may have seen fit to allow them). Thank God, Pat's chemical depression was cured through the skill of Dr William Sargant, to whom she went (on the advice of our friend Dr Martyn Lloyd-Jones) as one who was expert in curing chemical depressions by chemical means. Nor have we any doubt that Hugh is 'at home with the Lord' (2 Corinthians 5:8) and that God's plan for him *is being* fulfilled.

A new job

In the autumn of 1970 I was elected as a lay representative of the Diocese of London on the General Synod, which in that year took the place of Church Assembly; and then, when the Synod met in November, I was elected Chairman of the House of Laity. This added a considerable dimension to my work: four to five days, three times a year, actually in Synod; membership of its Standing Committee, Policy Sub-Committee and several other committees, including, of course, the House of Laity Standing Committee. I had asked for the approval of the University before I took on this very considerable load; and this was readily accepted as one form of the variety of voluntary service to the nation or community in which academics often take part. By 1970 my routine lecturing at the School of Oriental and African Studies had been taken over by others; and the few seminars in Islamic law which I still took need not always be on the same day. The administrative work of the Institute had grown enormously with our discussion groups, visiting professors, workshops, research fellowships and all that concerned the new building we had in mind. But John Boxhall was a most efficient and reliable Secretary, and I could usually keep up, with the able help of Shelagh Brown (my secretary and personal assistant) with all that concerned me personally.

The task of the Chairman of the House of Laity had, moreover, changed radically with the introduction of synodical government. Even in the Church Assembly, bishops, clergy and laymen had usually, of course, met and debated together; but the Convocations of Canterbury and York had continued to meet separately, especially to deal with matters of doctrine and liturgy. Much of this then had to be passed on to the House of Laity sitting alone, since under the Church Assembly legislation an alternative service, for example, could not be introduced unless it had finally been approved by two-thirds of the House of Laity as well as by the Convocations. This was a most unsatisfactory procedure, since we had not heard the preceding debates and had had no opportunity to express our opinion. All we could do, therefore, was to debate it all over again and then either accept it *in toto* or send it back to the Convocations with the request that they should reconsider certain points. And any such referral meant something like two years' delay in the relevant Service, with all the frustration this might entail.

An occurrence some two years previously will, I think, illustrate this point. The Convocations had approved a new Funeral Service which included some fourteen prayers for the dead, and the Evangelicals in the House of Laity had asked me to oppose these. But it so happened that, when the House of Laity met to debate this draft Service, I had to be abroad. So another member took my place and, in the event, we lost the vote each time by a very small margin. When, therefore, the Service again came before the House, I was asked if I would take over the opposition to these prayers. But I felt this was the wrong approach, and said I would speak on this subject only if they would trust me to do this in my own way.

This they agreed, and when the time came I took

an entirely new line. First, I said how deeply unsatisfactory it was if, in a united church, we decided matters of principle by two or three votes, which might well go one way or the other, and a large minority would go home with wounded consciences. Couldn't we do somewhat better than that? Suppose we Evangelicals had a new look at the whole question of 'prayers for the dead', instead of opposing them lock, stock and barrel? Thanksgiving for the lives of the departed we all thoroughly approved; and no member of the House, I hoped, thought that intercessions for the dead would 'change God's mind' about their eternal destiny. There remained at issue an intermediate category of prayers which seemed to us to call in question the doctrine of justification by faith. So could not we Evangelicals, for our brethren's sake, examine them afresh and see whether these largely optional prayers could be shorn of those elements which appeared to us to give official sanction to a weakening of that salient doctrine of the Reformation? And could not our Anglo-Catholic friends content themselves with more carefully worded prayers in an official liturgy, adding in their silent or personal prayers whatever they felt to be necessary and proper?

This approach received overwhelming support, both in speeches from Anglo-Catholic members and in the final vote. But the prayers to which many of us objected had already been approved by the Convocations. So the next step was to persuade the Archbishops to set up a small committee of clergy and laity, made up of both Evangelicals and Anglo-Catholics, to reconsider these prayers and make recommendations. This was agreed, the members were selected, the Bishop of St Edmundsbury and

Ipswich was appointed Chairman, and a rewording of each of the prayers was approved – I think unanimously. In the event, however, the Convocations accepted only two or three of these redrafted prayers and re-endorsed the original wording of the remainder. So I well remember what happened when the House of Laity next met, with this item, *inter alia*, on its agenda. It was introduced by Chancellor Wigglesworth, himself a staunch Anglo-Catholic who had no personal objection to these prayers. He simply said that it was his duty to re-introduce this draft Service; but, since the House of Laity had already overwhelmingly approved a new approach to all these prayers, with which the Convocations had not seen fit to agree, he proposed that we should turn to the next item on our agenda without any further debate. This was agreed, and the Service concerned dropped to the bottom of the sea and was never seen again.

A new procedure

Now, however, this very clumsy procedure was to be ended. In the Synod all motions were to be brought before the Houses of Bishops, Clergy and Laity together, where they would be debated (and then, if 'generally approved', revised) in open Synod, before a final vote. Sometimes the vote was collective and sometimes by Houses, according to the nature of the business concerned or the request of a sufficient number of members. As a result, separate meetings of the House of Clergy (to say nothing of the Convocations of Canterbury and York as such) became increasingly infrequent, and those of the House of Laity still more so, although the House of Bishops continued to meet with some regularity. In the Synod, moreover, the practice was ended according to which the Archbishop of Canterbury normally took the Chair throughout (except when relieved, from time to time, by the Archbishop of York or some other senior Bishop). Instead, a panel of chairmen was appointed to deal with all business other than those items which, under Standing Orders, must be presided over by one of the Archbishops.

In the Church Assembly it had been the normal practice for those who wanted to speak to send in their names and to indicate whether they were for or against the motion, and for the Archbishop to call 'Bishop X to be followed by Dr Y', and then 'Dr Y to be followed by Canon Z'; but this system was to be radically changed in the interests of the freedom and spontaneity of debates. People could still send in their names, but Standing Orders prescribed that, after the first speaker (as specified on the Order Paper), no-one who did not rise to his feet at the conclusion of the preceding speech was to be called by the Chairman. He then had to choose between all those who were upstanding. This was no easy matter – for he was supposed to give a certain precedence to those who had sent in their names. He also had to do his best to alternate between those who would be likely to speak for or against the motion (an almost impossible task), to give a fair crack of the whip to bishops, clergy and laymen, and to encourage speakers making their maiden speeches – without by any means ignoring those likely to speak with authority or special knowledge. He must do all this, moreover, in an assembly of some 550 persons, most of whom he did not know by name. And this task is both guided and sometimes complicated by a mass of

Standing Orders, some of which are by no means easy to interpret or apply.

So acting as Chairman was far from restful, as I discovered when I had to take the chair for some seven hours (not counting interludes) at the Revision Stage of the debate about the original Series 3 Communion Service. This was before the rule was introduced that, in such debates, members might raise on the floor of the Synod only those amendments that they had already sent in to the Revision Committee (and had, in many cases, had the opportunity to discuss with its members), but which that committee had seen fit to reject. So there were, I think, a number of reasons why many of us felt a sense of relief when it was decided that the panel of chairmen should be changed every few years – in regard to all except the two Archbishops.

When actually in the chair one is, of course, precluded from making a speech, except for the device by which the Archbishop of Canterbury, for example, used very occasionally to vacate the chair temporarily while he spoke for, or against, a motion. When not in the chair, however, there was nothing to keep the Prolocutors, or the Chairman and Vice-Chairman of the House of Laity, from making speeches. Of this liberty I made, I fear, a somewhat liberal use. But I did impose on myself a principle from which I seldom, if ever, diverged: that, although I would always vote in accordance with my conscience, I would abstain from making speeches which followed a distinctly 'party' line. This principle was not required by any generally accepted criterion, but it did, I believe, reinforce the fact that in my official capacity I did my best to be impartial. This stance was sometimes under considerable strain, but I think it was probably worth while. When chatting about the Synod recently with a bishop from a somewhat different ecclesiastical tradition, after we had both retired, I reminded him that I am, myself, 'a dyed-in-the-wool Evangelical'. 'I know', he replied; 'but we all trusted you' – and I *hope* this was because I tried to be fair-minded rather than because I sat lightly by matters of principle. But even in the matter of voting, of course, members of the Synod often feel compelled to support a motion they consider far short of their ideal, but which represents the best they can hope for in the circumstances.

International links

The following year another 'church' opportunity opened up, when I was appointed the lay representative of the Church of England on the Anglican Consultative Council. This is a comparatively small body, made up of bishops, clergy and lay representatives from all the different Provinces of the Anglican Communion, each delegation ranging from three to one according to the size of the Province concerned. The Archbishop of Canterbury is always its President, Bishop John Howe was at that time its Secretary General, and a Nigerian layman was elected Chairman. The Council met for the first time in Limuru, Kenya, for a residential conference lasting some twelve days – long enough for a body of about fifty delegates to get to know one another reasonably well. Even at this first meeting the Asian and African Provinces outnumbered those from the 'Old Commonwealth'; so although the former were in part represented by Europeans, at least half the delegates were of Asian or African descent. Meeting each day for worship and for meals, besides plenary and sectional debates and discussions, we soon came to understand each other's standpoint and concerns; and it was an enriching experience to hear the views of such a diverse group of men and women – including two or three 'youth' members and four or five selected 'Advisers'.

Like the Lambeth Conferences themselves, the Council, true to its name, is purely consultative, so its reports are in no sense authoritative. The basic object of the exercise is, of course, to hold the very widespread and disparate Provinces of the Anglican Communion together in between Lambeth Conferences, and to try to ensure that, in so far as possible, no Province goes off at a tangent without consulting its partners. To this end the visits of the Secretary General (in which capacity John Howe was at that time indefatigable), together with continual correspondence with him and his staff, made a major contribution. The Council also elected a small Standing Committee, on which for its first four years I was the Church of England representative; and we met in London for a few days in the intervening years, when the Council itself was not due to meet, to review the last meeting of the Council, take note of any developments, and plan its next meeting. It was soon clear that the advice of the Council was taken very much to heart in some Provinces; but I always felt that the Church of England itself treated both the Council and its advice with very scant respect.

The vagaries of memory – when not stimulated by some written record or by the recollection of others – have always intrigued me. There seems to be no particular reason why some incidents are vividly remembered and others forgotten, regardless of their intrinsic importance. Thus from those two weeks in Kenya a number of purely personal memories survive. There was the surprise I felt when, in a discussion about the distinctly controversial WCC grants to combat racialism, it became apparent that they were staunchly supported by all our African colleagues, including members of the Rwanda Revival. The fact that some powerful nations of the West had come alongside the weak and oppressed, in practical action rather than mere words, was likened by one African to the incarnation; and several emphasized how greatly this had aided the negotiations for peace in the Southern Sudan.

Then, too, there was the talk I had with Bishop (later Archbishop) Luwum about the very recent coup that had brought Idi Amin to power in Uganda in place of President Milton Oboeti. This had seemed at the time to many in England a change for the better; but Bishop Luwum already felt serious forebodings.

I vividly remember, too, the cordial greeting Bishop (later Archbishop) Hands of Papua New Guinea gave to our Kenyan night-watchman when he passed us as we stood talking just before bed. David Hands then told me that he had gone out the previous midday to share a meal with this night-watchman and his wife in their simple shack a few miles away in the bush. It was there, too, that I had the pleasure of meeting Bishop Lesslie Newbigin for the first time – when we were asked jointly to draft some resolution. And there was the Sunday when, after listening to a fine sermon from Archbishop Michael Ramsey in the Nairobi Cathedral, I was wafted away during the last hymn by our second daughter Janet (then employed as a psychiatrist by the Kenya Government) to slip into the Church of Scotland just in time to preach.

In January 1972 I paid my third visit to India (this time at the personal invitation of the Chief Justice, Mr Justice Hidayatullah), to give lectures, take part in a seminar, and generally advise whether Muslim personal law as applied in India was in need of reform, and how this could best be achieved. In the event I gave three lectures at the Indian Law Institute, took part in a weekend seminar to which Muslims from several parts of India were invited, and lectured at the Ministry of Justice and elsewhere.

I got the impression that there was a growing, if cautious, response from Muslims to my argument that a house which is in good order is much more likely to stand secure than one which is riddled with holes; and that, even if the time might eventually come when the Government of India would insist on a uniform civil code, their own law would be taken much more seriously into account in any such project if it had been suitably reformed. But my attempt to convince them suffered a sharp, and quite unnecessary, setback when Mr Justice Hegde, when taking the chair at one of my lectures, stated boldly that what he wanted was not the reform of Islamic law, but its abolition. This naturally increased the fear of the Muslim minority that they were in danger of losing their 'linguistic, educational and even legal identity'. On my return to England I wrote a paper outlining my suggestions, which was duly published by the Indian Law Institute.

A miscellany

Back at the Institute in London I was persuaded by Lord Longford to act as Vice-Chairman of his Study Group on Pornography. In this it was my task to chair the sub-committee which was to enquire into the moral, psychological, medical and social aspects of the subject – a committee on which a number of interesting people served, including a very popular novelist and an eminent psychiatrist. It fell to my lot to draft the sub-committee's report, under the title 'The effects and control of pornography'. The Group, of which Sir Frederick Catherwood was treasurer, eventually published a composite report, while individual members took part in a television interview with a well-known publisher, and in other incursions into the media.

In October 1972 I went on another trip to North America. The primary purpose was to give the Inaugural Lecture of what was termed 'The Bishop John McLean Lectureship of the Commonwealth and Continental Church Society to the University of Saskatchewan and the University of Emmanuel College'! Pat was able to accompany me on this tour, during which I lectured at three Canadian Law Schools and gave Christian talks in Vancouver, Saskatoon and Toronto. The Inaugural Lecture (together with another talk at Saskatoon) provided the seminal basis for a book I subsequently wrote under the title of *A Lawyer among the Theologians*. This was published in 1973.

Six months later I was at a residential conference at which Michael Ramsey, then Archbishop of Canterbury, was a fellow member. I knew him fairly well; and one day he put his hands on my shoulders and said: 'Norman, I have a confession to make to you.' 'What have you done?' I asked. 'Well, I've just finished writing a review of your latest book,' he replied. 'Have you been very unkind?' I asked him. 'No, but I've been rather naughty – rather light-hearted,' he said. 'What have you done?' I repeated. 'Well, I've said that I think you are rather a good theologian, but a very bad lawyer. Are you very angry with me?' For almost the only time in my life, the right rejoinder came to me at once, instead of half an hour later. 'Not at all,' I said; 'I think I ought to feel rather flattered. After all, you're much better qualified to assess a theologian than a lawyer, aren't you?' He went away chuckling in his inimitable way.

In December I paid another short visit to India to take part in an International Seminar on 'Religion, Morality and Law'. This was held in New Delhi and was jointly sponsored by the Islam and the Modern Age Society and the Indian Institute of Islamic Studies. My paper was entitled 'Morality and Law in Islam: the past and the present'; and I also gave a lecture at the Tagore Institute on 'Islamic Law in the Modern World'. In addition, I took the opportunity to respond to a long-standing invitation to pay a visit to the University of Kabul, for talks with the Faculty of Law and Administration and that of Islamic Law. The visit to India was financed by the Seminar, and that to Kabul by the British Council.

In the summer I started to write a book on *Law Reform in the Muslim World* which would, I hoped, summarize nearly thirty years' work on this subject and incorporate the substance of some fifty articles in various Journals.

In January 1973, the Institute suffered a grievous loss in the death of Sir David Hughes Parry, to whom

249

we owed so great a debt. He had been Director of the Institute from its inception until his retirement in 1959; and then, when Lord Birkett resigned from being Chairman of its Committee of Management in 1960, Sir David took over until his death. He was the ideal chairman. He never in any way tried to do my job, but always gave excellent advice when consulted, and his knowledge of the University of London and its ways was unrivalled. A Welshman of the old school, he addressed me as 'Director' and I addressed him as 'Sir David' to the end, although we were on excellent terms. When he had retired as Director we received a splendid bust by Mr David Wynne, which also graced the London School of Economics. With his fine features and somewhat unruly hair, through which he would periodically pass his hand, he must have been a superb model. We were very grateful when Lord Diplock consented to replace him as Chairman; and he again was an excellent choice.

Meanwhile the work of the Institute went on as before, but our new building got more and more delayed. This was not due to financial stringency, although this was acute, but to a protracted dispute between the architect and the builder over which we had no control. The date when this building was to come into use had continually to be postponed, and we eventually had to ask Her Majesty Queen Elizabeth the Queen Mother to postpone from 1975 till 1976 the date on which she had graciously promised to preside at its official opening. I was myself due to retire on 30 September 1975, since I should have reached the prescribed age of sixty-seven on the previous day. But the Committee of Management were kind enough to ask the Senate of London University if I could be granted another year in order to see the Institute into its new home; and this was duly approved by the Senate provided I became Professor Emeritus on the correct date. But this is to anticipate.

18

Up to retirement

The years 1974 and 1975 were years of both pleasant and tragic surprises. The pleasant ones came in 1974. About the first of these I had in fact been told at the end of the previous year, but it was on 25 January that I was given the honorary degree of Doctor of Divinity by St Andrews University. This was on the occasion of the installation of Lord Ballantrae as their new Chancellor, and Pat and I were invited up to what proved to be a most enjoyable occasion. We stayed with old friends, Professor and Mrs Malcolm Jeeves; were entertained to tea and lunch by Lord Ballantrae, whom I got to know quite well later and greatly admired: and had an impressive service in their Chapel, from the pulpit of which John Knox had once preached, followed by an equally splendid Ceremony in the afternoon and a most enjoyable evening.

Just before dinner a rather amusing incident occurred when those who had been given honorary degrees were to be photographed with the Chancellor and the Principal. The Chancellor was seated in the middle, with the Principal on his left and an empty chair on his right, on which one of the new graduates was to sit while the rest stood behind. All except me were old friends of Lord Ballantrae and were very well known: Lord Franks, Field-Marshal Sir Gerald Templar, M. Maurice Schumann and Mr Osbert Lancaster. When, therefore, they told me that the DD was 'the senior doctorate' and that I must take the vacant chair, I naturally expostulated. But they insisted; and it suddenly dawned on me that this solution would relieve them of a difficult problem of protocol, for how were they to decide the relative seniority of a Field Marshal, the former British Ambassador to Washington, and a former French Foreign Minister? So I gave in. At the dinner I sat opposite to Sir Gerald Templar and asked him whether he knew Lieut.-General Sir Arthur Smith. To this he promptly replied: 'Certainly I do. First-class soldier; first-class Christian.'

Unexpected honours

The other two pleasant surprises were that I was made a Queen's Counsel in April and was informed in December that I was to be knighted in the New Year Birthday Honours. Pat accompanied me to the House of Lords (but not to the subsequent visits to the Law Courts) in April, when I wore a motley of borrowed and hired regalia; and Pat and both our daughters came to Buckingham Palace when I was dubbed. This was the more poignant, in retrospect, in the light of the tragic surprises that were to follow, for in July of that year our two daughters both died, suddenly and totally unexpectedly, within three weeks of each other.

Hazel and Janet

Our elder daughter had four daughters of her own. She was an active Christian, running both 'Ladies' Coffee Mornings' and an occasional evening 'At home' (with an advertised speaker), to which her husband's medical colleagues and their wives, besides many other friends, were invited. But she had to have very painful operations on both of her knees, one of which had to be repeated. As a result she was laid up for some weeks, and was taking strong pain-killers. She was also taking sleeping-pills and was emotionally upset; and one night she took too many. The coroner recorded an 'open' verdict; and Dr Lloyd-Jones told me that her pain-killers, in the quantity she was taking, were enough to 'change her whole personality'. Normally she was a very attractive and happy young woman, with streaks of occasional melancholy. Her sudden death was a great shock, not only to us but also, of course, to her husband and four daughters.

Our second daughter, Janet, was unmarried. She had qualified as a doctor at University College Hospital in London and had then specialized in psychiatry. After four house jobs in England (two of them in psychiatry) she had gone out to pay a visit to Pat's parents in Kenya, as a result of which she had applied for, and got, a government appointment in Nairobi. This she enjoyed very much, but one night she had a terrible experience. Her ground-floor flat was broken into by two Africans who sexually mal-treated her for some hours, stole all her movable possessions and left her very severely shocked. As it happened, this shock was compounded by a case of disappointed love. I was able to see her very soon after, and Pat flew out to spend some days with her;

and then she came home. After several weeks with us we encouraged her to take a new job, since we felt that only so could she get back into the stream of life and of her chosen profession. So she applied for, and secured, a post in Bristol, where Alec and Beryl Motyer were very good to her; and she found a flat on the fourth floor of a building in Clifton.

At first she seemed happy in this job, although her nervousness showed itself in the fact that she got bolts fitted to all the windows, inaccessible although they were. She went away almost every weekend, either coming home to us or visiting a variety of friends. But a strange hang-up (which had, for years, inhibited her from writing *any* letters) now extended itself to an inability to keep proper reports of her patients. This may have been the case in Kenya; but it became very serious in Bristol, where general practitioners naturally demanded reports on patients whom they had sent into hospital. We did all we could to help her, as did Pat's doctor sister and others; but with very little effect. Then, one evening, a policeman called at our home in Hampstead, and I thought that I must have been driving too fast. But he came in, insisted that I should sit down, and told me that Janet had been absent from hospital for two or three days, so her chief had telephoned and then called. Finding that the door was locked and that he could get no answer he alerted the police, who found her body half-clothed, with her keys beside her, just inside the front door – between her bedroom and the bathroom – with a big bruise on her forehead.

At first sight it looked like suicide, but we found that rather difficult to believe, since she had sounded quite cheerful on the telephone shortly before this must have happened. A pathologist confirmed this impression and said that she had died of asphyxia during a faint caused by tripping up and banging her head very hard against the door; and the Home Office in due course concurred and said that various tests had shown no trace of drugs. This was a partial relief, but did little to temper the double blow.

As with Hugh, the death of our two daughters was even harder for Pat to bear than for me. She had borne them all; she had to rest a lot because of her persistent, if intermittent, backache; and she had all too much time to think. I, on the other hand, had all my normal academic work to do, to finish my book on *Law Reform in the Muslim World* (which was published in 1976 by the Athlone Press) and to prepare and deliver the next series of 'London Lectures on Contemporary Christianity' in November and December. As I have already said, Pat found it exceedingly difficult at first to speak about our bereavements, but after a time she told the Lord that she was willing to do this if he so willed; and since then she has been asked to do so repeatedly. Inevitably, bereavement in some form is the lot of almost all of us, sooner or later; and we can only try to follow in the footsteps of the apostle Paul in giving thanks to 'the Father of compassion and the God of all comfort, who comforts us in all our troubles, so that we can comfort those in any trouble with the comfort we ourselves have received from God' (2 Corinthians 1:3–4).

I was singularly ill-prepared by my own studies to give a series of lectures on so difficult and controversial a subject as 'Issues of life and death', much of which was concerned with topics such as genetic engineering, artificial insemination, birth control, abortion, transplant surgery, euthanasia, capital punishment, war, revolution and violence. This was a daunting task, especially for me; but the committee wanted the whole subject to be tackled by one person, rather than by a team of experts. For this my only qualification was that I had taken the chair at discussions on most of these subjects between those who had had practical experience in one or another of them, and that I knew where to look for expert advice. So I asked friends and acquaintances what I ought to read; wrote a tentative draft, got them to read it, correct any mistakes or misunderstandings, and discuss it with me; and then wrote my lectures. In this way I think I was able to avoid any serious mis-statements of fact, and to ensure that my material was reasonably up to date at the time of delivery. Being firmly based, for the most part, on practitioners' views, it largely – I hope – avoided the dogmatism of the ivory tower. The lectures were well attended, largely by doctors and nurses, and they were subsequently published, republished and translated.

Crown appointments

In September 1975 I was re-elected Chairman of the House of Laity of the General Synod for another five years. As it so happened I was deeply involved at that time with the question of Crown appointments, particularly to diocesan bishoprics. As early as February 1973, the Standing Committee had been instructed by the Synod to 'bring forward proposals to secure for the Church a more effective share' in the appointment of bishops (and, specifically, such proposals as would 'enable the Synod to decide whether or not in any new system of appointments the final choice should in its view rest with the Church'). The Standing Committee had discussed this subject at some length and had prepared a Report which set forth several alternative possibilities – for the Committee itself was not by any means of one mind on this subject. So at the July Synod I had been requested by the Standing Committee first to propose, on its behalf, 'that this Report be received' and then, in my own name, to move that the General Synod

'(i) affirms the principle that the decisive voice in the appointment of diocesan bishops should be that of the Church;

(ii) believes that, in arrangements to give effect to this, it would be desirable that a small body, representative of the vacant diocese and of the wider Church, should choose a suitable person for appointment to that diocese and for that name to be submitted to the Sovereign; and

(iii) instructs the Standing Committee to arrange for further consideration of these matters, including the administrative, legal and constitutional implications, and to report the results to the Synod at an early date.'

The debate on the first of these motions was a long one, with the speeches ranging in principle – as the custom is – over the substantive proposals and amendments that were to follow. As often happens, the Report as such was 'received' without opposition. Then, after a break, the Synod returned to the motion standing in my own name. The debate on this was shorter, but more detailed; several amendments were proposed, debated and eventually defeated;

and at the end of a long day the motion was carried by 270 votes against 70.

The next move clearly had to be an approach to the Government. But the Standing Committee decided that this must not be rushed, for three reasons: first, a general election was imminent, and we needed to know with whom we had to deal; secondly, Michael Ramsey was on the eve of retirement, and it seemed clear that we must wait until his successor was in office; and thirdly, we felt that Parliament must be given an interlude in which to recover from the Worship and Doctrine Measure, which had been the occasion of considerable controversy. Thus it was not until the new year that the Standing Committee commissioned Dr Donald Coggan (who had by this time succeeded Lord Ramsey) and me to ask for an appointment with the Prime Minister.

In due course we went to 10 Downing Street and had a fairly long talk with Mr (now Sir) Harold Wilson. This proved almost entirely fruitless, since the Prime Minister came back repeatedly to the subject of bishops in the House of Lords – although I distinctly remember telling him that the Church was not greatly concerned about this point. Presumably he wanted Christian opinion to be adequately represented in the Upper House, but there were other ways in which this could be achieved. What the Church was primarily interested in was the choice of its own chief pastors. Finally, the Prime Minister suggested that they should leave it to Sir Philip (now Lord) Allen (formerly Permanent Under-Secretary of State, Home Office) and me to work away at the problem; and to this the Archbishop agreed.

We had several meetings, each supported by a

small team, and eventually reached a solution which was acceptable both to the Archbishop and to the Prime Minister – and also to the Leaders of both the Conservative and Liberal parties (with whom the Archbishop and I had consultations). The essence of this solution was to give the Church about 80% of what it had requested, but to recognize that the Prime Minister, as the Crown's constitutional adviser, refused to have his role reduced to that of a mere rubber stamp. In the past the Prime Minister's Appointments Secretary and the Archbishops' Appointments Secretary had both made independent enquiries, as a result of which the Archbishop concerned had presented three names, *not* in order of preference, to the Prime Minister, who had made a practice of presenting one of these names to the Crown. But even this was only a matter of convention, for the Prime Minister had never formally undertaken to choose one of these names. Under the new proposals, by contrast, the two Appointments Secretaries were to work together, and be seen to work together, from the first; then a Crown Appointments Committee appointed by the Church was to present two names to the Prime Minister, putting them (if it so wished) in order of priority; and the Prime Minister would then present one of these names to the Crown.

There was, however, one proviso on which Mr Wilson insisted: namely, that in very exceptional circumstances the Prime Minister might feel compelled to come back to the Crown Appointments Commission for one more name. I clearly remember the three examples of such 'very exceptional circumstances' which he gave. I also remember reminding him that when, under these proposals, the Prime

Minister chose the second, rather than the first, of the two names submitted to him, this would be known to all the members of the Commission. If, therefore, this happened too often, the Commission would no doubt feel – and, if necessary, state – that these proposals were not being honoured in spirit. To this he assented.

My next task was to lead another debate in the Synod, in July 1976, recommending this agreement to its members as the best way forward under the circumstances that prevailed. But before this there was another problem: the relative timing of a statement in Parliament by the Prime Minister and of the relevant debate in the Synod. This was quite a difficult question. One suggestion was that the Standing Committee should be given the full facts, in strict confidence, on the first day on which the Synod met, that the Prime Minister should make his statement in Parliament on the following day, and that the Synod should then be asked to debate the matter later in the week. But it was felt that the Synod might in these circumstances feel that it was being rushed into a decision on a very important issue, without adequate time to give it the consideration it deserved. So it was eventually agreed that Mr Callaghan (who by then had succeeded Sir Harold Wilson as Prime Minister) should make a statement in Parliament on 8 June 1976, and that the Synod should debate the matter in July – with all the misconceptions that this would probably entail in the intervening weeks. In the event a number of letters were in fact published in the Press describing the Prime Minister's written answer in Parliament, to a question put down by the Leader of the Opposition, as 'a rebuff to the Church', 'half a loaf', 'an undersized carrot', 'a morsel of cake', 'little more than window dressing' or even 'no advance at all'. But no answer to these letters to the Press could be given, and no misconceptions publicly dispelled, in the weeks before the debate.

Space forbids any attempt to summarize the debate that eventually ensued. There was widespread support for the solution once it had been adequately explained and analysed; but there were, naturally, a number of trenchant criticisms raised and several amendments proposed. What most of these amendments amounted to was a grudging, or distinctly qualified, response to the Prime Minister's statement, introducing phrases such as 'a step in the right direction' or 'as a temporary agreement'. In contrast, I asked for a generous response to what was, beyond doubt, constitutionally speaking a generous statement – arguing that the Church ought to give it a fair trial and do its best to make it work. Should a scheme of union between the Church of England and any other Church or Churches be successful, this would obviously change the whole position. If, moreover, the State were at any time not to honour this agreement, in letter or in spirit, then the Church could raise the matter again, and from a much stronger position than had previously obtained. In the event all the amendments were lost, and the motion was carried by 390 votes to 29.

Developments at the Institute

But I must return to the Institute. The Ford Foundation, which had in 1971 renewed its grant to the Institute until 1975, later agreed to extend this until 1976, so that it would continue for a year after my expected date of retirement. So I must record my special gratitude to the Trustees for extending it for yet another year when my appointment as Director was similarly extended, since I was much concerned that the new Director should have at least a year to make his own plans and approaches before this invaluable assistance came to an end.

Over the years the Library had grown from some 57,000 volumes in 1959 to over 125,000 in 1975, while the number of serial publications currently received had increased from 855 to well over 2,000. The number of registered readers had also increased from some 400 to over 1,500 – coming from 65 different countries. In addition, the Institute had attracted an ever-growing number of distinguished visitors from abroad, to say nothing of the eminent scholars we had been able to invite, year by year, under the grant from the Ford Foundation. Our inter-disciplinary discussion meetings had also continued, and in my last year we had two similar discussions which were virtually limited to lawyers. These were introduced by Professor Archibald Cox, the former Watergate Special Prosecutor, and Judge Roger Traynor, the former Chief Justice of California, respectively. Judge Traynor's subject was particularly fascinating, for he told us how the American Appellate Courts had begun, on occasion, to give a judgment which itself upheld the interpretation of a statute which had previously prevailed, but at the same time served notice that it would not follow this interpretation in the future.

At long last our new building neared completion, and during November and December 1975 we were able to move our books into a purpose-built library extending over three floors, with further storage space in a basement. Then, just before Christmas, the administration moved in to 'Charles Clore House' (so named in honour of our principal benefactor), with its 'Hughes Parry' Council Chamber, its excellent Lecture Theatre, and its several seminar rooms. My own office was immense, with enormous glass windows facing east, south and west – with the result that, in the unusually hot summer that followed, the temperature reminded me forcibly of Egypt, since our plans for double glazing had had to be dropped. We were eventually able to open our doors to the public on 7 January 1976, after several alarms about increased fire precautions.

The highlight of 1976 was, of course, the formal opening of the new building by Queen Elizabeth the Queen Mother, then Chancellor of the University of London, in the presence of a most distinguished company. Her Majesty was greeted on arrival by the Mayor and Mayoress of Camden, the Vice-Chancellor and Principal of the University, and the Chairmen and Directors of the two Institutes. Inside the building the presentation line included the Lord Chancellor, the Lord Chief Justice, other senior judges, the architect and our principal benefactor. Her Majesty first unveiled a commemorative plaque in the main entrance hall and then entered the Hughes Parry Council Chamber for a brief ceremony in the presence of some 110 guests, together with about a hundred more to whom it was transmitted by closed circuit television in the Lecture Theatre immediately below. After this she met members of the staff of both Institutes and the building and planning team (with each of whom she shook hands and talked in her usual charming way).

A Reception had been arranged in the Library, for which Sir Charles Clore had kindly provided champagne. At this, more presentations were made, and Her Majesty became so involved in conversations, both with old friends and those who had never met her before, that the detailed timetable was soon forgotten. Then, just as I bade her goodbye, she presented me with a large coloured photograph of herself with the question, 'Do you think you could find some corner for this?' Needless to say, it now adorns the entrance hall to the building. I chanced to walk to the Underground that evening with a distinctly left-wing QC, who remarked: 'Well, if we had needed any advertisement for the British Royal Family, we have had it today!'

A delightful buffet lunch was arranged at the Institute in September to bid me farewell. Then, a few months later, I was asked to sit for a portrait, which was paid for by subscriptions from many old friends. Not having features in any way comparable with those of Sir David Hughes Parry, the decision was wisely taken to resort to the splash of colour provided by academic robes, and Mr Charles Hardaker did wonders with his very raw material. I had retired from the School of Oriental and African Studies at the end of the previous academic year, and was elected an Honorary Fellow not long after. I also resigned in 1976 from being Chairman of the Hamlyn Trustees, and was genuinely surprised when I was invited to give these lectures myself in 1978.

A full diary

While writing, I have just unearthed a small pocket diary for 1976, and I am astonished to be reminded of many personal engagements in the early months of that year which I had largely forgotten. In January, for example, I attended as much as I could of a missionary conference in Hastings at which the union of the Middle East General Mission, the Lebanon Evangelical Mission and the Arab Literature Mission (already linked with the LEM) was launched as the 'Middle East Christian Outreach'. As chairman of the MEGM London Council, I had been working towards this end for many months, since I firmly believed that the time had come when small missionary societies, working with the same doctrinal basis and broadly similar principles and practice in adjacent countries, should be united. This was partly to save expenses, partly to facilitate the interchange of personnel, and partly to present a united challenge to supporters in the 'sending' countries (loath though some of them always are to sacrifice the close family feeling of a smaller, and longstanding, society). It was a very good conference, part of which I had to miss in order to attend an important meeting in London. Nor was it long before the rightness of the mutual decision to amalgamate was amply justified by the fact that the MEGM had to withdraw its missionaries from Eritrea.

In the same month I preached in Liverpool Cathedral at the annual 'Judges' Service' on the evidence for the Christian faith, epitomized in the resurrection. I remember to this day how I could have kicked myself afterwards for not concluding with the remark that a judge must often go home in the evening, after listening to the arguments of counsel, saying to himself: 'I wish I could be sure what really happened; I wish I could put it to the test.' In the case of the resurrection, however, there is not only exceedingly strong historical evidence but the ever present possibility for any of us to 'put the risen Lord to the test'. Almost immediately, however, I had the opportunity to make this point in the course of one of the extra-curricular lectures sponsored by Imperial College in an extended lunch hour, in which I tried to demonstrate the essential validity of the Christian faith.

The next few months seem to have been equally busy. *Inter alia*, I gave a lecture at New College, Edinburgh; spoke at meetings in Birmingham and Warwick Universities; read a paper at a conference of the Society for the Study of Theology; gave an evening lecture in Bradford Cathedral; and spoke at meetings in Sheffield. Then, in late April and early May, Pat and I made another visit to the USA. This was primarily for me to lecture, speak or preach in Harvard, in Gordon College, Hamilton, in Wheaton College, Illinois and in Washington, D.C. But we also spent two delightful days as the guests of the Marshall-Wythe School of Law of William and Mary College, Virginia, where I was to receive a medallion. But this needs a little explanation.

The name of the Law School is derived from a combination of the names of its most illustrious alumnus, Chief Justice Marshall, with that of his law teacher, Professor Wythe; and for a decade or so it had become its practice to award a medallion every year to an American Lawyer – whether from the Judiciary, the Bar or the Universities. But in the American tri-centennial year they had decided to award two medallions, one to an American and the other to a lawyer from Britain. There could only have been one reason why this was presented to me, since I was in no sense a representative of British lawyers: namely, that the Institute had acted host to a very considerable number of American lawyers.

On our return home I had speaking engagements for several weekends. But I chiefly remember a continuing engagement: a Bible study, once a fortnight in term time, for academic, administrative and library staff in the vicinity of the Senate House of London University, led jointly for several years by Professor Donald Wiseman and me. From time to time, moreover, we invited a wider number of friends to a buffet lunch to hear a visiting speaker, and that summer our speaker was Bishop Stephen Neill.

A look back

In retrospect, I look back on some thirty years in the University of London – and, indeed, on my life as a whole – somewhat in terms of a patchwork quilt. I enjoyed excellent health, thank God, only temporarily marred by a bout of painful disc trouble and a 'coronary warning' (some of the symptoms of which recurred in the months before I retired, when the doctors decided that I must have had mild angina for several years). The first half of this time was centred on the School of Oriental and African Studies, where my pupils were almost all from overseas and predominantly Muslims. Later on, when we lived in Hampstead, we were often able to entertain a number of them to tea on Sundays; and some of them would then come with us to the evening service in All Souls, Langham Place.

When I moved (at first, half-time) to the Institute, the debt I owe to its staff is readily apparent from the numerous occasions when I was able to accept invitations from overseas. They were in fact eminently capable of running the Institute without me. And my own work, both administrative and literary (including several books and scores of articles) would have been impossible without the expert help of Shelagh Brown.

In my personal life I look back on times of great anxiety (centred on Pat's successive operations and Hugh's protracted illness) and the sadness of three bereavements. I realize now how much I failed, in one way or another, as a father, although I have treasured memories of a growing intimacy with Hugh. I gave innumerable lectures, talks, addresses and sermons, both at home and abroad, to University and College Christian Unions, at conferences and informal meetings, and in churches, chapels and (very occasionally) cathedrals. From time to time I was greatly encouraged by hearing of, and from, people who had been influenced, converted or helped; but I have no doubt these opportunities would have produced much more fruit if I had spent more time in believing prayer and had consistently walked more closely with my Lord.

In my earlier years as an academic I got several invitations to give a series of Bible Readings at conferences and elsewhere; and this sort of speaking has always, I think, been my first love. I also found 'Freshers' Squashes', as they were then called, very fruitful opportunities. But in recent years I have usually been asked to speak on 'apologetics', or to give talks which might, perhaps, best be classified as 'pre-evangelism'. I have once or twice been asked whether I would lead a University mission, but have never felt free even to consider this – partly because from 1947 to 1976 I was being paid to do something else. But it was also because, although I love to preach the gospel, I have certainly not received the gift of evangelism. Teaching or developing a reasoned argument – often with an evangelistic purpose – is much more my line. Nor have I ever felt worthy to speak about such subjects as prayer or worship, except in a very elementary way.

I wish I could look back on a life of steady progress in holiness, but I cannot. My life has been one of ups and downs, with times of spiritual renewal interspersed with times when I have been over-busy, spiritually impoverished or defeated by some elementary temptation. But God is faithful, and he has never let me go. Arid periods have always, by his grace, been followed by times of refreshment, and I can testify that no other joy can compare with that of Christian service. Far from finding it difficult to keep on switching from law to theology, moreover, it has been my experience that a routine commitment to the primarily intellectual challenge of an academic life has added zest to, and provided relief from, the much greater emotional involvement of speaking for Christ.

19

After retirement

Australia ∗ *The Hamlyn and Prideaux Lectures* ∗
Prince Charles ∗ *Many invitations* ∗ *A seizure*

The first few years after my retirement were almost as busy as before, except that I did not, of course, have my routine work at the Institute. We had decided to sell our fairly spacious house in Hampstead, now that our children were no longer with us, and to move to Cambridge, where we both had several friends and I knew some of the senior members of the Faculties of Law and Divinity. We had also opted for a flat rather than a house, chiefly because I did not want to have to do any more gardening!

On arrival in Cambridge I was almost immediately asked to help out by giving six lectures on Islamic law for an absent member of the Cambridge Law Faculty, of which I was made an honorary member. To my great pleasure I was also elected a member of the Trinity High Table. I have no record of interesting engagements in the next few months, but I remember spending a lot of time preparing for two series of lectures I had promised to give early in 1978.

Australia

There was, however, one outstanding event during 1977: my first visit to Australia. Pat and I had been invited to Australia and New Zealand more than once, but had previously felt unable to accept. So we had been greatly looking forward to visiting both countries on a tour of some eight weeks in the spring of 1977 (their autumn, of course). Some months before, however, we had come to the regretful conclusion that the journey would be too much for Pat, whose back was still giving her a lot of trouble. So I had written to say that the planned eight-week visit would be impossible: they must either get another speaker for all our engagements or I would go along for three weeks only, and pack into them as much as I could. This would cover my most important commitments in Australia: the annual 'Universities' Service' and a Memorial Lecture in Sydney Cathedral, four talks at a residential Clergy School, and other items in the diocese of Sydney. But it would preclude visits to New Zealand (chiefly to speak at a Summer School) and to other States in Australia, except for Canberra.

When I reached Sydney Archbishop Marcus Loane and Bishop Jack Dain were at the airport to meet me, and I spent the greater part of the next three weeks based on Marcus home, where he and his wife Patricia were wonderful hosts. The first two days were free, so I got the chance to rest a bit, go for a delightful walk with Marcus, which gave me a panoramic view of Sydney's wonderful harbour, and do a lot of preparation. Then, on Sunday, came the Universities' Service, which was attended by the Vice-Chancellors and some of the teaching staff of Sydney's three Universities.

The Dean of the Cathedral, who was an expert in

public relations, had made an appointment for me to meet representatives of the press and broadcasting company next day. The invitations which arose from this meeting, together with prior engagements, gave me a programme of some thirty-odd 'dates' during the next two and a half weeks. I have a number of happy memories. One is of an afternoon at Moore Theological College (which is associated with Sydney University), where I was entertained by the Principal, Canon Broughton Knox, and his wife, and spoke twice to his students. Another is of two visits to Menzies College, Macquarrie University, where the Master, Dr Alan Cole (an old friend) had invited me to give the first 'Menzies Memorial Lecture' one evening and to meet members of his staff over lunch for an informal talk. A further memory is of New College, in the University of New South Wales, where the Master, Canon Stuart Babbage, entertained me.

I preached in both the Pro-Cathedrals of the diocese, and in a church closely adjacent to the University of Sydney in which an old friend, Dr Howard Guinness, had ministered to students and others for many years. A literally flying visit to the Christian Union in Newcastle University was sandwiched between three or four broadcast interviews – one of them over the telephone to Melbourne, which I was very sorry not to be able to visit in person. The Clergy Conference was held in King's School, Sydney, where I was entertained by the Headmaster, and the four talks I gave there represented a tentative first draft of lectures on the incarnation I planned to give as the Bishop John Prideaux Memorial Lectures in Exeter early in the following year.

Immediately after the Clergy School I was due to fly to Canberra for a night – to make various contacts and to speak at two meetings. But the Australian air controllers were by then on strike, so flying was impossible. Very kindly, however, Bishop Don Robinson (now Archbishop of Sydney) drove me there and back in his car. This was a distinct bonus, since one gets so much more vivid an impression of the terrain by car than from the air, and we had plenty of time to talk. In Canberra I was delighted to be able to pay a call on Mr Sam Richardson (an old friend from the two visits to Nigeria in which he was Secretary to the 'Panel of Jurists'), now Principal of the large Canberra Polytechnic. Canberra reminded me strongly of both Washington and New Delhi. This is scarcely strange, since they are the only three capital cities I have ever visited which were designed as such. The view of Canberra from a vantage-point to which I was taken was most impressive.

Happily for me, the strike of the Australian air controllers was over just in time for my scheduled return home. Correspondence and travel between Australia and Britain had been impossible for several days, and there were many people waiting to fly to Europe. As a consequence, my plane from Sydney to London made stops at Melbourne, Singapore, Bahrein, Frankfurt and Amsterdam, which was rather tedious. Soon after I got home I resigned the chairmanship of the London Council of Middle East Christian Outreach, some thirty years after I had become chairman of its predecessors (the EGM and, subsequently, the MEGM). Attending monthly Council meetings in London in the evenings and getting back to Cambridge late at night was becoming increasingly difficult. I made one other overseas visit that year, primarily to give the Inaugural Lecture of a new series on Islamic studies at Ann Arbor, Michigan. Pat was able to accompany me, and the University gave us a wonderful welcome.

The Hamlyn and Prideaux Lectures

I cannot remember my activities during the remainder of 1977, although they must have included the three sessions of the Synod, its several committees and a number of speaking engagements. My major preoccupation was the preparation of the Hamlyn Lectures I was to give early the next year, since these lectures always have to be printed in advance, and to be actually on sale at the end of the last lecture. I had had considerable difficulty in finding a suitable subject, since I could scarcely lecture on Islamic Law in a series founded to bring home to the English people how fortunate they are to live under the Common Law – although, on second thoughts, a series of discourses on Islamic law might have had precisely this effect, had anyone been prepared to listen to them or to read them! Eventually I decided to speak on 'Liberty, Law and Justice', for three reasons. First, this was a subject in which I was genuinely interested. Secondly, it would allow me to include references to other systems of law. Thirdly, it brought the series of lectures right round again to the first of them all, given nearly thirty years before by Mr Justice Denning (now Lord Denning, and formerly Master of the Rolls) on 'Liberty under the Law'.

A lot more work also had to be done on the Bishop John Prideaux Memorial Lectures. They are given once every two years and are always sited in Exeter University, with a special invitation to the clergy of Devon. I had decided to take as my subject 'The Mystery of the Incarnation', since at that time – as also, I think, today – the person of Jesus is at the centre of theological debate. It was Professor John Hick's Presidential Address at a conference of the Society for Theological Studies that first prompted me to choose this subject. His address was subsequently printed as his personal contribution to *The Myth of God Incarnate* (which he edited). This book had provoked an immediate reply, by Michael Green and others, entitled *The Truth of God Incarnate*, while a major book by Professor C. F. D. Moule, *The Origin of Christology*, had been published at almost the same time as *The Myth* itself. This, in turn, was followed by *Theology and the Gospel of Christ*, much of which is concerned with Christology, by Professor Eric Mascall, and *God as Spirit* by Professor Geoffrey Lampe. There were some other fairly recent books on this subject which I had not previously read. So my Sydney lectures had to be substantially revised, expanded and re-written. In their final form they were published by Hodders that same year as *The Mystery of the Incarnation*.

The Hamlyn Lectures are more often than not given in London, but they periodically make the circuit of cities where there are major concentrations of lawyers – academic, practising, or both. They had been given in London three times in the previous four years, and it had been decided that those for 1978 should be given in Bristol, by courtesy of the Law Faculty of Bristol University. So I rashly decided that, since Exeter and Bristol are comparatively close together, and a date around the beginning of March was suitable for both series of lectures, I would deliver them virtually concurrently: Monday and Tuesday at Exeter for the Prideaux Lectures, and Thursday and Friday at Bristol for the Hamlyn Lectures; then Monday and Tuesday at Exeter again, followed this time by lectures

276

in Bristol on the Friday evening and Saturday morning. When I told some friends about this arrangement they comforted me by remarking that, should I get in a muddle and give lectures on law in Exeter and on theology in Bristol, no-one would recognize the mistake or be any the wiser!

In point of fact it was a very happy time. The University of Exeter stands in magnificent grounds, and proved to be most hospitable. Tea and cakes were provided each day, for the visiting clergy and others, just before the lectures, and a dinner party was given by Professor Porter and Dr Margaret Hewitt (two friends from the Synod) on the first Monday and by the Vice-Chancellor on the second. In Bristol, too, they were very kind, and Professor Pettit, the Dean of the Faculty of Law, gave a dinner party. I was also interviewed on the radio in Exeter, and had several speaking and preaching engagements in Bristol.

It is difficult to pick out occasions of particular significance from a positive welter of (to me) interesting engagements about that time. I paid my first visit to Louvain University to give a law lecture (*not* in French, or Flemish!); preached in two Oxford and four Cambridge College Chapels; gave three talks on the incarnation to a joint meeting of the Norwich Diocesan Evangelical Fellowship and the Fellowship of Catholic Priests; spoke at a conference of the Universities and Colleges Christian Fellowship on such varied subjects as 'The Christian Mind', 'Cross-Cultural Communication' and 'Legislator and Lawyer'; and gave lectures on Islam at a conference in All Nations Christian College. Other speaking engagements included a CICCU Bible Reading, a meeting for doctors and medical students at Nottingham, the Annual General Meeting of 'The Responsible Society' in London, a meeting in Essex University and a busy weekend at Malvern College for Girls. I find it impossible to know which of this very heterogeneous list made any lasting impact; and I always come back to the thought that, while one plants, and another waters, it is only God who makes anything grow (and it is often years later that one hears about it).

In the autumn Pat and I paid another visit to Nova Scotia, Harvard, New York and Washington, D.C. In Nova Scotia it was a new experience to participate with Mr Harley Smyth, a well-known neuro-surgeon from Toronto, in a 'mini-mission' under the aegis of the Rector of St Paul's, Halifax – the first Anglican Church founded in Canada by the early settlers. His plan was to involve not only his church members, the civic authorities and the business community, but also the Hospital and the Law Faculty of Dalhousie University. The central theme, for both lawyers and the medical profession, was 'The Sanctity of Human Life'. For me this meant preaching in St Paul's, giving two lectures in the Law School, speaking at a Businessmen's Lunch, and sharing with Harley Smyth in other meetings. We paid a visit to the Mayor, were entertained to lunch by the Lieutenant-Governor, and had interviews on radio and television. Pat and I also spent a night in St John, New Brunswick, where I preached in Stone Church and was interviewed on television.

In Harvard I had been asked to lecture on 'Morality and Law in Islam' and 'The Shari'a and Modern Life', and to speak more informally on 'Islamic Criminal Law' and 'Muslim Personal Law' at lunch and dinner meetings. Islamic law was at that time just beginning to hit the headlines. In New York I preached in Grace Church again, and in Washington we were both asked to speak briefly at a dinner and at a 'Prayer Breakfast' hosted by the International Christian Fellowship.

Later that year Pat had to have her third disc operation, this time in Addenbrooke's Hospital. While she was recovering there I had to go to Paris for a long-promised weekend as the guest of the Rural Dean and his wife, Eric and Edith McLellan. The Diocese of Europe and Gibraltar was about to send representatives to the General Synod in England, and I had been asked to speak about the nature and work of the Synod, preach, give a devotional talk at the Deanery Synod and speak at an evangelistic luncheon.

Prince Charles

On the very day when I brought Pat home from hospital Prince Charles came to Cambridge to give the Hugh Anderson Memorial Lecture at the Union. In most of the years since Hugh died this has been given by a leading politician from the Labour Party, since Hugh's leanings were distinctly left wing. But on this occasion the President of the Union had written to Prince Charles to ask if he would give it, and he was good enough to accept. Prince Charles had known Hugh at Trinity, where they were contemporaries, and had spoken at the Union when Hugh was President.

There is always a dinner before this Lecture to which Pat and I are invited, and this year it was a star occasion in Trinity Hall in honour of the Prince. It was sad that Pat was in too much pain to come, but she wanted me to represent the family. The Prince gave an excellent lecture and then answered with great skill a series of very predictable – and largely irrelevant –

questions. I still remember his answer to a distinctly loaded question as to whether he ever regretted having been born into the family in which he had in fact been born. To this, after a somewhat nervous laugh, he replied: 'No, not really. Because, you see, had I been born into any other family, I should not have had the opportunity to meet nearly so many interesting people by my time of life.'

Many invitations

In the earlier part of 1979 life went on much as usual. I was still Chairman of the House of Laity of the General Synod, and usually able to attend the dinners of a very interesting dining club named 'Nobody's Friends', to which I had been elected in 1974. These took place three times a year, to coincide with meetings of the Synod. The dinners were started over a hundred years ago by a wealthy Anglican businessman who used to send out invitations to his friends, saying that 'Mr Nobody invites you to dine with him'; and when he died his friends decided to continue these useful and pleasant opportunities for bishops, clergy and laymen to meet in such an informal way. Hence the name. I also attended periodical luncheons at which a few members of the Synod met interested Parliamentarians. Other engagements included preaching in Norwich Cathedral on their Education Sunday, giving the closing talk at a service in St Martin's-in-the-Fields to launch the publication by Hodders of the New International Version of the Bible, recording seven television 'Epilogues' for Dover TV, and addressing members of the staff of Southampton University on 'The Jesus of History: a Lawyer's View' as a preliminary meeting shortly before a University Mission.

Two events in that year stand out in my memory. The first was a series of lectures in memory of Professor Henry Drummond, who was a great influence in University circles at the time of the Moody missions in this country. These were given in the University of Stirling, where the Principal and his wife made us very welcome. I had been told that 'perhaps three topics in the area of Law and Comparative Religion might be appropriate'. So I chose 'The Law of God and the Love of God' as my subject, with the sub-title 'An Essay in Comparative Religion'. These lectures were subsequently expanded into a book published in 1980 by Collins under the title *God's Law and God's Love*.

The second outstanding engagement in 1979 was a twelve-day visit to Dallas, Texas, to give a series of Bible Readings at one of the Biennial Conferences of the Wycliffe Bible Translators and the Summer Institutes of Linguistics – to which they invite their leaders from all over the world for consultation and spiritual refreshment. In the daily Bible studies I tried to expound the letter to the Hebrews (largely with the help of a commentary by an old friend, Alan Stibbs); and I was also asked to speak at a Sunday service and to give some talks on Islam. Together with the need for much preparation, this programme proved to be a whole-time assignment, with only two outings. The first was to a downtown dinner, at which Professor Kenneth Pike sang a delightfully witty, yet very relevant, song of his own composition about the missionary call (followed by a special speaker). The other was my only experience of a Texan Rodeo, at which I was startled when the compère suddenly burst out into an extempore prayer. I had forgotten I was in the 'Bible Belt'.

Back at home, I gave one lecture in that year's series

of London Lectures on Contemporary Christianity. In this series, on 'Crime and the Responsible Society', several speakers participated, and the subject allotted to me was 'Criminal Sanctions'. I had decided to retire from the chairmanship of the House of Laity in the Synod's July group of sessions, so that its members could elect their new chairman when everyone knew all the possible candidates. I would be 72 when the new Synod met in 1980, and felt that 'Enough is enough'. The Synod gave me a splendid 'Farewell' with the Archbishop of Canterbury, the Chairman of the House of Clergy and the Vice-Chairman of the House of Laity making the sort of speeches normally reserved for an obituary; and I was so carried away that I made much too long and rambling a reply. Then, when the Synod rose, the House of Laity had arranged a delightful party for Pat and me, and they gave us a Commentary, a set of sherry glasses and a book of signatures. I had also been invited to give the Bible Study at this group of sessions.

A seizure

I was due in September to give three talks for the Archbishop of Wales at a conference for the clergy of his own diocese of Bangor. He had written to me saying that it was sometimes alleged that the Church of Wales was 'priest-ridden'; and that, while he was sure this was a gross overstatement, he had an uneasy feeling that there might be *some* substance in it! So would I come to give this the lie? But I had gone to the Institute some four days before this engagement, left it in plenty of time for my intended train, and then suddenly realized (on the escalator at King's Cross) that a previous train was just about to leave. So I rushed for it...and woke up in University College Hospital, having had a 'seizure'.

A young Registrar did a preliminary check-up, after which I telephoned to Pat (who had been told by a policewoman that I had been taken from King's Cross unconscious in an ambulance). The doctors suspected either coronary or neurological trouble, so I was put through several tests and told I ought to stay in hospital overnight. At first I refused, saying that I would go home by taxi and train; but when I added that I had a car parked at Cambridge station, the Registrar blew up and said I must not in any circumstances drive a car that night. So I succumbed, had more tests, and bedded down in the Casualty Ward.

Next day the big white chief came to see me, and made soothing noises when I said I wanted to go home. When, therefore, the Registrar came into the ward, I hopped out of bed and insisted on this, promising to have any further tests in Addenbrooke's Hospital in Cambridge. 'Well, we can't keep you here against your will,' he eventually conceded. 'I know that,' I replied; 'I happen to be a barrister' – and after that there was no more opposition. Our Vicar, Mark Ruston, happened to be free that day and very kindly drove down to fetch me home. The further tests I had to have at Addenbrooke's were again both cardiac and neurological, looking for a possible brain tumour. But after the last X-ray had been developed the consultant duly telephoned to say that he was happy to inform me that I still had a little brain left, and might go on the ten days' holiday that we had planned. Meanwhile, my meetings in Bangor had been cancelled for me by another friend, whose kindly attempts to telephone the Archbishop of Wales were nearly frustrated by the fact that he was listed only as the Bishop of Bangor.

After this episode quite a number of engagements had to be cancelled by doctor's orders. But I was able to accept an interesting invitation to visit Ampleforth, where I was let loose to speak to their 'Oxbridge Form' on the incarnation, and to answer questions. Other commitments followed: evangelistic talks at the Manchester University Business School and at a Businessmen's Dinner in Liverpool, a busy weekend in the Wirral, and a sermon in Bristol Cathedral at their annual 'Legal Service'.

During the November meetings of the Synod I was invited to a farewell dinner given by the Prime Minister in honour of Donald Coggan, who was about to retire from Canterbury. Presumably at his suggestion, this was a very ecumenical occasion. Although now a back-bench member of the Synod, I had got extremely tired, two days before, lugging some heavy luggage around London when I was twice unable to find a taxi. This was probably the reason why, on my return rather late from this dinner to the friends with whom I was staying, I had some fairly severe pain across my chest and down my left arm. So next day I left the Synod early and went home, where our doctor came round and called a cardiologist. An ECG again showed that no real damage had been done; but I was forced to cancel all engagements for six weeks and to rest quietly at home. This gave me the opportunity to do some writing, but I felt weak and spiritually depressed.

When speaking at Malvern in the autumn I had stayed overnight with a travel agent. So, early in 1980, I asked him if he could find us a two-week package tour to some hotel where there was a heated swimming-pool, which would be good both for Pat's back and for my rehabilitation – since walking still provoked that tingling down my arm. The result was a booking at Reid's Hotel, Madeira, in February 1980. This meant missing the February sessions of the Synod, but did us both a lot of good. Reid's is an ideal (and, we discovered, a very expensive) hotel, with two heated sea-water swimming-pools; and I must have taken a leisurely swim nearly ten times a day, interspersed with lounging and reading in the sun – preparing, *inter alia*, some Bible Readings I was to give at a conference of the Christian Alliance (of which Pat was then Chairman) soon after we got home. But when the time to leave came, the Portuguese air controllers were on strike, so we were given an extra three or four days at Reid's, on full pension (unlike the previous fortnight), by courtesy of Thomas Cook. This was delightful at the time but far from convenient, since I got home later than we had planned only to find that the proofs of *God's Law and God's Love* had been printed earlier than expected and were overdue for correction.

Unhappily, this coincided with a full programme, including four days at the Christian Alliance Conference, a sermon in Cambridge, a talk and a broadcast in Sheffield, and some meetings in the Isle of Man. Meanwhile, when awaiting the proofs, I had been getting on with a book I had been asked to write – a straightforward, non-academic book about the Bible. Entitled *God's Word for God's World* (Hodder), this was chiefly made up of illustrations (some from my personal experience, but mostly from my reading) of the power of the Bible in individual lives, in the community at large, and in missionary situations. All this, at the publisher's request, was very easy reading. Then, in the second part of the book, I tried to explain this power – and here I attempted to pack much too much into three short chapters. It was not a success.

In May I paid a week's visit to Wheaton College, Illinois to give their 'Commencement Address'. Wheaton is an Evangelical Liberal Arts College with high academic standards. As is customary in America, a Commencement Address coincides with graduation, and looks forward to the life on which the new graduates are about to embark. They also conferrred on me an honorary D.Litt. Soon after this our 'Cambridge Missionary Fellowship' (made up of some fifty CICCU members who had graduated in 1930 and 1931) held its Golden Jubilee in Ridley Hall. This was a wonderful opportunity to meet old friends, many of whom one had not seen for many years – although we had kept in some sort of touch by writing a letter twice a year (if we remembered!) to our noble secretary, who had them duplicated and circulated. With wives and widows it was quite a party, including Donald and Jean Coggan, Oliver Allison (for long Bishop of the Sudan) and a number of other missionaries, clergy, doctors and teachers. Just before the July sessions of the General Synod Lady Collins gave a party in London to launch *God's Law and God's Love*, at which I met a number of interesting people. Then, in September, I was able to give the talks at the clergy conference in Bangor which I had had to cancel at the last moment the year before.

20

Today

*Another book * Don Cupitt * Recent
activities * Our Golden Wedding*

By 1981 I had begun to cut down somewhat on travelling, but I still had a fairly full programme. One
commitment was to give a considerably increased
number of lectures to missionaries, missionary recruits
and others who were interested in Christian witness to
Muslims. Some of these were at a course on non-
Christian religions run by the Worldwide Evangelization Crusade in Bulstrode, some at a special course on
Islam held at All Nations Christian College in Ware,
and others at Patrick Sookhdeo's 'In Contact Minis-
tries' in East London. All these visits now seem to have
become yearly events. I remember, too, a 'once off'
commitment which involved recording seven video
tapes on Islam for Operation Mobilisation. For these I
requested a live audience as a precaution against the
danger of nodding off – as I did once, for a few seconds,
while giving an afternoon lecture at the Inns of Court
Law School! I was also able to accept numerous
invitations to preach, lecture or speak informally –
including, that year, four weekends in Oxford.

One interesting task which came my way was to
collaborate with Dr Graham Leonard (in his capacity

as Chairman of the Board for Social Responsibility) and with Keith Ward (then Dean of Trinity Hall, Cambridge and a philosopher by training) in giving advice to the Archbishop of Canterbury about what reply he should make to a 'Working Paper' issued by the Law Commission. This paper invited comments on their discussion about whether the Common Law crimes of blasphemy and blasphemous libel should be abolished or replaced. Hitherto, these offences had been virtually confined to matters concerning the Christian faith in general – and even, in the more distant past, the Church of England in particular. So were they not, perhaps, incongruous with the principle of freedom of speech as understood today, and inequitable in what was now a polyglot society? Our advice was to the effect that freedom of speech could be kept within the bounds of decent controversy, and need not degenerate into vilification or scurrilous abuse. Might not the present law be replaced, therefore, by an enactment making it an offence to publish matter 'knowing that it was likely to insult or outrage' the feelings of the adherents of any religious community? The Archbishop approved our memorandum and forwarded it, under a covering letter, to the Law Commission.

Unhappily, Pat was beginning to suffer severe pain from an arthritic joint in her right foot, and some trouble in her right cheek had been diagnosed as quite a deep skin cancer. Providentially, we were able to arrange for the two necessary operations to be performed under the same anaesthetic, one surgeon working at one end of her body and another at the other! She is half Irish, and found the nuns in the Hope Nursing Home witty, congenial and attentive.

Since my retirement we had made it a practice to

take an overseas holiday in winter rather than summer. So in January 1982 we went on a two-week package tour to Agadir, Morocco (having come to the reluctant conclusion that it would be self-indulgent to go to Reid's Hotel for a third time). Just before the end we received a telegram informing us that my sister Dolly, who had been in a Nursing Home for some weeks, had died (at the age of eighty-one). We got home the day before her funeral.

Another book

Months before, I had been invited to give three lectures at Cardiff University College during the Lent term, 1982, on Ethics – the precise subject being left to my discretion. Then, soon after this invitation, Michael Green had asked me to write a volume on 'The Example of Jesus' for a series of books (to be called 'The Jesus Library') of which he was to be General Editor; but I felt wholly unworthy to tackle such a subject. So it was agreed that I should write a book for this series on 'The Teaching of Jesus' and should give the Cardiff lectures on 'The Ethical Teaching of Jesus' – which would provide the substance of three chapters in the book. As a consequnce I had been studying this subject, off and on, for some time, and had found it a daunting challenge. By instinct I tend to turn much more frequently to the New Testament letters, so it was very good for me to have to study the Gospels in a way I had never done before. I spent most mornings reading in Tyndale House Library, which could provide almost all the books which I needed to consult, and I often went there again after tea.

We went to University College, Cardiff, during the last week in February, and greatly appreciated the welcome and hospitality we received. In the three lectures on 'The Ethics of Jesus' I attempted to cover his teaching in regard to 'The Law and the Prophets', Personal Ethics and Social Ethics. I was also asked to address their Theological Circle on 'The Christological Debate', and had commitments in Swansea, Aberavon and Aberystwyth.

Don Cupitt

Back in Cambridge, I was waylaid next Sunday by the President of the 'Rousseau Society' – of which I had never previously heard. It was a recently formed undergraduate society which invited two dons to speak, for ten minutes each, on their different views about some chosen subject, to question each other about it, and then to answer questions 'from the floor'. They had recently had two such meetings on subjects in the field of economics, and had now planned one, for the very next day, in which Don Cupitt and Keith Ward, the Deans of Emmanuel College and Trinity Hall respectively, would speak about 'God without Myth'. Unhappily, Keith Ward had got laryngitis, so would I take his place?

This seemed an almost impossible task at such short notice, for I had not read Don Cupitt's last two books, and I still had to do some preparation for a difficult discussion in London next day. But the President was very insistent, and it seemed cowardly to refuse. So he brought me a copy of Cupitt's latest book and I flipped through a few pages that evening, and meant to read more on my way back from London. When I got into the train at Liverpool Street, however, I was dismayed to find that I had forgotten to put the book in my brief-case. But on this occasion I am inclined to think that my forgetfulness was providential, since I spent the time in prayer and thought instead of reading, and decided to give a personal confession of faith rather than attempt any detailed reply to whatever Cupitt might say. I got back to Cambridge just in time to dine with the committee of the Society and with Cupitt, whom I had met only twice before.

Don Cupitt is a very good communicator, but I found what he said that evening singularly unconvincing. It should, I think, have been entitled 'Symbol without Substance' rather than 'God without Myth'. He has described himself as 'a Christian Buddhist', which presumably means that he is an atheist who regards the teaching of Jesus as ethically superior to any other, and 'God' as no more than a postulate which sums up a spiritual man's aspirations. When I had given my *confessio fidei* his first remark was that, had he been speaking as a theologian, he would have said something not wildly different from me; but as a scientist or philosopher in today's world this was impossible. It was clear, however, that many of those present (who were far more numerous, apparently, than at previous meetings) found his position extremely difficult to understand. In the subsequent discussion he deprecated intercessory prayer on the ground that this amounts to trying to 'manipulate God'. It was only contemplative prayer for which he had any use. I replied that I, too, deprecated any idea of 'manipulating God' and agreed about the value of contemplative prayer; but I added that I did believe that there was Someone who listened.

A few weeks later Keith Ward asked me to write a preface to a manuscript he had written as a reply to Cupitt. Ward had been converted from atheism to what he describes as 'fairly orthodox Christian faith' when already teaching philosophy at a British university. His book (which answers Cupitt on his own professional grounds) was published by SPCK under the title *Holding Fast to God: a reply to Don Cupitt*. Its blurb states that Ward regards Cupitt's book *Taking Leave of God* as 'completely wrong. Almost every position he holds is, in my view, mistaken', and describes Ward's reply as 'argued with rigour by a philosopher, unmistakably contemporary and taking full account of scientific and critical knowledge'. Unhappily for us, Ward has now left Cambridge to become F. D. Maurice Professor of Moral and Social Theology at King's College, London.

Recent activities

In February 1983 we had planned to go on a visit to California instead of our usual package tour. We were to be the guests of our friends, Professor and Mrs Robert Bartel, for three weeks, during two of which I was to give some lectures in Santa Barbara and in Berkeley, followed by a week's holiday. But we regretfully decided that Pat was not fit for the long journey from Cambridge to Santa Barbara, and I telephoned Bob Bartel accordingly. He said that my engagements in Santa Barbara, which had not been advertised, could be cancelled, since I felt very loath to leave Pat for three weeks. But the Dean of New College, Berkeley, telephoned to ask me if I could fly direct to San Francisco, for seven days, to fulfil commitments in Berkeley which had been widely advertised.

A conference for lawyers and law students had been jointly sponsored by the (American) Christian Legal Fellowship and New College, and a series of other engagements had been arranged: a talk on 'Do all religions lead to God?', two sermons in a Covenant Church and one in New College Chapel, a talk to the Christian Union of Berkeley University, interviews with the 'Spiritual Counterfeit Project' and with Radix Magazine, and a talk to a group deeply concerned with overseas students. I stayed for the first four days with the David Adeneys, which was a renewal of a very old friendship. David had been on the CICCU Executive Committee with me more than fifty years before; he had done a splendid job for the Overseas Missionary Fellowship and the International Fellowship of Evangelical Students, and was now combining the leadership of 'Prayer for China' with being the chaplain of New College and President of the IFES.

Pending the publication of *The Teaching of Jesus* by Hodders in September 1983, I had been working on an enlarged and updated second edition of a book I wrote some fourteen years ago for the IVP under the title *Christianity and Comparative Religion*. In its new form it is now entitled *Christianity and World Religions: the Challenge of Pluralism*. In the intervening years many books had been published on inter-faith dialogue; and the former emphasis on syncretism (the attempt to reconcile conflicting creeds and construct a unified religion) had been largely superseded by pluralism (the insistence that there are many different ways to God). As a result, parts of this book were not only revised and rewritten but wholly new, with numerous references to, and quotations from, the work of Hans Küng, John Hick and Lesslie Newbigin, for example. When I had finished this I turned to a new, and substantially revised, edition of another book of much the same vintage. Formerly published as *Christianity: the Witness of History*, it has recently been republished by the IVP as *Jesus Christ: the Witness of History*. Books which discuss 'the Christ Event' – the person, teaching, death and resurrection of Jesus, together with their implications – seem to follow each other in an unending stream, and the new title is a much more accurate reflection of the substance of the book – besides indicating that it is more than a reprint.

Our Golden Wedding

Anyone who has read this book as far as this will conclude that I now spend much more time writing (together with the reading that this necessarily entails) than in travelling around to speak at a plethora of meetings; and this is, indeed, the case. In May 1983 Pat and I celebrated our Golden Wedding, when our son-in-law gave a splendid dinner for a number of close relatives and a few local friends (including two former Presidents of the CICCU). This was in the ideal setting of the Old Kitchen at Trinity, of which he, too, was a member. It was wonderful to look back on fifty years of God's faithfulness, although we also remembered with deep regret how often we had failed him. In terms of our wedding text God had indeed been our guide for over fifty years, and he would continue to be so 'even unto death'. Next day the twenty-first birthday of our youngest granddaughter, Susan, was also celebrated in Cambridge; in July 1984 our second granddaughter, Jenny, was married; and in January 1985 her elder sister (by some twenty minutes!) produced our first great-granddaughter.

I have cut down especially on single meetings which involve a lot of travel. This is partly, no doubt, because now that I am old (and have twice had to cancel engagements over some weeks) I do not get so many invitations. But it is also because I get much more tired than I did, still have to watch my angina (although this is, thank God, much less troublesome than it was two or three years ago) and do not want to leave Pat too much alone. I still, however, preach quite often in churches or college chapels, speak to a variety of Christian Unions, and occasionally have the chance to give a series of Bible studies. Lectures on Islam continue at the three conferences to which I have already referred, and this year visits to London Bible College were added, to help out in an emergency. The CPAS has asked me to remain as their President until they reach their 150th anniversary in 1986, and the BCMS and the Fellowship of Faith for Muslims have not yet seen fit to replace me, although I have suggested this several times. But none of these offices involves any real work.

Pat and I live in a somewhat geriatric and very friendly block of flats, and we are much concerned to share our faith with our neighbours. So Roy Clements, the pastor of a local Baptist church, recently agreed to come and speak informally to most of them one evening, after refreshments, on 'Why Christmas?'; and we hope to do the same sort of thing again. For some of us it often seems strangely difficult to embark on a personal talk about the things of God with colleagues, neighbours or acquaintances without some starting-point. This was, indeed, precisely what CICCU sermons used to provide in my student days, since it was both easy and natural to ask a friend, whom one had persuaded to come, what he thought of it. If he said that he was impressed, this opened the door to a talk about what he was going to do about it; and if his reply was unfavourable, that was a ready-made opportunity for a discussion. In my later years I am sadly conscious that I have always found it easier to speak at meetings than to make openings for profitable talk with individuals, and that I have had many personal contacts which I have failed to follow up in any effective way.

As I write I am now seventy-six, so I have long since reached the time of life when one looks in *The Times* to see which of one's friends have died, rather than got married or had a baby. I was recently at an 'Assembly' in Trinity to which all those who 'came up before 1928' were invited. One of those present was Bishop Stephen Neill, who was in Cambridge for the last year of his prize Fellowship when I came up as a freshman in 1927 – and was, perhaps, the most brilliant man I have known personally. But now he, like several of my friends, has gone to be with the Lord he loved and served. Only last year I had the privilege of speaking at a memorial service for Miss E. G. R. Swain, for many years headmistress of Clarendon School. I had got to know her fairly well when I was Chairman of her Council for more than a decade – to say nothing of the time when our two daughters, and subsequently two of our granddaughters, were her pupils. Pat had known her even before she became headmistress; and we both regard her as one of the comparatively small number of authentic 'saints' we have known personally.

At times since I retired I have experienced bouts of spiritual depression – times when I have longed, and prayed earnestly, for a much more vivid awareness of the love of God being 'poured into [my] heart by the Holy Spirit, whom he has given us' (Romans 5:5). I have also had a greater realization than ever before, I think, of the way in which I have so often failed to live, witness and pray as I should have done, and of the times when I have fallen captive to 'the sin that so easily entangles' (Hebrews 12:1). But I can testify to a growing experience of the riches of the 'new covenant': a perfect forgiveness, a longing to 'know the Lord' in a more vital, personal way, and a greater awareness that he is 'writing his law' on my heart and mind (Hebrews 8:10–11).

I often think of Christina Rossetti's poem:

Does the road wind up-hill all the way?
    Yes, to the very end.
Will the day's journey take the whole long day?
    From morn to night, my friend.

But is there for the night a resting-place?
    A roof for when the slow dark hours begin.
May not the darkness hid it from my face?
    You cannot miss that inn.

Shall I meet other wayfarers at night?
    Those who have gone before.
Then must I knock, or call when just in sight?
    They will not keep you standing at that door.

Shall I find comfort, travel-sore and weak?
    Of labour you shall find the sum.
Will there be beds for me and all who seek?
    Yea, beds for all who come.

Epilogue

On towards the goal

As Christians, our goal is sure and can never be frustrated. It is God's eternal purpose that all who are genuinely 'in Christ Jesus' will ultimately be 'conformed to the likeness of his Son, that he might be the firstborn among many brothers' (Romans 8:29). That is the 'glory' to which our Pioneer is bringing all God's adopted sons and daughters. They have already, by his grace, 'crossed over from death to life' (John 5:24), for there will be 'no condemnation' for them at the end of the road, and no possibility of 'separation' from his love along the way (Romans 8:1 and 35). We have been set free from the tyranny as well as the guilt of sin; and although sin still lurks in our 'bodily members', and 'so easily entangles' us in thought, emotion, word and deed, we eagerly await the Saviour who will one day 'transfigure the body belonging to our humble state, and give it a form like that of his own resplendent body, by the very power which enables him to make all things subject to himself' (Philippians 3:21, NEB).

While, however, we continue to look forward to that culmination of our adoption, 'the redemption of our bodies' (Romans 8:23), we already enjoy the status and privileges of the 'many sons' whom God, 'for whom and through whom everything exists', is 'bringing to glory' (Hebrews 2:10). As John puts it: 'How great is the love the Father has lavished on us, that we should be called children of God! And that is what we are!... Dear friends, now we are children of God, and what we will be has not yet been made known. But we know that when [Christ] appears, we shall be like him, for we shall see him as he is. Everyone who has this hope in him purifies himself, just as he is pure' (1 John 3:1–3).

As we anticipate that day, we need continually to remember that we died to sin – and to the law of God which at one and the same time defines, condemns and aggravates it. We 'died' to these 'through the body of Christ, that [we] might belong to another, to him who was raised from the dead, in order that we might bear fruit to God' (Romans 7:4). The very reason why we have been 'released from the law' is that we might serve God 'in the new way of the Spirit, and not in the old way of the written code' (Romans 7:6). So the 'fruit' we should bear consists both in the progressive transformation of our characters as we contemplate and reflect the glory of the Lord (2 Corinthians 3:18; Galatians 5:22–23), and in a life of unselfish service and faithful witness to others. There are so many whom we meet and to whom we speak, or could speak, who have never heard, understood or responded to the invitation that the Saviour has commissioned us to give in his name, since he 'committed to us the message of reconciliation' and made us his 'ambassadors' (2 Corinthians 5:18–20).

Throughout most of our lives (speaking for myself) we are so absorbed in the activities of the present and our plans for the future here on earth that we do not think nearly enough about the 'inheritance that can never perish, spoil or fade' which is 'kept in heaven' for us – and for which we are ourselves being 'shielded by God's power until the coming of the salvation that is ready to be revealed in the last time' (1 Peter 1:4–5).

Meanwhile, there is still 'very much land to be possessed'. Looking back, I realize that things that once meant a good deal to me, and goals to which I used to aspire, were in themselves of little real value. I spent a lot of time acquiring qualifications and a certain degree of knowledge and status that did, indeed, give me many spiritual opportunities which I could, I know, have put to more effective use. I often think of what Patricia St John, in 'The Alchemist', terms 'the sum of life's lost opportunities'. But I thank God that

> He seeks no second site on which to build,
> But on the old foundation, stone by stone,
> Cementing sad experience with grace,
> Fashions a stronger temple of His own.[1]

So there must be 'no looking back'. There is a *much* deeper sense than I have ever yet experienced in which I long to 'gain Christ' and to 'know him and the power of his resurrection and the fellowship of sharing in his sufferings' (Philippians 3:8–10). So I want to forget 'what is behind' – failures as well as successes, opportunities that were lost as well as those that, by God's grace, were taken. Instead, 'straining towards what is ahead', I want to 'press on towards the goal to win the prize for which God has called me heavenwards in

[1] Quoted from *Verses* (CSSM, 1953) in Timothy Dudley-Smith, *Someone who beckons*, pp. 70f.

Christ Jesus' (Philippians 3:12–14). As the years go by, we inevitably fight a losing battle against decreasing resilience of body, retentiveness of memory and power of concentration. But we can still aspire to be so 'strengthened' inwardly by the Holy Spirit that 'Christ may dwell in [our] hearts through faith' and that we may be enabled to grasp, with all God's people, 'how wide and long and high and deep is the love of Christ ... that surpasses knowledge – that [we] may be filled to the measure of all the fullness of God' (Ephesians 3:16–19).

We can all echo Bishop Frank Houghton's words:

> Thou who art love beyond all telling,
>   Saviour and King, we worship Thee.
> Immanuel, within us dwelling,
>   Make us what Thou wouldst have us be.
> Thou who art love beyond all telling,
>   Saviour and King, we worship Thee.